Demographic Gaps in
American Political Behavior

Demographic Gaps in American Political Behavior

PATRICK FISHER
Seton Hall University

WESTVIEW
PRESS
A Member of the Perseus Books Group

Westview Press was founded in 1975 in Boulder, Colorado, by notable publisher and intellectual Fred Praeger. Westview Press continues to publish scholarly titles and high-quality undergraduate-and graduate-level textbooks in core social science disciplines. With books developed, written, and edited with the needs of serious nonfiction readers, professors, and students in mind, Westview Press honors its long history of publishing books that matter.

Find us on the World Wide Web at www.westviewpress.com.

Every effort has been made to secure required permissions for all text, images, maps, and other art reprinted in this volume.

Westview Press books are available at special discounts for bulk purchases in the United States by corporations, institutions, and other organizations. For more information, please contact the Special Markets Department at the Perseus Books Group, 2300 Chestnut Street, Suite 200, Philadelphia, PA 19103, or call (800) 810-4145, ext. 5000, or e-mail special.markets@perseusbooks.com.

Library of Congress Cataloging-in-Publication Data

Fisher, Patrick (Patrick Ivan)
  Demographic gaps in American political behavior / Patrick Fisher.
    pages cm
  Includes bibliographical references and index.
  ISBN 978-0-8133-4596-3 (paperback) — ISBN 978-0-8133-4597-0 (e-book) 1. Political participa-
tion—Social aspects—United States. 2. Political culture—United States. 3. Political socialization—
United States. 4. Demography—Political aspects—United States. 5. Income—Political aspects—
United States. 6. Religion and politics—United States. 7. Women—Political activity—United States. 8.
Men—Political activity—United States. 9. Race—Political aspects—United States. 10. Age—Political
aspects—United States. I. Title.
  JK1764.F528 2014
  323'.0420973—dc23
                            2013050469

10 9 8 7 6 5 4 3 2 1

Contents

Preface

I have long been fascinated by the intricacies of American elections. Even as a first-grader I recall being captivated by the Jimmy Carter–Gerald Ford election and remember being shocked the day after the election when I woke up and found out that Carter had won the election—after all, Ford had been leading when my parents forced me to go to bed on election night. Needless to say, these days I do not go to bed early on election night: I live for presidential and congressional elections. It is like the Super Bowl, World Series, and Olympics combined in one intense night every four years.

For the first part of my career as a political scientist, my research focus was primarily on the federal budget process, a topic on which I wrote two books: *Congressional Budgeting: A Representational Perspective* (University Press of America, 2005) and *The Politics of Taxing and Spending* (Lynne Rienner, 2009). Even as I was writing about budgetary politics, however, I found myself continually being drawn to the minutiae of American elections, and after getting tenure at Seton Hall University, I thought it was the right time to finally concentrate on my interest in American political behavior.

I got the idea for writing a book on the demographic gaps in the American polity from the *New York Times* article "In Politics, the 'God Gap' Overshadows Other Differences," published on December 9, 2006. While reading this fascinating article by Peter Steinfels, I found myself wondering how other demographic gaps would compare to the "god gap" and the preliminary concept for this book was born. My initial foray into the study of "gapology" was research on the age gap in US politics, which resulted in a couple of articles published in the journal *Society*. After a considerable amount of positive feedback on my age gap findings, I was encouraged to make the plunge and write this book analyzing a number of different demographic gaps in American politics. I hope you will find these gaps—which tell us so much about American politics—as interesting as I do.

Of course, no body of work is done without the help of others, and I want to acknowledge all the invaluable support I received in the undertaking of this project. I was awarded a University Research Council Award by Seton Hall University in 2011 in support of my research on this book and wish to thank the university for its commitment to me in this research endeavor. I express gratitude to Michael Taylor and Jeffrey Togman, my colleagues in the Department of Political Science at Seton Hall, for all the moral support they have given me through the years. Once I decided to make gapology my research focus, I annually taught senior seminar courses at Seton Hall on the topic, and I wish to acknowledge all my senior seminar students, who so usefully served as a laboratory of ideas for this book. I particularly want to recognize Kaitlyn Aurilio and Tyler Marandola, two stellar students of mine who provided substantial help in my research on this project. I thank Ada Fung and Anthony Wahl at Westview Press for all their support. I sincerely value the opportunity offered to me by Westview to write this book and appreciate all the critical work Ada and Anthony provided me. Finally, I want to thank the peer reviewers who took the time to offer their insightful feedback: Matt Guardino (Providence College), Whitt Kilburn (Grand Valley State University), Seth McKee (University of South Florida), John McNulty (Binghamton University), Jeffrey Stonecash (Syracuse University), Costas Panagopoulos (Fordham University), and others who wished to remain anonymous.

Illustrations

TABLES

Introduction to Gapology

The Concept of "Gapology"

This work will investigate the "gapology" of American politics. Gapology, simply put, is the study of political "gaps," or divides. Though the concept of gapology can be used to denote the differences between viewpoints (e.g., liberal or conservative) and situations (e.g., married or single), my focus will be the study of marked political disparities between groups (e.g., male or female) in the United States.

One's demographic background has the potential to greatly influence how one views politics and behaves politically. As such, this book will examine the political beliefs and behavior of different demographic groups in the United States. By studying American political culture from a demographic perspective, I will endeavor to come to a greater understanding of how Americans conceptualize the political universe. How are different demographic groups politically distinct in American democracy? Why are they distinct?

Americans are divided on a wide array of political divisions that go beyond the "red" (Republican or conservative) and "blue" (Democratic or liberal) state classification that has become so ingrained in popular discourse. Media coverage has disproportionately focused on the red state versus blue state divide, leaving the impression that American political behavior is determined by place or residence. This, however, ignores the numerous other divides in American political behavior. What it means to be red or blue is much more complex than geography. There are considerable demographic political divisions—what I will refer to as gaps—that differentiate red America from blue America. The many political gaps in the United States distinguish the political behavior of Americans and are extremely useful in understanding the political divides within the United States today.

The central mantra of this book is that the gaps in American political behavior are not only intrinsically fascinating but also informative. People unquestionably respond to gaps. Americans perceive themselves as belonging to one group or another, and there is widespread acknowledgment that these group memberships affect political beliefs and voting choices. The focus of gapology is on the demographics of the American polity.

There are certainly factors other than demographics that influence one's political beliefs; partisan identification and ideology are obvious factors that have independent effects on political behavior. Compared with other countries, however, political activism in the United States has often been built more around group identities and less around broad ideologies.[1] As a result, group identities have a significant impact on one's political beliefs. A key principle behind studying gapology is that political attributes such as one's partisan identification and ideology are influenced considerably by demographics. Americans' "left" and "right" self-identifications, in fact, are usually symbolic, attached to group loyalties.[2] Though gaps represent oversimplifications of the complex reality of political behavior, the utility of gapology is that it connects something of undeniable importance with key characteristics of everyday life.[3]

Gapology assumes the importance of socialization in determining Americans' political views. Group differences are a product of shared experiences, which vary considerably from group to group. People do not learn about politics in a vacuum; political behavior is learned through the process of political socialization. The learning of specific orientations to politics and experience with the political system are extremely important in understanding one's political beliefs.[4]

By the time one enters college, one's partisanship tends to be rather stable.[5] Party identities are quite stable relative to attitudes, in part because partisans defend their identities by adopting "lesser of two evils" justifications.[6] Children acquire partisan attachments through early socialization and develop emotional attachments to a party, even though they may not be aware of any conflict between their party identification and their positions on various issues. One's family plays the most critical role in the fixing of attachments to political parties and on beliefs on issues.[7] Based on the nature of relationships with their parents, children begin developing value orientations at a very early age, understanding morality either as strength and discipline or as compassion for the less strong. Offspring of families with high levels of political interest also tend toward a higher degree of psychological involvement in politics.[8]

Though political orientations typically begin to form in childhood—shaped through one's socialization environment, genetics, and development of personality traits—political attitudes can be transformed when public policies directly affect citizens' lives. Victims of crime, for example, participate in politics more than comparable nonvictims.[9] The Vietnam War draft lottery reoriented the political views of young men who received a lottery number. Males holding low lottery numbers became more antiwar, more liberal, and more Democratic in their voting compared to those with high numbers, which protected them from the draft. Low-number young men were also more likely than those with safe numbers to abandon the party identification they had held as teenagers. Vulnerability to being drafted not only structured attitudes toward the Vietnam War, but also provoked a cascade of changes in basic partisan, ideological, and issue attitudes.[10]

From the perspective of gapology, political socialization is most important in regard to group membership. The idea of a group influencing its members could seem contradictory. A group, after all, is only the sum of its individual members. Yet groups affect the individuals in them. The reality of a group can be psychological, and that reality can change behavior. In the course of a campaign, for example, there may be talk of the "black vote," "women vote," "youth vote," and so forth. These groups are not obviously political: they did not come into being as a result of politics.[11] Yet the group shapes the politics of its members because they psychologically identify with that group.[12]

Social groups help voters organize the political world, and social networks moderate the effect of elite discourse on public opinion.[13] People use mental shortcuts to make sense of things, including politics, about which they have limited information. Politically significant group identities are widespread among Americans, and group members' policy preferences cut across generations. Similarities in life experiences lead to similarities in political outlook.

People who conceptualize politics from a group-benefit perspective tend to be abstract in their evaluations and in the substantive content of the criteria they employ. They evaluate candidates and parties in terms of their sympathy and hostility toward particular groups in society.[14] Some members are very attached to a group, others less so. Although everyone may be in the group in name, certain members will be strongly pulled by the group, while others may actually feel nothing for the group. Thus, even though all members carry the same group label, they can differ substantially in their psychological attachment to it. The more identified one is with the group, the closer one will adhere to the group norm.[15] As a result, those who identify strongly with a particular group are more likely to be affected politically by that group membership.[16]

Americans increasingly identify with various social groups as opposed to political parties.[17] Yet even though Americans are more likely than they were to identify themselves as Independent as opposed to Republican or Democratic, party loyalty today is much higher than it was thirty years ago, especially among Democrats.[18] Most Americans, of course, are not formal members of a political party. But they do feel some psychological affiliation to a party, and that strongly shapes their political behavior. Official party activists compose a very small group, but the group that is psychologically attached to a party is large.[19] The primary motivation for voting today, in fact, is partisanship, not civic duty as it had been in the past. As partisanship has increased, Americans have become more political, as they are more likely than before to talk to their friends and neighbors about politics and display yard signs and bumper stickers, while also donating money to the parties and candidates in record numbers.[20] This reinforces the importance of group membership.

Gapology relies on the idea that political culture—the predominant pattern of ideas, assumptions, and emotions regarding political processes—shapes the socialization experiences of groups, which in turn leads them to have different political belief systems. Differences in societal experiences alter citizens' cultural orientations.[21] Political culture exercises a psychological grip that contributes in important ways to the well-being of a relevant group.[22] It is a common mistake to try to explain the diversity of everyday behavior in the United States on the grounds of uniformity in shared national values. Even though the United States is a single nation, Americans do not constitute a single political culture.[23]

The United States in Red and Blue

Since 2000 presidential election-night media coverage has been dominated by the coloring of each state red or blue depending on which party's candidate carries that state's electoral votes. Blue states where the Democratic Party is dominant include those in New England (such as Massachusetts), the Northeast (New York), the Midwest (Illinois), and the West Coast (California). The strongest red states tend to be located in the South (such as Alabama), the Great Plains (Nebraska), and the Mountain West (Utah). This red-blue color scheme for differentiating Republican and Democratic support is relatively new. Historically, the use of colors to indicate partisan support was arbitrary. *Time* magazine, for example, favored Democratic red and Republican white in the 1976 election between Jimmy Carter and Gerald Ford and then later reversed those colors for Ronald Reagan and Jimmy Carter in 1980. Gradually, the color scheme became more formalized, but it was not until 2000 that red for Republican and blue for Democrat became the standard. The red state–blue state dichotomy has now become entrenched in the political lexicon.[24] Figure 1-1 displays the Electoral College maps for the 2008 and 2012 elections in light gray (often shown in red,

FIGURE 1-1   Electoral College Maps of 2008 and 2012 Presidential Votes

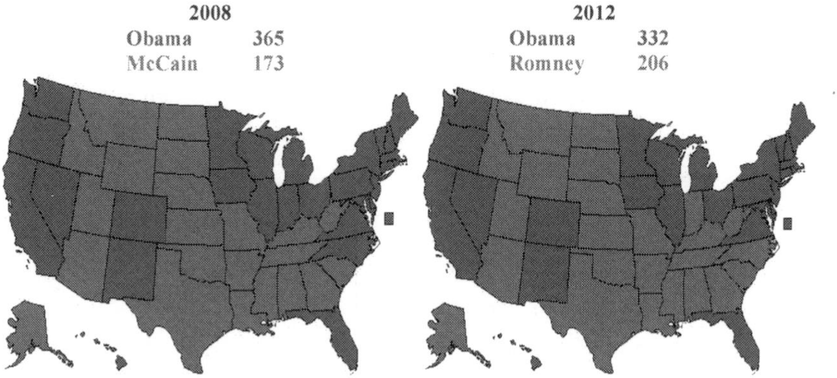

2008		2012	
Obama	365	Obama	332
McCain	173	Romney	206

Source: National Election Pool exit polls, 2008 and 2012.

where the Republican nominee for president won the state) and in dark gray (often shown in blue, where the Democratic nominee won the state). These maps—that is, the actual Electoral College vote count—will be used as a baseline when I discuss hypothetical Electoral College maps for specific demographic groups in Chapters 2 through 7.

The increasing political polarization in America along a red-blue divide is partially the result of a greater media emphasis on cultural issues and resulting cultural divisions. Findings suggest a widening and deepening of a cultural-values-based realignment of the American electorate. For red America, moral traditionalism has exerted a stronger influence on vote choice through party identification; more morally traditional citizens have become more Republican. The growing importance of values and the cultural divide has served to nationalize citizen's vote choices, with voters more willing to cast their ballots in state and local elections on the basis of national issues that usually are only thought to affect presidential vote choice.

The gaps on cultural issues are in part the result of the fact that Americans have become increasingly divided along religious lines. Religious polarization is associated with a growing schism on cultural issues, especially abortion and gay marriage. The religious cleavage between the parties has grown over time as the Republican Party has become more traditionally religious and the Democratic Party more secular. The more often one attends religious services, the more likely one is to vote Republican, and this so-called god gap is growing (I will analyze this in detail in Chapter 3).

This has not always been the case. In 1960, for example, regular church-goers were actually more Democratic in their vote for president.[25] Today, committed evangelicals, who have distinct political attitudes and who live disproportionately in the red states of the South, increasingly align themselves with the Republican Party: in 2012 Republican Mitt Romney won more than three-fourths of the white evangelical vote. As the Republican Party has become more influenced by the religious right, the geographical base of the party has moved to the South. This in turn has influenced how the American polity is conceptualized here and abroad. A popular post-2004 election map that circulated on the Internet had the United States divided in two: "The United States of Canada" (blue states joined to Canada) and "Jesusland," representing red states.

It would be wrong to suggest, however, that the red-blue divide does not have any economic underpinnings. As I will demonstrate throughout this book, economic issues play a crucial role in delineating the gaps of American politics. It is commonly believed, for example, that the primary reason that the gender gap has emerged with women disproportionately supporting Democratic candidates is due to the prominence of social issues such as abortion. Yet as I will demonstrate in detail in Chapter 4, the gender gap has emerged in large part because the Democratic Party has become associated with an activist government that supports the economically vulnerable and disadvantaged and with a less belligerent foreign and defense policy.

Gapology is centered on the idea that Americans are becoming more polarized politically and that to a significant degree this polarization can be appreciated through comparison of the political preferences of different groups. Polarization can be defined as a commitment to a candidate, an issue, or an ideology that sets people in one group definitely apart from people in another group.[26] Of course, polarization is a subjective judgment. For some people a 10 percent difference in the preference of a socioeconomic group may be sufficient to conclude Americans are polarized, whereas for others that same difference denotes a lack of polarization.[27] I will not argue that polarization begins with some arbitrary percentage difference in a group's preferences. Rather, the goal of this book is to indicate that on a number of aspects of political preferences there are important differences—gaps—between groups. Whether or not these gaps indicate polarization can be debated. But these gaps are critical to any attempts to come to a greater understanding of the American polity.

Much of the logic of the contemporary red state–blue state divide rests on the premise that the nation's escalating polarization is evident geographically. Overall, blue states tend to be getting "bluer," or more Democratic, and red states are getting "redder," or more Republican. Presidential vote tallies in more states, for example, have strayed from the national norm: presidential candidates' margins in more and more states have widened. Due to the winner-take-all nature of the Electoral College, relatively few states (about one-third of all states in recent president elections) are considered swing states that could potentially go red or blue. This is a noticeable shift from a generation ago. In the close election of 1976 (which Jimmy Carter won by 2 percentage points nationally), twenty states with 299 Electoral College votes were decided by a margin of less than 5 points. By 2004 the relatively close election nationally saw only ten states with 106 electoral votes decided by a margin of less than 5 percentage points. This number was cut in half in the similarly close presidential election in 2012 (which, like 2004, saw the incumbent win by about 3 percentage points), as only five states with 85 electoral votes were decided by 5 points or less: Ohio, Florida, Colorado, Virginia, and North Carolina. In the four presidential elections from 2000 to 2012, forty of the fifty states supported the same party.

Red and blue states, therefore, are becoming more politically distinct from each other. The emergence of a more partisan and polarized electorate is a product of long-term realignment and social change. The growing intensity of partisanship within red and blue states is creating parties with increasingly distinct identities. Divisions between red and blue America are increasingly ideological. This has important consequences because state policies tend to reflect the ideological sentiment of state electorates.[28] The red state–blue state dichotomy, however, measures only some of the polarization in the country. Many states are themselves deeply divided internally between liberal and conservative areas. Voters are also polarized in different ways within different states.

Partisan and ideological polarization is greatest among those individuals whose beliefs and behavior most closely reflect the ideals of those paying the closest attention to politics. It is politically engaged citizens who are the most polarized in their political views.[29] The emergence of the Tea Party, for example, provided conservative activists with a new identity as it energized disgruntled middle-class conservatives. In 2010 Tea Party activism reshaped many Republican primaries and enhanced voter turnout for Republicans in the general election. The result is that the Tea Party has pulled the national Republican Party farther toward the right.[30] Some Americans may be turned off by the sharp ideological divisions between the parties, but more Americans appear to be excited and energized by the choice between a consistently liberal Democratic Party and a consistently conservative Republican Party. As a result, the size of the engaged public has been increasing and becoming a substantial portion of the American electorate.[31] This polarization makes the study of gapology even more compelling as it has led to greater distinctions in groups' political behavior. Greater polarization has made the gaps between groups more remarkable.

A Culture War?

The greater levels of polarization in the country have led to suggestions that a "culture war" is taking place in the United States between red and blue America. This notion that the country has culturally divided into separate red and blue groups based on religious traditionalism versus religious progressivism has become commonplace. I once went to a bookstore that had a reading section on American politics that was systematically divided between red and blue, with books advocating the red viewpoint on one side of the table and books defending blue ideology on the other side of the table. One advertisement for Dell computer had "the Republican chose Blue" and "the Democrat chose Red." This belief that red America has a different set of values from blue America has become fashionable in political humor.

As humor columnist Dave Barry joked, red staters are "ignorant racist fascist knuckle-dragging NASCAR-obsessed cousin-marrying road-kill-eating tobacco-juice-dribbling gun-fondling religious fanatic rednecks," whereas blue staters are "godless unpatriotic pierced-nose Volvo-driving France-loving leftwing Communist latte-sucking tofu-chomping holistic-wacko neurotic vegan weenie perverts."[32]

Though Dave Barry's stereotypes are no doubt hyperbolic, there are indeed cultural differences between Democrats and Republicans that transcend politics. Part of this difference can be seen in consumer behavior. Car brands most likely to be driven by Republicans, for example, are Porsche, Jaguar, Land Rover, and GMC, whereas car brands most likely to be driven by Democrats are Volvo, Subaru, Mazda, and Volkswagen. Cultural difference is also reflected in choice of recreational activities. The most Republican activities are waterskiing, volunteer work, snowmobiling, and ice-skating; the most Democratic activities are dancing, gardening, bicycling, and cross-country skiing. Democrats and Republicans also have different television-sports-watching habits. The most Republican television sporting events are NASCAR, college football, and the National Hockey League; Democrats are much more likely to prefer the Women's National Basketball Association, the National Basketball Association, and major league soccer.[33]

Despite widespread acceptance of this idea of a culture war, some argue that its existence is much exaggerated. One of the leading critics of the culture war concept is political scientist Morris Fiorina, who argues that reports of a culture war are mostly wishful thinking. This myth, he argues, is the result of misinterpretation of election returns, lack of hard examination of polling data, misrepresentation by issue activists, and selective coverage by the media.[34]

To critics, the culture war has always existed more in the minds of journalists and political activists than in the lives of ordinary Americans.[35] Rather, the culture war is waged by limited interests on narrow policy fronts under special political leadership, and a broader cultural division in the country is largely not the case.[36] Much of what is considered popular polarization of the public on cultural issues may in fact simply be a result of an increase of partisan and institutional polarization. It has been suggested that the candidates, not the voters, are the ones who are polarized. Polarized alternatives, after all, can produce the appearance of polarized citizens.[37] It has been suggested, for example, that much of the contemporary polarization in American politics is due to the Republican Party shifting markedly to the ideological right.[38] Consequently, the divisions in American politics exist because politicians pose a false choice between individualism and community even though Americans actually prefer both.[39]

Polarization at the elite level, however, is largely a reflection of polarization among the politically engaged segment of the American public.[40] Central to Fiorina's argument is the belief that the American public is largely nonideological. Yet as I will establish, demographic groups do have distinguishable ideological beliefs that make them distinct from one another. If Fiorina's hypothesis were correct, groups would not be worth studying because their political preferences would largely be the same. All the gaps I will analyze, however, have unique political attributes.

A new political culture is transforming American politics as social issues are increasingly distinguished and emphasized relative to economic issues.[41] Yet as articulated previously, it would be a major mistake to discount the influence of economic issues on political behavior. Rather, both economic and social issues have a considerable impact. The United States still has a class-based politics, but one in which cultural issues sometimes appear to trump class concerns. Inequality is increasing, and class political divisions are now greater than a generation ago. At the same time, cultural issues are now more prominent, and there is growing polarization between the parties on cultural issues. Groups are steadily moving toward greater partisanship, and that division is driven by differences in class and culture.[42]

The notion of a culture war is central to gapology's concerns. The idea of a culture war suggests that different groups of Americans have distinct political preferences. Though differences on cultural issues might not be worthy of the hyperbolic term "war" and it is wrong to suggest that cultural issues now regularly trump economic issues in importance, groups have strongly different preferences on social issues. And these differences are coming to define American politics more and more.

The Gapology of American Politics

The objective of this book is to demonstrate the importance (or lack thereof) of each gap in regard to vote choice and public policy preferences. My analysis will be derived in part from data from exit polls conducted by the National Election Pool, a consortium formed by NBC, ABC, CBS, CNN, Fox, and the Associated Press.[43] I will also rely on data from the American National Election Studies (ANES), especially the 2008 and 2012 datasets. The ANES conducts national surveys of the American electorate in election years and has carried out an unbroken series of national election studies since 1952. It has become an invaluable resource for political scientists studying the American electorate as it helps to inform the nation about itself, exploring the causes and consequences of voting behavior and electoral outcomes.[44]

My purpose in analyzing exit polls and ANES data is twofold. First, I want to investigate how important particular demographics (i.e., gaps) are in determining vote choice. Second, I want to examine how one's demographics affect ideological and public policy preferences. The objective is to ascertain the level by which demographics impact voting behavior as well as general political beliefs.[45]

I will analyze the following gaps: (1) income, (2) religion, (3) gender, (4) race, (5) age, and (6) geography. Though there is a plethora of potential gaps that we could look at, these were chosen because of their prominence in the American political scene. These gaps often are referred to in discussions of American politics, and political data on these demographic groups have been collected for decades.

I will start this investigation of specific gaps in Chapter 2 by examining the income gap, traditionally one of the most important (if not the most important) divides in American politics. The difference in political behavior between those with low income and those with high income has been noteworthy for much of American history and is still extremely relevant as class divisions in American politics have been growing. Of all the gaps I will investigate in this book, it is the income gap that possess the largest differences on economic issues relative to social and cultural issues.

Political commentators often argue that today the religious gap, the topic of Chapter 3, has become the most important cleavage in American politics. Religious traditionalism is indeed a strong predictor of political behavior. The religion gap reflects the political significance of religious beliefs. High levels of religious commitment expose individuals to specific types of information that in turn differentiate people's political beliefs. The religious gap is likely to become even more prominent in the future due to the fact that even though the country as a whole has become more secular, those who regularly worship have become more conservative politically. The religion gap, therefore, may lead to even greater political polarization in the future.

In Chapters 4 and 5 I will look at two of the most obvious gaps in American politics: those along gender and race lines. Of all the gaps I will analyze in this book, the gender gap has historically received the greatest attention from political scientists. Yet as I will demonstrate, the gender gap is not nearly as pronounced as other gaps I will examine. Despite popular belief to the contrary, the gender gap is largely the result of economic issues, not social issues such as abortion. Whereas the gender gap may be overrated as a political division in American politics, race may actually be underrated. Race is far and away the most significant gap studied here. There is a substantial gap in the political behavior of whites and minority racial and ethnic groups in the United States. This large gap has existed since the 1960s, and recent elections do not indicate any attrition in the race gap.

A gap that has traditionally received considerably less attention is the age gap, the topic I will examine in Chapter 6. Though a discernible difference among age cohorts in their political preferences has not historically been a consistent feature of American politics, the age gap has recently emerged as one of the country's most noteworthy divisions. In 2008 and 2012 the age gap was considerably larger than it had ever been before: Barack Obama won the under-30 vote by a staggering 34-point margin in 2008 and a reduced by still historically impressive 23-point margin in 2012. Much of the significance of the age gap relies on the possibility of long-term generational effects on vote choice. Historically, the generation in which one comes of age politically can play an important role in structuring one's political views throughout life. The main significance of today's age gap, therefore, is that it may differentiate generations politically over the course of their lives.

The last gap I will investigate, in Chapter 7, is the geography gap. Politically, where people live is as important as it ever was. Localities have real and significant cultural and political differences that in some cases deviate markedly from the national norm. The geography gap is a consequence of the heterogeneous nature of American political culture. One aspect of geographical divisions that I will analyze is the regional gap, the difference in political behavior between those living in different regions of the country. My focus will be on how political attitudes in the South vary from those in the rest of the country. Sectionalism has always been a prominent feature of American politics, and a significant regional gap existed before the country was even born. Southerners have long had distinct political beliefs, and southern exceptionalism is still a marked feature of the American political landscape. Another geographical characteristic of American politics that will be examined is the urbanism gap, the difference in political behavior between those living in urban, in rural, and in suburban areas. There is a strong relationship between population density and partisanship, and the existence of an urbanism divide is one of the oldest concepts in the study of American politics.

Finally, in Chapter 8, I will attempt to piece the gaps together. The gaps do not exist in a vacuum and consequently are not completely independent from one another. There is an important correlation in the United States, for example, between race and income. Yet though the different demographic gaps examined in this book are certainly intertwined, each is distinct and has an independent effect. Some gaps, however, are more politically prominent than others. Whatever the angle of my approach (income, religion, gender, race, age, race, or geography), indicators suggest that political divisions are evolving in such a way that the future of American politics may be markedly transformed. The enormous demographic change the country is undergoing has left both major political parties in a state of transition.

For each chapter I will look at the evolution of each group's political behavior since 1980. The 1980 presidential election, between incumbent president Jimmy Carter and Republican challenger Ronald Reagan, was chosen as the starting point for my data analysis because this election is widely seen as a catalyst for much of the differences between the parties' coalitions of support in contemporary American politics. Many of the demographic differences in the parties' bases of support today became pronounced after this seminal presidential election. Before 1980, for example, there was no gender gap between the parties: men and women for the most part were indistinguishable politically. Since 1980, however, the gender gap has consistently been a prominent feature of American politics.

After examining the history of each gap, I will focus in each chapter on the political dynamics of the gap in 2008 and 2012. Obama's impressive victories in these elections—it was only the second and third time a Democratic presidential nominee received more than a majority of the vote since 1964—suggests a potential change in the demographic bases of support for the parties. Though for each gap studied here the direction of the gap was consistent with what it had been during the previous decade, in some cases the magnitude of the gap was considerably larger. The age gap, for example, was considerably larger in 2008 and 2012 than ever before. This unquestionably has important implications for the future of American politics.

Though how groups tend to vote is an important indicator of political preferences, my concept of gapology denotes more than just vote choice. As such, I will analyze a number of questions from the ANES regarding public policy preferences in 2008 and 2012 to gain a greater appreciation of groups' political differences. For every chapter I will analyze group preferences on economic policy (opinions on government services, health care, aid to the poor, and Social Security), preferences on domestic and foreign policy (immigration, gun control, environment, and defense spending), and preferences on values (moral standards) and social issues (gay marriage, abortion, and the death penalty). The importance of public opinion in influencing public policy can be vividly demonstrated in the implementation of the death penalty. Institutional arrangements in the United States allow public support for the death penalty to influence political decisionmaking more directly than is the case in European countries.[46] Unlike most countries that abolished the death penalty, which they did through countermajoritarian political initiatives, the strong receptivity of American political leaders to the public implies that the country will abolish the death penalty only after a change in public opinion.[47]

I will also consider the consequences of turnout among different groups.[48] Because not all demographic groups turn out to vote at the same rates, certain groups are advantaged politically by their relatively higher participation rates. Some gaps, therefore, may be more or less relevant politically due to varying turnout dynamics among groups. Wealthier Americans, for example, always turn out to vote at higher rates than poorer Americans, and this undoubtedly has important consequences for the nation's economic policy (and, as we will discover, for noneconomic policies as well).

In such a large and diverse country, gapology helps us to understand what it means to be American. To be German or Japanese denotes an ethnicity as well as a country of citizenship, but because there is no "American" ethnicity, what it means to be American is much more complex. Though American politics has always had important geographic differences, those who analyze American politics are increasingly focusing on other demographic gaps to gain a better understanding of political behavior. There is evidence that Americans, too, are increasingly more aware and interested in political differences among groups. More election analyses, for example, include tabulations of the demographics of the vote.[49]

Gapology also has important implications for public policy. In a pluralistic democracy like the United States, group competition is critical to an understanding of public policy outcomes. Different groups' policy preferences, therefore, offer important insights into how coalitions in American politics are created. The winners and losers in public policy are determined not only by the size of respective groups, but also by the level and intensity of groups' policy preferences. In addition to outcomes, group preferences demonstrate fascinating attributes of the American political environment. Policy preferences—as well as vote choice—are in fact closely tied to other deep value systems in American culture.

Demographically, the United States is undergoing significant changes, and a central premise of this book—one that I will address in depth in the conclusion—is that there are important political consequences associated with the nation's changing demographics. Because groups have distinct political preferences, the fluidity of the nation's demographics will inevitably affect the nation's politics. Simply put, some groups are increasing in political influence while other groups' political power is shrinking. Demography, therefore, is destined to have a marked impact on the future of American politics.

Notes

1. Raymond A. Smith, *The American Anomaly: U.S. Politics and Government in Comparative Perspective,* 2nd ed. (New York: Routledge, 2011), 112.

2. Christopher Ellis and James Stimson, *Ideology in America* (New York: Cambridge University Press, 2012).

3. Laura R. Olson and John C. Green, "Introduction—'Gapology' and the Presidential Vote," *PS: Political Science and Politics* 39 (2006): 443–447.

4. Gabriel Almond and Sidney Verba, *The Civic Culture* (Boston: Little, Brown, 1965).

5. Patrick Fisher, "The Emerging Age Gap in U.S. Politics," *Society* 45 (2008): 504–511.

6. Eric Groenendyk, "Justifying Party Identification: A Case of Identifying with the 'Lesser of Two Evils,'" *Political Behavior* 34 (2012): 453–475.

7. V. O. Key, *Public Opinion and American Democracy* (New York: Knopf, 1961), chap. 12.

8. David Barker and James D. Tinnick III, "Competing Visions of Parental Roles and Ideological Constraint," *American Political Science Review* 100 (2006): 249–263.

9. Regina Bateson, "Crime Victimization and Political Participation," *American Political Science Review* 106 (2012): 570–587.

10. Robert Erikson and Laura Stoker, "Caught in the Draft: The Effects of Vietnam Draft Lottery Status on Political Attitudes," *American Political Science Review* 105 (2011): 221–238.

11. Michael S. Lewis-Beck, William G. Jacoby, Helmut Norpoth, and Herbert F. Weisberg, *The American Voter Revisited* (Ann Arbor: University of Michigan Press, 2008), chap. 11.

12. Angus Campbell, Phillip E. Converse, Warren E. Miller, and Donald E. Stokes, *The American Voter* (New York: Wiley, 1960).

13. Carin Robinson, "Cross-Cutting Messages and Political Tolerance: An Experiment Using Evangelical Protestants," *Political Behavior* 32 (2010): 495–510.

14. Paul Lazarfeld, Bernard Berelson, and William McPhee, *The People's Choice* (New York: Columbia University Press, 1944).

15. Lewis-Beck et al., *American Voter Revisited,* chap. 11.

16. Bernard Berelson, Paul F. Lazarfeld, and William McPhee, *Voting: A Study of Opinion Formation in a Presidential Campaign* (Chicago: University of Chicago Press, 1954).

17. Mark P. Petracca, "The Rediscovery of Interest Group Politics," in *The Politics of Interests,* ed. Mark P. Petracca (Boulder, CO: Westview Press, 1992), 3–31.

18. Alan I. Abramowitz, *The Disappearing Center* (New Haven, CT: Yale University Press, 2010), chap. 5.

19. Lewis-Beck et al., *American Voter Revisited,* chap. 11.

20. Abramowitz, *Disappearing Center.*

21. Charles Lockhart, "American and Swedish Tax Regimes," *Comparative Politics* 35 (2003): 379–397.

22. James Johnson, "Why Respect Culture?," *American Journal of Political Science* 44 (2000): 405–419.

23. Aaron Wildavsky, *Federalism and Political Culture* (New Brunswick, NJ: Transaction, 1998), 49.

24. Tom Zeller, "One State, Two State, Red State, Blue State," *New York Times,* February 8, 2004.

25. American National Election Studies Time Series Cumulative Data File, www.election studies.org.

26. James Q. Wilson, "How Divided Are We?," *Commentary,* February 2006, 15–21.

27. Morris Fiorina, *Culture War?: The Myth of a Polarized America* (New York: Pearson Longman, 2005).

28. Robert S. Erikson, Gerald C. Wright, and John P. McIver, *Statehouse Democracy: Public Opinion and Policy in the American States* (Cambridge: Cambridge University Press, 1993).

29. Abramowitz, *Disappearing Center.*

30. Vanessa Williamson, Theda Skocpol, and John Coggin, "The Tea Party and the Remaking of Republican Conservatism," *Perspectives on Politics* 9 (2011): 25–43.

31. Abramowitz, *Disappearing Center,* chap. 2.

32. James Q. Wilson, "Politics and Polarization," Tanner Lectures on Human Values, Harvard University, Cambridge, Massachusetts, November 2, 2005.

33. "The Politics of Leisure," *New York Times,* December 6, 2004.

34. Fiorina, *Culture War?*

35. Alan Wolfe, *One Nation, After All* (New York: Viking Penguin, 1998).

36. Geoffrey Layman and John C. Green, "Wars and Rumours of Wars: The Contexts of Cultural Conflict in American Political Behavior," *British Journal of Political Science* 36 (2006): 61–89.

37. Fiorina, *Culture War?*

38. Thomas Mann and Norman Ornstein, *It's Even Worse Than It Looks: How the American Political System Collided with the New Politics of Extremism* (New York: Basic Books, 2012).

39. E. J. Dionne, *Our Divided Political Heart* (New York: Bloomsbury, 2012).

40. Abramowitz, *Disappearing Center.*

41. Terry Nichols Clark, "The Presidency and the New Political Culture," *American Behavioral Scientist* 46 (2002): 535–553.

42. Mark D. Brewer and Jeffrey M. Stonecash, *Split: Class and Cultural Divides in American Politics* (Washington, DC: CQ Press, 2007).

43. Exit poll data for 2012 were collected by Edison Research for the National Election Pool. The survey was based on questionnaires completed by 26,565 voters leaving 350 voting places throughout the United States on Election Day and by 4,408 telephone interviews with early and absentee voters. In 2008 the exit polls were conducted by Edison/Mitofsky; in 1996 and 2000, by Voter News Services; in 1992, by Voter Research and Surveys; and in earlier years, by the *New York Times* and CBS News.

44. The ANES is an excellent source of data on the political beliefs of American citizens, offering a range of questions much more varied than exit polls due to limitations of its sample size (2,322 in its 2008 preelection wave and 2,102 in its 2008 postelection wave). Some groups, however, are oversampled to get a statistically significant sample for that group (in 2008 both African Americans and Latinos were oversampled). Consequently, the ANES data throughout this book are corrected in the aggregate by weighing of the data. The preelection sample weights are the product of the household nonresponse adjustment factor by age and education, and the postelection sample weights are adjusted for attrition.

45. Throughout this book, unless otherwise differentiated, with the exceptions of the sections of Chapters 2–8 that deal with public policy preferences and are based on analysis of ANES data, data that refer to how demographic subsets of the population voted are based on exit polls.

46. T. Alexander Smith and Raymond Tatalovich, *Cultures at War: Moral Conflicts in Western Democracies* (Toronto: Broadview Press, 2003), chap. 7.

47. Sagnmin Bae, "The Death Penalty and the Peculiarity of American Political Institutions," *Human Rights Review* 9 (2008): 233–240.

48. When possible, I use turnout data from the Census Bureau, which estimates actual voter turnout among different demographic groups as well as the voting-age population as a whole. For Chapters 4–7 I use Census Bureau estimates. The Census Bureau does not estimate turnout on the basis of religion and has only recently begun to release turnout data by income level, so for Chapters 2–3 I use data from the American National Election Studies that denote self-reported voter turnout. Because these data are consistently higher than actual voter turnout as determined by the Census Bureau, readers should use only the turnout data for the purposes of comparison within the particular gap, not across the different gaps.

49. Olson and Green, "Introduction."

2

The Income Gap

Income and American Political Behavior

Political scientists have heavily investigated the relationship between income and political behavior and have found that income has often proven to be a very good predictor of partisanship.[1] The income gap—the difference in the political behavior of those with low income and those with high income—has been a prominent feature of American politics for more than a century. Historically, wealthier voters leaned more toward the Republican Party while poorer voters leaned more toward the Democratic Party. As I will demonstrate in this chapter, this is as much the case today as ever before. The income gap is unquestionably one of the most important—if not the most important—divides in contemporary American politics.

Relatively few Americans are willing to label themselves lower class or upper class.[2] Despite this tendency to shun overt class consciousness, however, American politics has a long history of being divided along income lines going at least as far back as William Jennings Bryan's "Cross of Gold" nomination speech in the presidential campaign of 1896.[3] Following the Great Depression, the political preferences of the rich and of the poor diverged as less affluent Americans became a pillar of the Democratic Party due to their support of Franklin Delano Roosevelt's New Deal policies. The 1930s witnessed ideological conflicts over the role of government that resulted in significant class political divisions. Poor and lower-income Americans became strong supporters of the Democratic Party.

Even though a large income gap existed in the decades following the Great Depression, by the 1950s the parties were not nearly as polarized on ideological and class grounds. Rather, the major differences in the party electoral bases became more regional than class based. There was only a small difference in how poorer and wealthier Americans voted in presidential elections during the 1950s: 42 percent of whites in the bottom third of the income distribution voted for the Democratic presidential candidate during the decade, and 38 percent of those in the upper third voted for that same candidate.[4] A similar trend could be seen in House elections in the 1950s. As income in US House districts declined, the Democrats' likelihood of winning the seat increased, indicating the Democrats were more successful among the lower classes, but this relationship was largely due to the fact that most low-income districts were in the South, which was still overwhelmingly Democratic.[5]

After declining in the 1950s, the income gap increased once again during the 1960s and 1970s.[6] Since 1960 the working class without exception has been more likely than the upper classes to favor the Democratic candidate for president, though this relationship has varied in its magnitude from election to election.[7] In recent decades the political preferences of individual voters have become increasingly related to their incomes, with high-income voters more likely to vote for Republican presidential candidates and low-income voters increasingly voting Democratic.[8] Class divisions in American politics, therefore, have actually been increasing since the 1960s, not decreasing as is commonly believed.[9]

That the Democrats increased their appeal to the less affluent and the Republicans to the more affluent is a result of the fact that both the constituencies and concerns of the parties changed considerably. The parties, while moving apart ideologically, have also become more homogeneous internally on economic issues.[10] As the Republican Party became more conservative, its electoral base moved from the Northeast to the South and West and its political strength became much more heavily based in more affluent areas. At the same time, Democrats are much more unified on economic issues today than they were in the 1960s and 1970s when the party was split among northern Keynesian and southern conservative camps.[11] This unity is largely a result of a switch of partisan allegiances in the South. As the South moved from a one-party system dominated by the Democrats to a two-party system, the region saw a dramatic increase in the income effect on vote choice. Outside the South, however, the income effect has leveled off since the 1990s.[12]

As Figure 2-1 demonstrates,[13] since 1980 the income gap has been relatively wide. From 1980 to 2012 the poorest third of the population supported the Democratic presidential candidates by margins ranging from 12 to 40 percentage points, while a majority of the wealthiest third of the population supported Republican presidential nominees in every election except for 2008. For every presidential election from 1980 to 2012, the poorest third of the population voted strongly Democratic for president and the

FIGURE 2-1   Partisan Vote for President by Income

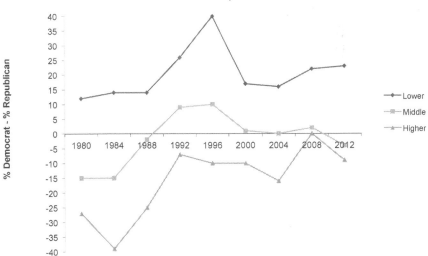

Source: ANES, 1980–2004; exit polls, 2008–2012

middle third's partisan vote preference was in between the poorest and the wealthiest. Since 1980 the largest income gaps occurred in 1984 and 1996, when Ronald Reagan and Bill Clinton, respectively, won reelection. The smallest income gap occurred in Barack Obama's initial victory in 2008.

Class Divisions and the Income Gap

At the individual level, income is an important predictor of how Americans vote, as it has been for decades. Generally, the higher one's income, the more likely one is to vote Republican. The wealthy have long been more supportive of Republicans because the party is perceived to be supportive of economic policies (especially tax policies) that work to the benefit of the upper classes.

Political divisions on the basis of income are a consequence of the Republican and Democratic parties differing sharply in their concern for class issues.[14] As political scientist Larry Bartels states, "While American politics is increasingly about cultural issues, it continues to be primarily about economic issues."[15] High-income voters' tendency to identify with and vote with the Republican Party relative to low-income Americans, who disproportionately support the Democrats, is an aftereffect of the different fiscal policies favored by the parties.[16] Though this has been the case since the Great Depression, as the parties have become more differentiated in economic policies, they have cued the voters to vote more on the basis of income. The parties are now ideologically farther apart on economic issues than they have been at any time since World War I.[17]

Differences on tax policy in particular have come to increasingly define the parties.[18] Ideologically, the tax debate in the United States revolves around the question of equity versus efficiency. Democrats support progressive taxation measures where the more affluent pay at higher rates as a means to curtail the growing inequality in the distribution of income. Republicans, in contrast, argue that high marginal rates on upper tax brackets stifle innovation and initiative. Over the past generation it is Republicans who have been winning the political debate on taxes: the federal tax system has unquestionably moved in a less redistributive direction as the wealthy pay a lower percentage of their income in taxes than at any time since the election of Franklin Roosevelt as president.

One's income level does not always define policy preference, but it does give an ideological framework for looking at the political universe. Despite the tradition of limited government in the United States, after the Great Depression skilled and blue-collar workers became more likely to believe in an activist government than professionals and white-collar workers did.[19]

That the United States has smaller class divisions than might be expected is partly due to the individualistic nature of American political culture. Relatively speaking, the less affluent are not negative about their situation in the American economy.[20] At the same time, of course, voters can care about matters other than income. Class divisions, therefore, may be relatively muted in the United States simply because voters put a higher priority on noneconomic issues.

Race and the Income Gap

Race strongly influences the income gap. Among whites, economic status has become more important in structuring presidential voting behavior over the past half century: the gap in Democratic support between upper-income whites and lower-income whites has increased since the 1950s. White voters in the bottom third of income distribution have become more loyal in their support of Democratic presidential candidates during this time, whereas those in the higher third have become more likely to support Republicans.[21]

This suggests that, even though Democratic presidential candidates have lost support among white voters over the past half century, those losses have been concentrated among relatively affluent white voters. The net decline in Democratic identification among poor whites during these years is entirely attributable to the Democratic Party's loss of its once dominant position in the South. Although the erosion of Democratic identification among low-income whites is entirely concentrated in the South, the growing disparity in Democratic attachments between lower-income whites and higher-income whites appears in both the South and the rest of the country.[22] Thus, even though culture may have displaced class as an analytical

category in American political debate, class is still unquestionably an extremely critical component of American politics.[23]

Individual Versus Aggregate Behavior

An ironic feature of the income gap in the United States is the difference between individual and aggregate behavior. At the individual level, the more
income one makes, the more likely one is to vote Republican. But this is not
the case at the aggregate level: it is the Democrats who do better in wealthier states. Blue states have higher average incomes than red states. This does
not mean, however, that wealthier people are more Democratic. Democrats
win the rich states, but rich people tend to vote more Republican. Even
though the rich states have become more strongly Democratic over time,
rich voters have remained consistently more Republican than voters on the
lower end of the income scale.[24]

The poor people in red states tend to be Democrats, and the rich people
in blue states tend to be Republicans, but the wealthiest states tend to be disproportionately Democratic. The poor people in most Republican-leaning
states tend to be Democrats, while the rich people in most Democratic-
leaning states tend to be Republicans. Income matters, but geographical
context also matters. Individual income is a positive predictor and state average income is a negative predictor of Republican voting. Of the wealthiest ten states, only one (Alaska) voted Republican for president in either
2008 or 2012, and of the poorest ten states, only one (New Mexico) voted
for Obama. This trend can also be seen at the county level. Some of the
lowest-income counties in the United States cast overwhelming Republican
votes. These highly Republican but relatively poor counties can be found in
a number of states, including Georgia, Illinois, Colorado, Maryland, Michigan, Minnesota, New York, and Texas.[25]

In low-income states such as those in the South, richer people are significantly more likely to vote Republican. In richer states, however, income is
not as strong a predictor of individual votes. Within any state, Republican
support increases with income; at the same time, the Democrats do better
in richer states. This is partly due to the fact that wealthy people in wealthy

states are socially and economically more liberal than rich people in poor states. In poor states, rich people are very different from poor people in political preferences. The cultural differences among the states are a result of the differences among the richer people in these states. Being in a red or blue state, therefore, matters more for rich than for poor voters. As a result, economic issues are more salient in poorer states. Conversely, in richer states voters are more likely to follow noneconomic cues. Thus, contrary to public perception, it is richer Americans in richer parts of the country who are most likely to vote based on cultural issues. Culture and religion are more important predictors of vote choice among the rich than among the poor. The country is thus polarized in two ways: economically between the rich and the poor and culturally between upper-income Americans in red areas and those in blue areas.[26]

The Income Gap in the 2008 and 2012 Elections

The income gap in the 2008 and 2012 presidential elections was generally similar to what it had been for decades: the likelihood of voting Republican steadily increased with family income. Even though Obama won 60 percent of the vote of those making less than $50,000 in both 2008 and 2012, he won only 49 percent of those making more than $50,000 in 2008, a figure that dropped to 45 percent in 2012. One aspect of the income gap in 2008 and 2012 that differentiates it from previous elections is that the vote of those making more than $50,000 varied very little as income went up. In fact, Obama won close to the same percentage of the vote among those making more than $100,000 than he did among those making between $50,000 and $100,000. In every other presidential election since 1980, the wealthiest group measured in exit polls voted strongly for the Republican nominee, never giving him less than 55 percent of the vote. To put it in perspective, when George H. W. Bush won the presidency in 1988 by 7 points nationally, he carried those making more than $100,000 by a 2 to 1 margin. Thus, from a historical perspective, Obama did very well for a Democratic presidential candidate among the wealthy, especially in 2008.

The size of the income gap in 2008 and 2012 varied significantly by state. The largest income gap in both elections occurred in Mississippi. Following Mississippi generally were other southern states, particularly in 2008. The smallest income gaps generally occurred in western and New England states. Oregon, in fact, had a reverse income gap in 2012 (the only state to do so in either 2008 or 2012), as Oregonians with a family income of more than $100,000 were actually more likely to vote for Obama than Oregonians with a family income of less than $50,000. The wide income gap variation at the state level in both 2008 and 2012 contradicts previous findings that most states have cleavages on the order of that for the United States as a whole.[27] Within-state income stratification appears to be more a red state phenomenon as red states—especially those in the South—generally have larger income gaps than blue states.

Beginning with the civil rights movement, there was a change in partisanship in the South from inverse class polarization, in which higher-income individuals were more likely to vote Democratic, to the normal class polarization seen in the rest of the country. Class-based partisanship is not only a reality in the South, but it is also now considerably stronger in the South than in the rest of the country.[28] In 2008 and 2012 the gap between high- and low-income voters was greater in the South than in any other region, but because high-income voters in the South were much more supportive of the Republican presidential nominee than nonsouthern high-income voters were, McCain and Romney, respectively, won the region easily.[29]

State differences in income stratification are almost entirely a result of differences in how the wealthy vote. Nationally, a rise in income at the individual level leads to an increasing tendency to vote Republican. But this is not the case for every state. When we compare the extreme income gaps in 2012 of Mississippi and Oregon, what is most notable is that though there is a huge difference between the states' vote among those making more than $100,000—in 2012 Obama won 64 percent of this income group in Oregon but only 23 percent in Mississippi—there is very little difference between the states among those making less than $50,000: in 2012 Obama won 59 percent of this income group in Oregon, close to his 54 percent tally among this group in Mississippi. In most states both the Republican and Democratic parties move to the left or right depending upon the ideological composition of the state. In Oregon, however, the Democrats are relatively liberal and the Republicans relatively conservative.[30] This reinforces the notion that income is not the primary determinant of ideology. It is the poorer eastern part of Oregon that is the most conservative and the base for the Republican Party in the state. In Mississippi those identifying themselves as Democrats are relatively conservative, reinforcing the political stratification of the state on the basis of income.

In both 2008 and 2012 if only poor people's votes had been counted, Barack Obama would have won in an electoral landslide, and if only rich people's votes had been counted, the Republican candidate (John McCain in 2008, Mitt Romney in 2012) would have won overwhelmingly. Figures 2-2, 2-3, and 2-4 display Electoral College maps in 2008 and 2012 for different income groups.[31] Of those with a family income of less than $50,000, Obama won forty-three states in 2008 and thirty-eight states in 2012, with the states McCain and Romney won among this income group consisting of only 39 and 65 Electoral College votes, respectively (see Figure 2-2).

FIGURE 2-2   Electoral College Maps of 2008 and 2012 Presidential Votes: Income < $50,000

2008		2012	
Obama	499	Obama	473
McCain	39	Romney	65

Source: Exit polls, 2008–2012.

FIGURE 2-3   Electoral College Maps of 2008 and 2012 Presidential Votes: Income $50,000–$100,000

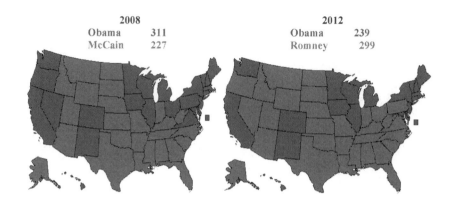

<table>
<tr><td>2008</td><td></td><td>2012</td><td></td></tr>
<tr><td>Obama</td><td>311</td><td>Obama</td><td>239</td></tr>
<tr><td>McCain</td><td>227</td><td>Romney</td><td>299</td></tr>
</table>

Source: Exit polls, 2008–2012.

Among middle-class Americans with family incomes between $50,000 and $100,000, the Electoral College map looks much as it does for the electorate as a whole in 2008 (see Figure 2-3). Among all the states that Obama won in the 2008 general election, he won all in this income group with the exceptions of Florida, Indiana, and North Carolina. The map for 2012, however, makes clear that Obama did noticeably worse among this middle-class group, as he lost a number of states among this group that he won overall, including Florida, Nevada, Ohio, Oregon, Pennsylvania, and Virginia.

Among those making more than $100,000 a year, the results look quite a bit different from the actual Electoral College maps of 2008 and 2012 (see Figure 2-4). Outside the Democratic base of the Northeast and West Coast, Obama won only a handful of states among this income group in 2008 and none in 2012, and overall McCain and Romney won states totaling a solid majority of the Electoral College in both elections.

The economy unquestionably played an important role in both the 2008 and 2012 presidential elections. In both elections the economy was much on voters' minds, and in 2008 economic issues helped to decide the election for Obama. A traditional economic retrospective voting theory—voters

FIGURE 2-4   Electoral College Maps of 2008 and 2012 Presidential Votes: Income > $100,000

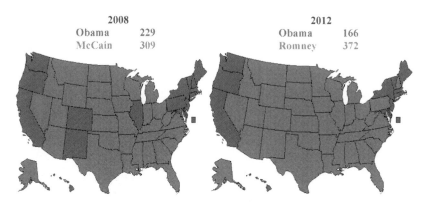

2008		2012	
Obama	229	Obama	166
McCain	309	Romney	372

Source: Exit polls, 2008–2012.

disapprove of past economic conditions and vote against the government—serves well as an explanation for Obama's 2008 victory. According to 2008 exit polls, those who believed that they were better off than they had been four years previously voted 60 percent for McCain, while those who believed that they were worse off voted an overwhelming 71 percent for Obama. Of those who were "very worried" about the direction of the nation's economy the next year, 60 percent voted for Obama, while those who were "not too worried" voted 69 percent for McCain. As a voter's assessment of national economic conditions in 2008 migrated from "ok" to "much worse," the probability of an Obama vote rose as much as 43 percent, given conscious attribution of economic responsibility to the Republican incumbent. Further evidence of economic voting in 2008 can be seen with voters' views of the importance of unemployment. Those who saw reducing unemployment as a first priority overwhelmingly supported Obama. Those who gave it a low priority supported McCain by a large margin.[32] This is consistent with the finding that higher unemployment tends to increase the vote shares of Democratic candidates.[33] As the incumbent president with a muddling economy in 2012, however, Obama could not look to economic conditions to bolster his candidacy: of the more than three-fourths of the electorate who said that the economy was either "poor" or "not so good," he won only 38 percent of that vote.

None of the economic problems that shadowed the 2008 and 2012 presidential elections were distributed evenly throughout the nation. Some places fared poorly, while others were comparatively untouched. For example, the nation's housing crisis was not geographically uniform because the rapid rise of housing prices was uneven. Also, the national jobless rate reached a much higher level than the national average in some locales, notably Nevada. The depth of the recession in particular states in 2008 may have played a role in the Obama victory. Of the six states voting for Bush in 2004 that had an unemployment rate of 9.4 percent or higher as of March 2009, five switched in the 2008 election to the Democratic ticket: North Carolina, Nevada, Florida, Indiana, and Ohio. The only holdout was South Carolina.[34]

Income and Public Policy Preferences

As is the case with vote choice, there is a clear ideological divide in the United States on the basis of income. Those in the lower third of the income range tend to identify themselves as being to the ideological left of other incomes, whereas those in the higher third of the income range disproportionately see themselves as being to the ideological right (see Figure 2-5). Though the differences are not dramatic, there is a correlation with income level and ideological self-identification: the wealthier one is, the more conservative one tends to view oneself. In 2008 the mean ideological leanings of the middle third were almost precisely between the views of the lowest third and the wealthiest third, which is a bit to the right of center, but from 2008 to 2012 the middle third moved to the right more than the other income groups and in 2012 was much closer to the upper third ideologically than to the lower third. This is a change from the 1970s, when the middle class was clearly segmented into relatively straightforward liberal, conservative, and centrist groups. By the 1990s, however, this clear segmentation had largely broken down as middle-class Americans increasingly considered themselves conservative.[35]

FIGURE 2-5   Income and Ideology

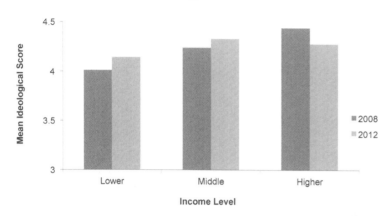

Definition: Self-Identification Scale from 1 to 7, with 1 = most liberal and 7 = most conservative.
Source: ANES 2008 and 2012 datasets.

At the same time, there is only a small difference among those in differ-ent income groups in regard to their concern for equality.[36] There is no clear relationship between class and concern for equality broadly defined; in fact, those with lower incomes are the least likely to be concerned with equality. Thus, even though class divisions have intensified since the 1970s, concern for inequality has not become differentiated on the basis of income. This is a consequence of "equality" being interpreted broadly; racial and gender equality, for example, may be what many Americans associate with the term "equality." Specific concern for economic inequality, however, is strongly re-lated to income, as we can see by looking at economic policy preferences by income group.

The Income Gap in Economic Issues

The income gap is undeniably most pronounced on economic issues (see Fig-ure 2-6). Views on income redistribution are significantly influenced by one's income, and as a result economic distribution and politics in modern democ-racies are intimately related.[37] Today there are large preference gaps between low- and high-income Americans on economic issues. Some economic is-sues, such as preferences on aid to the poor and health insurance, may be directly related to respondents' differing economic interests. Other economic

FIGURE 2-6   The Income Gap: Economic Issues

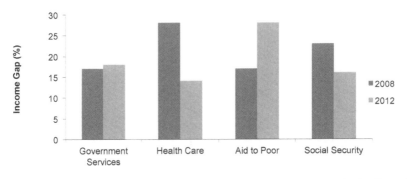

Definitions: Income gap = largest differential among lower, middle, and upper thirds of household income. Government services = government should provide more services. Health care = favor universal health insurance. Aid to poor = aid to the poor should be increased. Social Security = favor Social Security invested in stocks and bonds.
Source: ANES 2008 and 2012 datasets.

issues, however, appear to have an indirect connection to economic interests as reflected in the greater appeal of free markets to the affluent and the greater openness of low-income Americans to government regulation.[38]

On economic issues, wealthier Americans are more libertarian, seeking a less activist government. On government services in general, Americans in the higher third of family income are noticeably less likely than those in the lower third to believe that the government should provide more services. These figures are closely related to views on aid to the poor, as wealthier Americans are far less generous regarding increasing aid to the poor. There is also a strong relationship between income and support for universal health insurance as poorer Americans are much more likely to favor universal health insurance than wealthier Americans, though possibly as a consequence of political fallout from health care reforms (so-called Obamacare) enacted in 2010, this relationship was not as strong in 2008 and 2012. This is consistent with a previous finding that low-income Americans are more likely to support employer health insurance mandates.[39]

That those in the lowest third of income would be more supportive of universal health insurance is not surprising because lower-income Americans are the least likely to have health insurance. The same logic can be applied to Social Security. Lower-income Americans—who disproportionately rely on the income the program provides in retirement—are staunchly supportive of Social Security. There is little support among lower-income Americans for privatizing elements of Social Security. In both 2008 and 2012 less than three-tenths of those in the lower third of income favored putting Social Security in stocks and bonds. Among those in the higher third—who are much less likely to rely on the program's benefits after retirement—about two-fifths in 2008 and 2012 supported at least partial privatization of Social Security. Thus, with Social Security—as is the case in health insurance—economic self-interest tends to mean that people with higher incomes have more conservative views and those with lower incomes have more liberal views.

Although there is little difference among income groups regarding their concern for equality broadly defined, there are substantial differences in the beliefs, values, and policy preferences among income groups with regard to economic issues and economic equality. There are important ideological underpinnings to this, as people who identify themselves as liberal tend to place a higher priority on achieving social and economic equality.[40] This disparity is also due in part to different beliefs about the ability to succeed in the United States. In 2004, for example, while 66 percent of those who voted for George Bush believed that everyone had the "opportunity to succeed in America," this figure was only 17 percent for John Kerry voters.[41]

The enormous economic inequality that existed prior to World War II declined measurably after the war. This was the result of an increase in real incomes that was experienced disproportionately by lower-income groups. At the same time that inequality was declining, government was enacting policies (such as increasing funds for the food stamp program, creating Medicare and Medicaid, and creating the Pell Grant program) designed to create a safety net and reduce economic risk. The consequence was a widespread belief that political divisions based on class were no longer politically significant.[42] The story of postwar America was largely seen to be the story of a new social reality of affluence that changed Americans' political values.[43]

Since the 1970s, however, there has been an unmistakable rise in inequality.[44] It began increasing in the 1970s as the affluent began experiencing significant growth in incomes while those with more modest incomes were realizing no growth. This concentration of income gains at the top of the economic ladder was the result of major policy shifts in favor of those at the top.[45] It may also have been a consequence of elected officials being unresponsive to the policy preferences of low-income citizens,[46] though this conclusion is disputed by some.[47] Economic inequality has been found to be self-reinforcing because it generates political inequities that prevent the poor from using the democratic process to push for government action that would increase their well-being and reduce economic inequities.[48]

Regardless of causation, this increase in inequality has resulted in a number of economic divides in American society, including differences in the quality of (and access to) education, health care, and pensions. As inequality has intensified, class divisions have increasingly influenced Americans' vote choice.[49] This escalating income inequality keeps economic issues relevant, allows polarization to continue,[50] and corresponds with a more conservative public mood on economic issues that has worked to the advantage of the Republican Party since Ronald Reagan's election in 1980. A conservative public mood tends to lead to Republican control of the presidency, which leads to conservative economic policies, which in turn lead to increased inequality.[51]

To a large extent, the American public is aware of this increase in inequality. In the 2008 ANES survey, respondents from all income groups overwhelmingly said that inequality was larger than it had been twenty years earlier.[52] Yet that does not mean that upper-income Americans want government to try to rectify it. As their policy preferences on economic issues demonstrate, upper-income Americans are far from supportive of the government adopting egalitarian economic policy measures. The perception that inequality was getting worse and that it was being met with indifference by the wealthy was the dominant ethos of the Occupy Wall Street protest movement that began in 2011. Proclaiming, "We are the 99 percent," Occupy Wall Street protesters asserted that the top 1 percent in income were unfairly advantaged in the American political and economic systems. On the other end of the political spectrum, the dislike of redistribution programs by the relatively well-off financially can be seen in the dramatic rise of the Tea Party as an electoral force after Barack Obama was elected and began promoting egalitarian measures. Not only are Tea Party supporters, who tend to be wealthier than other Americans on average, inclined to think that economic issues should take precedence over social issues, but these supporters also are strong opponents of the government adopting policies to help reduce economic inequality.[53]

The Income Gap in Domestic and Foreign Policy Issues

Wealthier Americans, however, are not always more conservative than other income groups.[54] On immigration, for example, higher-income Americans are actually the least likely to support a reduction in immigration levels, and as a result the income gap on immigration is not that large (see Figure 2-7). Yet on gun control and environmental regulation, wealthier Americans do tend to lean to the right of those with lower incomes, though not to the degree that exists on economic issues. This suggests that on noneconomic domestic policy, wealthier Americans are not consistently more conservative than others, and when they do lean to the right of other income groups, it is not nearly

FIGURE 2-7   The Income Gap: Domestic and Foreign Policy Issues

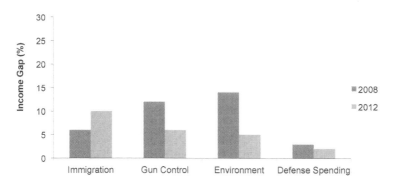

Definitions: Income gap = largest differential among lower, middle, and upper thirds of household income. Immigration = immigration levels should be reduced. Gun control = buying a gun should be made more difficult. Environment = favor increased regulation to protect the environment. Defense spending = defense spending should be reduced.
Source: ANES 2008 and 2012 datasets.

to the degree that exists in economic policy. The income gap, therefore, tends to be greater on economic issues than on noneconomic domestic policy.

The Income Gap in Values and Social Issues

A similar lack of polarization on income grounds can be seen in defense spending, an issue on which there is not much of a difference in policy preferences among the varying income groups. Higher-income Americans are inclined to be slightly more supportive of defense cuts than other income groups, but the diminutive differences among the income groups indicate that Americans' views on defense spending do not appear to differ significantly on the basis of income.[55]

Previous findings suggest that high-income Americans, though more conservative on economic issues, tend to be more liberal on social issues.[56] On creationism and stem cell research, for example, there are large preference gaps between high- and low-income Americans.[57] This relationship can also be seen on abortion (see Figure 2-8). Those in the wealthiest third are less likely than other income groups to believe that abortion should never be permitted or permitted only in cases of rape and incest, while the poorest third are the most likely to take the prolife position. This is consistent with previous findings that poorer Americans are less supportive of abortion rights than the more affluent are.[58] Paradoxically, women of lower incomes tend to be stronger in their opposition to the right to an abortion even though most women who obtain an abortion are of low income.[59]

Those with higher incomes, however, are not consistently more liberal on some contentious social issues. Those with higher incomes tend to be less tolerant of people with different moral standards. Upper-income Americans' moral traditionalism can be seen in their views on gay marriage, where those in the higher third of the income range were less likely to support gay marriage than those in the lower third. Thus, on two of the most contentious social issues of the day—abortion and gay marriage—upper- and lower-income Americans have preferences in opposite ideological directions: those of higher income were the most supportive of abortion rights by a small margin, and those of lower income were the most supportive of gay

FIGURE 2-8   The Income Gap: Values and Social Issues

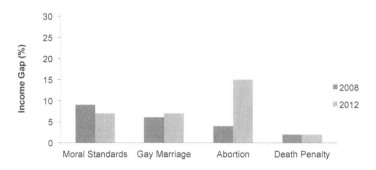

Definitions: Income gap = largest differential among lower, middle, and upper thirds of household income. Moral standards = should be more tolerant of people with different moral standards. Gay marriage = agree that gays should be allowed to marry. Abortion = abortion should never be permitted/permitted only in cases of rape and incest. Death penalty = favor death penalty.
Source: ANES 2008 and 2012 datasets.

marriage (albeit by a small margin). The lack of a discernible relationship between social issues and income is reinforced by the fact that on another divisive social issue—the death penalty—there is virtually no difference between this issue and income level. The core values of Americans thus appear to be similar regardless of income.[60] On the one hand, the relatively higher education levels of those with higher incomes might push them to more liberal positions on social issues. On the other hand, that those with higher incomes are more religious than those with lower incomes may push them in a more conservation direction on social issues: in both 2008 and 2012 those in the lower-income third were about 8 points more likely never to attend religious services than those in the upper-income third.[61]

Regardless of causation, the income gap is clearly much more pronounced on economic issues than on domestic policy and social issues. To many this would seem to be logical: people are simply reacting to their own economic best interests.

Yet despite the strong relationship between income and economic policy preferences, many allege that cultural issues—not economic issues— are becoming the principle mechanism by which Americans decide how to vote. By increasingly raising issues related to moral traditionalism, the

Republican Party has redefined itself. This has led people to openly question whether this shift has been good for the party and for the country. In his book *What's the Matter with Kansas?* journalist Thomas Frank suggests that the much-proclaimed culture war is simply a means to an end for the Republicans. The primary goal of Republicans, he argues, is to pass legislation beneficial to the wealthy and the powerful interests that support them, but the party needs the culture war to keep the support of voters whose economic interests suffer with Republican policies.[62] Republicans thus have duped poorer Americans into voting against their own economic interests by framing politics on the basis of cultural wedge issues. To Frank, the successes of the conservative movement derive from the fact that low- and moderate-income voters vote not according to their pocketbooks but according to social issues.

This argument is supported by the actions of Republicans after winning the 2004 presidential election. Instead of focusing on moral issues, they first initiated bankruptcy reform and championed Social Security privatization, issues that were hardly discussed at all during the campaign. A problem with Frank's argument, however, is that working-class Americans—even in Kansas—are actually even more relatively committed to the Democratic Party than in the past.[63] Income, in fact, is a good predictor of partisanship even among socially conservative Christians: low-income Christians do not completely ignore their economic interests and as a result do not support Republicans as much as Christians with higher incomes do.[64]

The Education Gap

Education, like income, is a measure of social status. At first it may seem redundant once we have taken income into account because income is highly correlated with education level. Yet the years of education one has dictate neither one's occupation nor one's perception of that occupation's prestige. Those with many years of formal education may work in blue-collar professions, and those with little formal education may become successful business entrepreneurs.

Formal education provides citizens with the tools for doing democracy. More formal education increases the likelihood of citizens engaging in individual political actions such as voting and trying to influence the vote. Education increases the amount of raw information made available, in conjunction with intellectual tools to organize this information. Education also instills a sense of civic responsibility, the idea of voting as a duty. At the same time it imparts a feeling of confidence in one's ability to understand politics and to do something about it.[65] As the proportion of college graduates in the voting-age population increases, the electorate may well become more ideologically sophisticated, possibly generating greater interest in politics.

Certainly, education influences one's views on a number of important public policy issues. Among the largest education divides is in regard to gay rights. The educational effect on gay rights, however, differs considerably by partisan identification. For self-identified Democrats, views of homosexuality are highly dependent on education level, but for Republicans there is little relationship with education.[66]

There is a substantial education gap in contemporary American politics, but, importantly, the education gap is considerably different from the income gap. Whereas with income the more money one makes, the more likely one is to vote Republican, there is not a linear trend with education and partisanship. Rather, Democrats tend to do best among those with the highest and the lowest levels of education and Republicans do best among those in the middle of the education spectrum (see Figure 2-9). Thus, whereas the income gap is linear, the education gap is curvilinear. Since the 1980s those with a postgraduate education have become significantly more likely to support Democrats and have become the most likely to support Democratic presidential candidates. In 1988 the Democratic presidential nominee, Michael Dukakis, lost postgraduates by 2 percent, but Barack Obama won this group by 18 points in 2008 and 13 points in 2012, easily his best group education-wise. Republican presidential candidates, in contrast, have done best among those with some college or a bachelor's degree (but not a postgraduate degree): in every presidential election since 1980, these education levels have given the most support to the Republican nominee.

FIGURE 2-9   Partisan Vote for President by Education

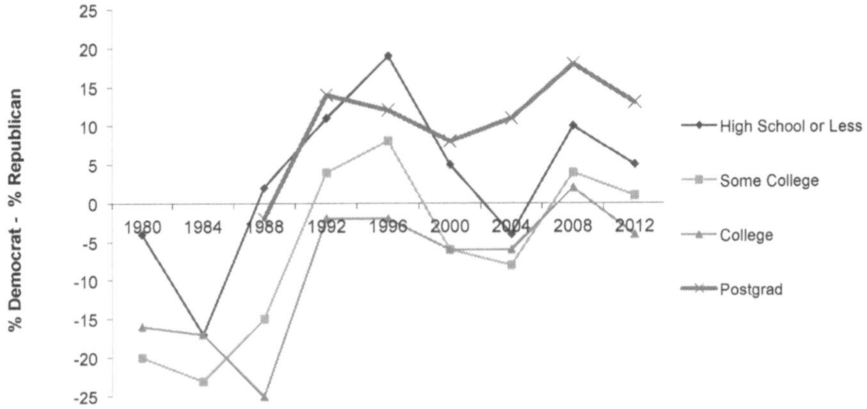

Source: Exit polls, 1980–2012.

The Democrats' strength among well-educated voters is strongest among those with household incomes of less than $75,000—the incomes of teachers, social workers, and nurses. The Republicans still disproportionately have the support of high-income voters, but these are conservatives of a different sort than a generation ago.[67]

At the state level in 2008 and 2012, of the ten states with the highest proportion of college-educated adults, all ten voted for Obama. Of the ten states with the lowest proportion of college-educated adults, Obama won only two (Indiana and Nevada) in 2008 and one (Nevada) in 2012. The three states with the lowest proportion of college-educated adults—West Virginia, Mississippi, and Idaho—were all states Obama lost badly both years.

The Significance of the Income Gap

It may be that some people's policy preferences, particularly those of the rich, matter more than others'.[68] The relative political power of those with higher incomes versus those with lower incomes can be vividly seen in voter turnout rates: those in the higher third of income consistently vote at rates considerably higher than those in the lower third (see Figure 2-10). In every presidential election from 1980 to 2004, those in the higher-income third had self-reported voter turnout rates at least 24 points more than those in the lower-income third. Though Barack Obama's presidential runs encouraged poorer Americans (particularly poorer African Americans) to vote at higher rates in 2008 and 2012, the difference in voter turnout rates between the higher-income third and lower-income third was still in double digits. This is consistent with previous findings that working-class identifiers in the United States consistently display lower levels of involvement in politics.[69] High abstention and large differences between the rates of electoral participation of richer and poorer citizens are caused by high levels of economic inequality.[70] Citizens of states with greater income inequality are less likely to vote, and that inequality increases income bias in the electorate.[71] That richer Americans are more likely to vote indicates the political importance of politicians appealing to them and suggests the possibility of a public policy class bias in favor of the interests of the wealthy.

Such a trend—which is unique to the United States among industrialized democracies—has the potential to magnify inequality if public policy is made for the relative benefit of those with higher incomes because they are more likely to politically participate. This class bias in American politics has increased as inequality has become more pronounced. Part of the increased class bias in voter turnout results from a decline of unions.[72] This

FIGURE 2-10   Voter Turnout Rates in Presidential Elections by Income

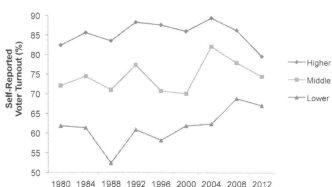

Source: ANES, 1980–2012.

class bias, however, is not uniform across the country: states with restrictive voter registration laws are much more likely to have an upper-class turnout bias.[73] Though higher overall turnout has been found to benefit the Democrats, Democratic advantages from higher turnout have steadily ebbed since 1960.[74] This has occurred even as income inequality in the United States has grown, suggesting the increasing prominence of noneconomic issues in voter choices.

The relative importance of noneconomic issues in understanding the income gap, however, is a matter of much debate. Economic issues obviously play an important role in the income gap: the wealthy tend to favor economically conservative measures that would benefit them individually. On some noneconomic issues, however, wealthier Americans are to the left of other income groups; as noted previously, this is the case with abortion, for example.

The relative importance of economic issues vis-à-vis noneconomic issues poses interesting dilemmas for the Republican and Democratic parties. The Republican Party contains both socially conservative and socially liberal groups, though both historically tended to be probusiness. The increasing dominance of social conservatives, however, has reshaped the Republican Party, driving some social liberals away from the party. At the same time, many economically liberal but socially conservative Americans have moved from the Democrats toward the Republicans.

Until 1980 populists and big business had been at loggerheads at least since the Andrew Jackson administration. William Jennings Bryan's "Cross of Gold" speech at the Democratic Convention of 1896 symbolized the opposition of southern and western Populists to the eastern financial interests that supported Republican William McKinley for president. Later, Bryan's fundamentalist attack on evolution at the Scopes trial symbolized a commitment among many Populists to conservative social ideology. With the election of Reagan as president in 1980, Republicans were able to form a marriage of convenience between populists and economic conservatives, in opposition to the federal government as sponsor of the social changes of the 1960s and 1970s. Thus, the Republican Party put together and has maintained a coalition that includes both populists and probusiness interests, both Bryan and McKinley. Although George W. Bush reflected McKinley's economic views, he was closer to Bryan in social values.[75]

It has been suggested that the decreasing significance of economic issues might cause the Republican Party to adopt policies analogous to those proposed by Bryan in 1896: populist and anticorporate.[76] The Democratic Party might then appeal to probusiness social liberals, with the party taking on the mantel of Abraham Lincoln. Though such a realignment of the electorate might on its face seem to work to the benefit of the Democrats, this would not necessarily be the case as it might cost the Democrats the votes of poorer voters. The Democrats have developed a substantial electoral base in recent years due to the increase of inequalities in American society. Not only has the distribution of income become more unequal since the 1970s, but inequalities among communities—of tax burdens, of access to higher education, of health care and pensions—have also grown considerably. Less affluent Americans have not necessarily been sharing in the nation's prosperity. The result is that lower-income Americans have become more Democratic in their partisan preferences.[77] Consequently, the historic populist image of the Democrats still holds true today: most Americans, even evangelical Christians, still view the Democrats as the party of the people.[78]

A less pronounced income gap would imply that noneconomic issues have trumped economic issues as the main division between the Democratic and Republican parties. This would suggest the creation of a partisan realignment in which the parties would be defined largely by their stances on noneconomic issues. This, however, remains far from the case today. Simply put, the income gap unquestionably remains an important feature of American politics. Despite the popular stereotype of Barak Obama, Nancy Pelosi, and other Democrats representing wealthy elites, from an income perspective the base of the Democratic Party remains those with lower incomes. The income gap is in part a result of cultural divides among those of different levels of income. Economic issues, however, still continue to be the primary motivating factor in determining the political preferences of the wealthy relative to the poor.

Notes

1. Nolan McCarty, Keith T. Poole, and Howard Rosenthal, *Polarized America: The Dance of Ideology and Unequal Riches* (Cambridge, MA: MIT Press, 2006), 98–101.

2. Michael S. Lewis-Beck, William G. Jacoby, Helmut Norpoth, and Herbert F. Weisberg, *The American Voter Revisited* (Ann Arbor: University of Michigan Press, 2008), 338–342.

3. William Jennings Bryan delivered the "Cross of Gold" speech when accepting the Democratic nomination for president in 1896. In his address, Bryan decried the gold standard, concluding the speech by proclaiming, "You shall not crucify mankind upon a cross of gold."

4. Mark D. Brewer and Jeffrey M. Stonecash, *Split: Class and Cultural Divides in American Politics* (Washington, DC: CQ Press, 2007), 73–75.

5. Jeffrey M. Stonecash, *Class and Party in American Politics* (Boulder, CO: Westview Press, 2000), 45–47.

6. Andrew Gelman, *Red State, Blue State, Rich State, Poor State* (Princeton, NJ: Princeton University Press, 2008), 46–48.

7. Lewis-Beck et al., *American Voter Revisited*, 342–343.

8. McCarty et al., *Polarized America*, chap. 3.

9. Stonecash, *Class and Party*.

10. Gary C. Jacobson, *A Divider, Not a Uniter: George Bush and the American People* (New York: Longman, 2007), 24.

11. John Coleman, *Party Decline in America: Policy, Politics, and the Fiscal State* (Princeton, NJ: Princeton University Press, 1996).

12. McCarty et al., *Polarized America*, chap. 3.

13. Throughout this book, time series figures such as Figure 2–1 represent the Democratic presidential candidates' percentage of the vote minus the Republican presidential candidates' percentage of the vote, meaning that "net" votes for the Republicans are below the 0 line and "net" votes for Democrats are above the 0 line.

14. Jeffrey M. Stonecash, "The Income Gap," *PS: Political Science and Politics* 39 (2006): 461–465.

15. Larry Bartels, *Unequal Democracy* (New York: Russell Sage, 2008), 86.

16. John W. Burns and Andrew J. Taylor, "A New Democrat?: The Economic Performance of the Clinton Presidency," *Independent Review* 5 (2001): 387–408.

17. Keith T. Poole and Howard Rosenthal, *Congress: A Political-Economic History of Roll Call Voting* (New York: Oxford University Press, 1997).

18. Patrick Fisher, *The Politics of Taxing and Spending* (Boulder, CO: Lynne Rienner, 2009).

19. V. O. Key, *Public Opinion and American Democracy* (New York: Knopf, 1961).

20. Brewer and Stonecash, *Split*, chap. 4.

21. Bartels, *Unequal Democracy*, chap. 3.

22. Ibid.

23. Adolph Reed Jr., "The 2004 Election in Perspective: The Myth of 'Cultural Divide' and the Triumph of Neoliberal Ideology," *American Quarterly* 57 (2005): 1–15.

24. Gelman, *Red State, Blue State*.

25. James G. Gimpel and Jason E. Schuknecht, *Patchwork Nation: Sectionalism and Political Change in American Politics* (Ann Arbor: University of Michigan Press, 2003).

26. Gelman, *Red State, Blue State.*

27. McCarty et al., *Polarized America,* 103–106.

28. Richard Nadeau, Richard G. Niemi, Harold W. Stanley, and Jean-Francois Godbout, "Class, Party, and South/Non-South Differences," *American Politics Research* 32 (2004): 52–67.

29. Thomas F. Schaller, *Whistling Past Dixie* (New York: Simon and Schuster, 2006), 206–208.

30. Nate Silver, "Oregon: Swing State or Latte-Drinking, Prius-Driving Lesbian Commune," May 17, 2008, www.fivethirtyeight.com.

31. Unfortunately, the National Election Pool that was conducted by Edison Research for the 2012 elections did not conduct exit polls in all states, as it had in 2008. As a result, for states without 2012 exit polls, 2008 exit polls were used and adjusted for 2012 assuming a uniform shift across all groups for all Electoral College maps throughout this book.

32. Michael S. Lewis-Beck and Richard Nadeau, "Obama and the Economy in 2008," *PS: Political Science and Politics* 42 (2009): 479–483.

33. John R. Wright, "Unemployment and the Democratic Electoral Advantage," *American Political Science Review* 106 (2012): 685–702.

34. Nate Silver, "Do Blue States Have Higher Unemployment Rates?," April 12, 2009, www.fivethirtyeight.com.

35. Joseph Gerteis, "Political Alignment and the American Middle Class, 1974–1994," *Sociological Forum* 13 (1998): 639–666.

36. According to author calculations of responses to questions V083248 and V085165 in ANES 2008 dataset, 48 percent of those in the lower third of family income thought we "should worry less about equality" while 42 percent of those in the middle third and 45 percent in the higher third agreed with this statement.

37. John E. Roemer, "Distribution and Politics: A Brief History and Prospect," *Social Choice Welfare* 25 (2005): 507–525.

38. Martin Gilvens, "Preference Gaps and Inequality in Representation," *PS: Political Science and Politics* 42 (2009): 335–341.

39. Ibid.

40. John T. Jost, "The End of the End of Ideology," *American Psychologist* 61 (2006): 651–670.

41. Brewer and Stonecash, *Split,* 82.

42. Stonecash, "The Income Gap," 461–465.

43. Brink Lindsey, *The Age of Abundance* (New York: HarperCollins, 2007).

44. Fisher, *Politics of Taxing.*

45. Jacob S. Hacker and Paul Pierson, "Winner-Take-All Politics: Public Policy, Political Organization, and the Precipitous Rise of Top Incomes in the United States," *Politics and Society* 38 (2010): 152–204.

46. Bartels, *Unequal Democracy.*

47. Joseph Daniel Ura and Christopher R. Ellis, "Income, Preferences, and the Dynamics of Policy Responsiveness," *PS: Political Science and Politics* 41 (2008): 785–794.

48. Nathan J. Kelly and Peter K. Enns, "Inequality and the Dynamics of Public Opinion:

The Self-Reinforcing Link Between Economic Inequality and Mass Preferences," *American Journal of Political Science* 54 (2010): 855–870.

49. Stonecash, "The Income Gap," 461–465.

50. Andrew Gelman, *Red State, Blue State,* chap. 8.

51. Nathan Kelly, *The Politics of Income Inequality in the United States* (New York: Cambridge University Press, 2009).

52. There was essentially no difference among those with lower, middle, and higher incomes on the question of whether or not the income gap was more or less than twenty years before, with 83 percent of lower incomes, 82 percent of middle incomes, and 80 percent of higher incomes agreeing that the income gap had grown.

53. Vanessa Williamson, Theda Skocpol, and John Coggin, "The Tea Party and the Remaking of Republican Conservatism," *Perspectives on Politics* 9 (2011): 25–43.

54. Ura and Ellis, "Income, Preferences," 785–794.

55. Peter K. Enns and Christopher Wlezien, "Group Opinion and the Study of Representation," in *Who Gets Represented?,* ed. Peter K. Enns and Christopher Wlezien (New York: Russell Sage, 2011), 1–25.

56. Gary Miller and Norman Schofield, "The Transformation of the Republican and Democratic Party Coalitions in the U.S.," *Perspectives on Politics* 6 (2008): 433–450.

57. Gilvens, "Preference Gaps," 335–341.

58. Brewer and Stonecash, *Split,* 167–169.

59. Melody Rose, *Safe, Legal, and Unavailable? Abortion Politics in the United States* (Washington, DC: CQ Press, 2007).

60. Saundra K. Schneider and William G. Jacoby, "A Culture of Dependence? The Relationship Between Public Assistance and Public Opinion," *British Journal of Political Science* 33 (2003): 213–231.

61. Author calculations of ANES 2008 and 2012 datasets.

62. Thomas Frank, *What's the Matter with Kansas?* (New York: Metropolitan Books, 2004).

63. Bartels, *Unequal Democracy.*

64. McCarty et al., *Polarized America,* 98–101.

65. Lewis-Beck et al., *American Voter Revisited,* 348–352.

66. Andrew Kohut and Bruce Stokes, *America Against the World* (New York: Henry Holt, 2006), 211–212.

67. Gelman, *Red State, Blue State,* 27–29.

68. Enns and Wlezien, "Group Opinion," 1–25.

69. Katherine Cramer, M. Kent Jennings, and Laura Stoker, "The Effects of Social Class Identification on Participatory Orientations Towards Government," *British Journal of Political Science* 34 (2004): 469–495.

70. Eric E. Schattschneider, *The Semisovereign People: A Realist's View of Democracy in America* (New York: Holt, Reinhart, and Winston, 1960).

71. Frederick Solt, "Does Economic Inequality Depress Electoral Participation? Testing the Schattschneider Hypothesis," *Political Behavior* 32 (2010): 285–301.

72. Jan E. Leighley and Jonathan Nagler, "Unions, Voter Turnout, and Class Bias in the U.S. Electorate, 1964–2004," *Journal of Politics* 69 (2007): 430–441.

73. James Avery and Mark Peffley, "Voter Registration Requirements, Voter Turnout, and Welfare Eligibility Policy: Class Bias Matters," *State Politics and Policy Quarterly* 5 (2005): 47–67.

74. Michael D. Martinez and Jeff Gill, "The Effects of Turnout on Partisan Outcomes in U.S. Presidential Elections," *Journal of Politics* 67 (2005): 1248–1274.

75. Miller and Schofield, "The Transformation," 433–450.

76. Ibid.

77. Stonecash, *Class and Party*.

78. Stephen P. Nicholson and Gary M. Segura, "Who's the Party of the People?: Economic Populism and the U.S. Public's Beliefs About Political Parties," *Political Behavior* 34 (2012): 369–389.

3

The Religion Gap

Religion and American Political Behavior

Religion has long been an important feature in American politics. From the nation's founding, religion has influenced Americans' political choices and churches have been an important source for political learning.[1] As early as 1800 Thomas Jefferson had to deal with accusations that he was an atheist, in the late 1800s William Jennings Bryan invoked biblical themes to support his Populist economic prescriptions, and in 1928 and 1960 Al Smith and John Kennedy, respectively, faced strong anti-Catholic sentiments in their presidential runs.[2] The cultural and social conflicts of the 1960s and 1970s marked a turning point in the role religion played in American politics as religiosity, or how religiously devout one is, as opposed to religious denomination, increasingly came to be seen as the moral foundation for political choices. In contemporary American politics the religion gap burst forth with the election of Ronald Reagan as president in 1980 when the Christian right became mobilized and the traditionally passive role of Baptists and evangelicals in politics ended. Since then religion has played a focal role in American politics, and what it means to be a Democrat or a Republican today is increasingly defined on the basis of religiosity.

Americans are much more likely than Europeans to say that religion is very important in their lives.[3] Consequently, Americans largely expect their elected representatives to be religious as well. Sixty-three percent of Americans have indicated that they would be less likely to support a candidate who doesn't believe in God, and only 3 percent claimed they would be more likely to support such a candidate.[4] One of the most underrepresented groups in Congress, in fact, comprises individuals who claim no religious affiliation.[5] Americans today tend to care less about sectarian affiliation and more generally about whether the candidate believes in God and how that lends itself to a moral framework.[6]

It is thus important to distinguish between two kinds of religious variables: one for group membership and another for beliefs and behavior. There are thus two different types of religion gaps: one based on religious affiliation and another based on actual religiosity. Today the religion gap defined on the basis of worship attendance has become one of the most significant points of division in American politics. Religious traditionalism is a strong predictor of political behavior, at least as strong as traditional independent variables such as social class, occupation, and income.[7] High levels of religious commitment foster particular connections between religion and politics by exposing individuals to special kinds of information.[8]

Religious Affiliation

Historically, any discussion of a "religion gap" in American politics would have focused on the political distinctions among different religious affiliations. Throughout American history voting was shaped by distinct loyalties among different religions. In the mid-twentieth century mainline Protestants supplied most of the Republican Party's leaders and its most loyal voters, while Catholics, Jews, and other religious minorities constituted the backbone of the Democratic Party.[9] The relationship between presidential vote and denomination began to erode in the 1970s. However, since Ronald Reagan was elected president in 1980, vote by religious group has tended to be relatively stable: Protestants have tended to favor Republican presidential candidates, Jews have supported Democratic presidential candidates (usually by overwhelming margins), and Catholics have been a key swing group that in all nine elections from 1980 to 2012 voted more Democratic than Protestants but less than Jews did (see Figure 3-1).

FIGURE 3-1   Partisan Vote for President by Religious Affiliation

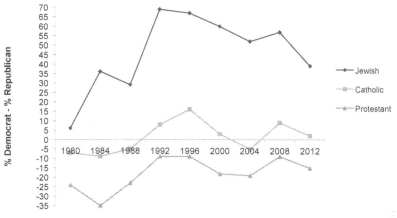

Source: Exit polls, 1980–2012

There is, of course, considerable difference in the relative political importance of religious groups. In 2012 Protestants made up 53 percent of the electorate, while Catholics were 25 percent, Jews (both religious and secular) constituted 2 percent, other faiths made up 7 percent, and those with no religious affiliation were 12 percent. Protestant and Jewish congregations have been losing market share in terms of membership, whereas Catholics, Mormons, and other religions have been gaining.[10]

The potential for religiously based political mobilization among church members is to some extent a function of the type of goals members of the laity attach to their religious beliefs and affiliations. To the extent that clergy can influence the collective missions of their respective congregations, clergy may be able to influence the political behavior of their congregations.[11] At the same time, the more parishioners feel "religiously different" from their neighbors, the greater is their congregational involvement.[12]

Scholars of religion and politics have historically distinguished between mainline Protestants and evangelical Protestants. The former include members of the following churches: Episcopal, Lutheran, Methodist, and Presbyterian. These denominations tend to be theologically moderate. The latter include members of these churches: Assemblies of God, Baptist, Church of Christ, Church of God, Church of the Nazarene, and Pentecostal. These

denominations tend to be theologically conservative.[13] The relationship between the orthodoxy of Protestant denominations and political behavior
has changed considerably, with members of evangelical denominations becoming more Republican relative to their counterparts in mainline denominations.[14] Mainline Protestants, once a strong Republican constituency,
have moved toward the Democrats, producing their highest level of support
for Democrats in recent times. Evangelical Protestants have become one of
the most loyal Republican constituencies.[15] This, however, is a relatively new
development. As late as 1976 Jimmy Carter won 46 percent of the white
evangelical vote.[16]

White evangelicals unquestionably have distinct political attitudes.[17] They
support Republicans as if doing so were an article of their faith: more than
70 percent of white evangelicals align themselves with the Republican Party.
The rise of evangelicals as a political force and their emergence as the main-
stay of the Republican Party have transformed the party. White evangelicals
are approaching a degree of political solidarity within the Republican Party
nearly on par with African Americans and the Democratic Party.[18]

Certainly, the churchgoing habits of those who consider themselves
Protestant varies considerably, and this is reflected in their political views.
In 2012 Protestants who attended church weekly (15 percent of the electorate) voted 70 percent for Mitt Romney while Protestants who did not attend
church weekly (14 percent of the electorate) gave him 55 percent of their
vote. At the same time, there are also important differences between the
political attitudes of black and of white Protestants. Although Obama won
more than 42 percent of the overall Protestant vote, he won only 30 percent
of the white Protestant vote.

The tendency of evangelicals to support Republicans varies according
to social context. Evangelical Christians are spurred to vote Republican in
communities with a greater share of secularists.[19] Public concern with family
decline increased after 1980, with high levels of concern with this decline
concentrated among evangelical Protestants who attended church regularly.[20]
In 2004, for example, evangelicals were at the heart of George W. Bush's reelection coalition, and many apparently cast their ballot for Bush because of

his opposition to gay marriage.[21] Republicans have increasingly used highly selective cues to appeal to religious conservatives. Because these cues are so specific to evangelical culture, however, they pass generally unnoticed by other voters and thus allow Republican candidates to avoid broadcasting very conservative issue positions that may alienate more moderate voters.[22]

A significant number of Americans regard being patriotic and Christian as the same thing. Conservative Protestants have more pride in America than do any other religious or nonreligious social group. Among the roughly one-quarter of Americans who belong to conservative Protestant churches, a large majority believe that the country was founded on Christian principles. Most of these people furthermore think that Christian morality should be the law of the land.[23]

This implies that the faith gap in the United States is large. Religion can become a cultural tag in which the enemy is those not like "us."[24] This, however, cuts both ways. Candidate religious affiliation, for example, plays a role in vote choice because it provides voters with an information cue that allows them to apply social stereotypes of religious affiliations. Voters stereotype evangelicals as more conservative than other candidates, all else being equal. The conservative ideology stereotype in fact puts evangelical candidates at a disadvantage by creating a greater distance between them and the average voter.[25]

Catholics, unlike Protestants, have historically favored the Democrats. The Catholic vote as a distinctive Democratic bloc, however, has vanished as Catholics have become far less reliably Democratic today than they were prior to the 1970s. As a result, Catholics have changed from a stalwart Democratic constituency to a key swing constituency. Yet Catholic religious identification still produces a statistically significant, though small, tendency to vote Democratic in presidential elections.[26] Of the ten states with the highest proportion of Catholics, Barack Obama won nine in both 2008 and 2012, losing only Louisiana in both years.[27] Catholics have swung back to the Democrats in recent years because of the rising number of Hispanic voters who are Catholic. In 2012 Obama won the vote of one-half of Catholics overall even though he won only two-fifths of the white Catholic vote.

Frequent church-attending Catholics have tended to favor Republicans: the Republican presidential candidate won this group in every election from 1980 to 2004, even favoring Methodist George W. Bush over Catholic John Kerry in 2004.[28] In 2012 Catholics who attended mass weekly (11 percent of the overall electorate) gave Obama 42 percent of the vote, a margin that pales compared to his margin among less religious Catholics: Catholics who did not attend weekly (13 percent of the electorate) voted for Obama by a 14-point margin. Compared to Protestants, American Catholics are relatively liberal, even on social issues. For example, although Catholic teaching opposes same-sex marriage, American Catholics support gay marriage more strongly than do Protestants and states with relatively large Catholic populations are more likely to accept homosexual relations.[29]

Anti-Catholicism has long existed in American politics, going back to the nation's founding. The first major-party Catholic nominee for president, Al Smith of New York, got trounced in the 1928 race in part due to the reluctance of many Americans to vote for a Catholic. In 1960 John F. Kennedy became the first (and to date only) Catholic to be elected president, an election in which religion played a major role as some questioned Kennedy's fitness for office on the grounds of his Catholicism. The degree that religious biases played in the election can be seen by the fact that Protestants were more likely to vote for Richard Nixon in communities where Catholics were congregated and Catholics were more likely to support Kennedy in communities where Protestants had a greater share of the population.[30]

Yet one of the most important changes in American politics over the past generation is the evaporation of political differences between Catholics and Protestants. The historical tension between Catholics and Protestants has largely disappeared, as demonstrated by the fact that John Kerry's Catholicism was barely an issue in his run for the presidency in 2004. The likelihood of a general anti-Catholic bias no longer predicts political party identification.[31] White evangelicals today have positive feelings toward Catholics—significantly warmer feelings than those of the religiously nonaffiliated or of secularists toward Catholics.[32] This is partly the result of the increased prominence of abortion as an issue, as evangelicals and devout Catholics share similar antiabortion views. The growth of evangelicalism within the Republican Party has been accompanied by an increase for the party in the percentage of the vote received from regularly attending Catholics.[33]

In 1960 among non-Catholics, those who were religiously more observant were significantly less likely to support John Kennedy. Among Catholics, however, religious commitment in 1960 was associated with much stronger levels of support for Kennedy.[34] Today, however, more observant Catholics vote similarly to religious non-Catholics. Whereas Kennedy did best among Catholics who regularly attended church, Obama and other recent Democratic presidential nominees have done better among Catholics who attended church infrequently.

Kennedy won more than 80 percent of the Catholic vote in 1960, but the next Catholic presidential nominee, John Kerry, did no better among Catholics than among the population as a whole, winning less than 50 percent of the Catholic vote. Essentially, Catholics have so fully assimilated into the larger American culture that they are no longer a distinctive political group.[35]

Jews, in contrast, definitely remain a distinctive political group. In every presidential election since 1984, the Democratic candidate has won more than two-thirds of the Jewish vote. Jews have been solidly in the Democratic camp since the Franklin Roosevelt administration, when they were an important part of his New Deal coalition.

Anti-Semitism has certainly worked against Jewish candidates in the past, but it is much more muted than it used to be. The nomination of Joseph Lieberman as the Democratic vice presidential candidate in 2000, for example, was not unlike John Kennedy's breaking the political barrier against Catholicism. But unlike 1960, in which Kennedy's Catholicism remained controversial, Lieberman's Jewish faith was generally not controversial.[36] Lieberman's religious affiliation did not hurt Al Gore in the 2000 election. Evangelical Christians were found to have had as positive a feeling toward Jews as toward Catholics or mainline Protestants in that election. In fact, of those who could identify both Lieberman's and Gore's religious affiliation,

Christian fundamentalists felt significantly warmer toward Lieberman than Gore, a Southern Baptist. Disapproval of Lieberman came not from Christian fundamentalists but from secularists, who complained that his public professions of faith and piety blurred the line between religion and politics.[37]

Mormons are at the other end of the political spectrum from Jews. Mormon voters are even more Republican than Jewish voters are Democratic. Mormons were overwhelming Republican even before the party's nomination of Mitt Romney, a former Mormon bishop, in 2012. In 2008 John McCain won 76 percent of the Mormon vote, only slightly less than the 78 percent that Romney carried in 2012.[38] In Utah, where Mormons are three-fourths of the population, Obama won less than 20 percent of the Mormon vote in 2008. Of the one-quarter of the Utah electorate that was not Mormon, however, Obama won nearly 80 percent of the vote.

The differences in the parties' composition can also be seen in the religious affiliation of those who voted in the 2008 presidential primaries: whereas Mormons made up 90 percent of the Republican primary voters, they made up only 37 percent of the Democratic primary voters in Utah.[39] Voters with no religious affiliation made up 24 percent of the Democratic primary voters in Utah and only 2 percent of the Republican primary voters. Utah politics, therefore, is extremely polarized by religion, and the religion gap in Utah is larger than anywhere else in the country. In Utah the majority of the Mormon population is overwhelmingly Republican while the majority of the non-Mormon population is overwhelmingly Democratic.

Religiosity

Though the religious affiliation gap has long been a defining characteristic of American politics, today the more noteworthy political feature of religion is the religiosity gap. Religion's influence on elections had long been assumed to operate through communitarian ties, with the particular values of different religions generating different voting patterns. Differences within religious groups, however, are now more politically significant than differences among religious groups.[40] Decades ago the Protestant-Catholic affiliation split constituted a dividing line, with Protestants favoring Republicans and

Catholics preferring Democrats. Today, however, the Protestant-Catholic religious affiliation dichotomy is a much weaker measure of religion's influence on political beliefs. Rather, religious commitment and religious belief have more significant effects on political beliefs than religious affiliation does.[41] Instead of being divided along the lines of religious denomination, Americans are increasingly divided by religious devotion.

The religious division between Democrats and Republicans has grown over time, with Republicans becoming more traditionally religious and the Democrats becoming more secular. The current division of the Republican and Democratic parties along religious lines was seen as early as 1972, but this religious cleavage has grown in recent years. The Democratic Party now draws its support disproportionately from the ranks of religious liberals and secularists. Not only is religious replacement within the parties occurring, but also within religious groups Democrats are becoming more culturally liberal relative to Republicans.[42] The religion gap is a logical consequence of the extremely different worldviews of the very religious versus the secularists. The very religious believe that the Bible embodies truth; secularists cannot comprehend that belief. The very religious believe that the Bible tells them how to live; secularists think that humans make morality. The gulf between the two is enormous and is increasingly being played out in the political arena.

Figure 3-2 demonstrates the strong correlation between how often one attends religious services and presidential vote choice: the more often one worships, the more one is likely to vote Republican.[43] This has not always been the case; in 1960, for example, regular churchgoers were actually more Democratic.[44] Since Ronald Reagan was elected president in 1980, however, those who attend religious services at least weekly have strongly supported Republican presidential candidates. Those who never worship have tended to strongly support Democratic candidates. In the 1980s there was only a miniscule difference between those who never attended religious services and those who occasionally did, but since Bill Clinton's initial victory in 1992, those who never attend religious services have been noticeably more Democratic in their presidential preferences than those who occasionally do. Yet those who are occasional worshippers have since 1992 consistently given a majority of their votes to Democratic presidential candidates, making these voters closer in their political preferences to those who never attend religious services than to those who regularly do. This suggests that the real religious divide in the United States today is between those who are regular worshippers and those who are not, not between those who never worship and those who at least occasionally do.

The impact of religious commitment on vote choice is thus growing, with very committed individuals becoming increasingly more likely than their less religious counterparts to vote Republican.[45] Although the genesis of the religion gap lies with Reagan's election, it took about a dozen years to take hold in the mass public.[46] It was not until 1992 that a sustained gap in voting behavior between frequent and less frequent worshippers emerged and the religious attendance gap arose as a clear feature of American voting behavior. Since the Clinton administration, people who are more devout—regardless of denomination—are generally more likely to favor Republicans. At the same time, there is a strong relationship between religious commitment and political engagement. Republican gains among religious white

FIGURE 3-2   Partisan Vote for President by Religious Attendance

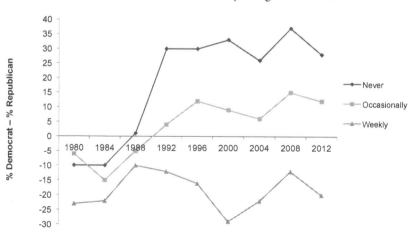

Source: ANES, 1980–1996; exit polls, 2000–2012.

voters have been concentrated among the most politically sophisticated members of the religiously devout.[47]

This increasing political polarization based on religious attendance—often referred to as the "god gap"—came as a surprise to those who had been arguing that secularization in the political sphere was the inevitable wave of the future. Having assumed that religion was retiring to private life, some have became anxious about the emergence of religious faith as a political force.[48] Conservative religious leaders, wanting to maximize their political influence, have argued that the emerging religion gap is evidence that electoral success may depend on a candidate's wooing more religiously observant voters. Whereas the Republican Party is increasingly the home of those encouraged about the public power of religion, the Democratic Party is increasingly the home of voters inclined to a secular worldview.[49] The god gap terminology has attracted attention and controversy because it suggests that Republicans have become the party of America's "believers" and Democrats the party of its "nonbelievers."[50]

Secularists first appeared as a political force within the Democratic Party in 1972. Previously, there was a commitment among elites in both parties to the traditional Judeo-Christian teachings regarding authority, sexual mores, and the family. As the Democratic Party became more secular, however, the Republican Party moved in the other direction and began to be seen as more hospitable to religious traditionalists and less appealing to more secular Republicans.[51] What was at first an intraparty culture war among Democratic elites during the Vietnam War era became by the 1980s an interparty culture war.[52] By the 1980s, therefore, disputes pitting religious "traditionalists" against religious "modernists" had restructured the larger American religious traditions. Traditionalists in all communities began to find more in common with each other than with modernists in their own traditions. Consequently, traditionalists have gravitated toward the Republicans and modernists toward the Democrats.[53]

Secularists today are an important component of the Democratic Party. In terms of their size and party loyalty, secularists are as important to the Democratic Party as organized labor is. Just as the Republican Party has been criticized for being too supportive of fundamentalists, the Democrats have been criticized for being too sympathetic to uncompromising secularists. This poses risks for the Democrats because many more Americans express unfavorable attitudes toward those with no religion than toward evangelical Christians.[54]

The Religion Gap in the 2008 and 2012 Elections

There was an extensive gap in the two-party vote on the basis of religious attendance in the 2008 and 2012 presidential elections. The more religious one was, the more likely one was to vote for the Republican presidential candidate. In both 2008 and 2012 while Obama won three-fifths of the vote of those who never attended religious services, he won less than two-fifths of the vote of those who attended religious services weekly. Though the number of voters in 2008 and 2012 who attended religious services weekly was more than twice the number of those who never attended, Obama won those who occasionally attended services by a large margin, and this group made up more than 40 percent of the electorate in both elections.

Unquestionably, the Republican and Democratic parties are today divided along religious lines. This is particularly evident in the polar extremes of those who are very religious and those who are not religious. Those who considered themselves to have "no religion," for example, gave Obama 75 percent of their vote in 2008 and 62 percent in 2012. At the other extreme, white evangelicals, who composed about 25 percent of the total electorate, gave McCain and Romney about 75 percent of their vote. In every state in the country, white evangelicals voted overwhelmingly for the Republican presidential nominee. Obama's best showing among white evangelicals in any state in either election was the 35 percent he took in Minnesota and Wisconsin in 2008. Of the ten states with the highest proportion of white evangelicals, Obama won only two in 2008: North Carolina and Indiana. These turned out to be the only states he won in 2008 but lost in 2012. The four states where the majority of the electorate was white evangelicals

FIGURE 3-3   Electoral College Maps of 2008 and 2012 Presidential Votes: Non-"White Evangelical" Vote

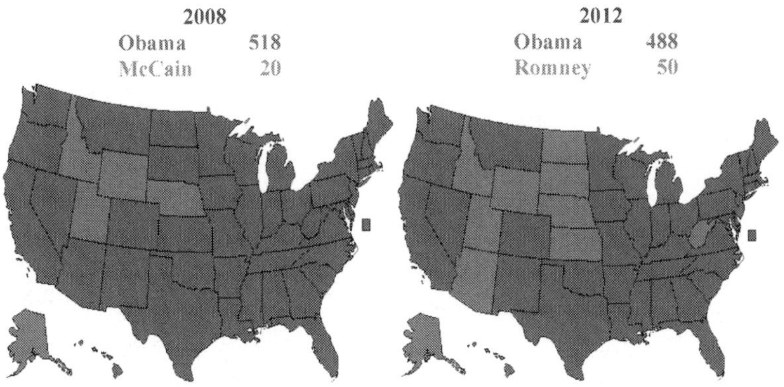

2008		2012	
Obama	518	Obama	488
McCain	20	Romney	50

Source: Exit polls, 2008–2012.

(Arkansas, Oklahoma, West Virginia, and Tennessee) were among the states where the Republicans made the biggest gains from 2004 to 2008.[55]

How important white evangelicals have become to the Republican Party can be seen in Figure 3-3. In an electorate without any white evangelicals, McCain would have won only five small states (worth a total of 20 Electoral College votes) in 2008 and Romney would have won ten states (with a total of 50 Electoral College votes) in 2012. In other words, without the overwhelming support of white evangelicals, McCain and Romney would have lost by a landslide.

States more religious than the national average overall were much more likely to give McCain and Romney their Electoral College votes. Obama won only three states in 2008 (Florida, Indiana, and Virginia) and two states in 2012 (Florida and Virginia) where the percentage of residents who said that religion was very important in their lives was higher than the national norm. At the other extreme, McCain and Romney won only four states (Alaska, Montana, Wyoming, and Arizona) where residents were less religious than the national average.[56]

FIGURE 3-4   Religious Attendance and Ideology

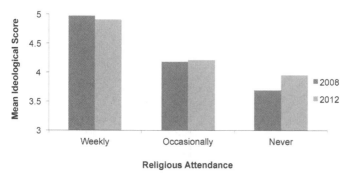

Definition: Self-Identification Scale from 1 to 7, with 1 = most liberal and 7 = most conservative.
Source: ANES 2008 and 2012 datasets.

Religion and Public Policy Preferences

The partisan religion gap bears a strong association with ideology. As Figure 3-4 demonstrates, weekly attendees of religious services see themselves as considerably more conservative than those who attend less than weekly. Those who never attend religious services tend to identify themselves as being relatively left of center. The mean ideological score for occasional attendees is about the average for all Americans.

The ideological preferences of regular worshippers are consistent with their views on equality. Those who attend religious services on a weekly basis are more likely to believe that the country should worry less about equality than those who occasionally or never attend religious services.[57] Whereas a majority of those who worship weekly believed that we should worry less about equality, of those who attended religious services less than weekly only about two-fifths agreed with this sentiment. This is consistent with findings that conservative white Protestants are more likely to prefer individualistic, rather than structural, explanations for racial inequality.[58] One explanation for the exceptionally high religiosity in the United States is that it is one of the world's most unequal postindustrial societies. Exceptionally high levels of economic insecurity in the United States differentiate it from relatively secular Europe.[59]

FIGURE 3-5   The Religion Gap: Economic Issues

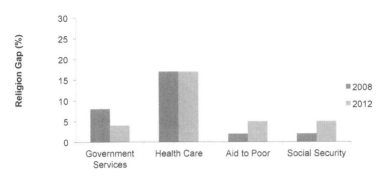

Definitions: Religion gap = largest differential among those who attend religious services weekly, occasionally, and never. Government services = government should provide more services. Health care = favor universal health insurance. Aid to poor = aid to the poor should be increased. Social Security = favor Social Security invested in stocks and bonds.
Source: ANES 2008 and 2012 datasets.

The Religion Gap in Economic Issues

Associated with beliefs on equality, religious attendance appears to influence views on some economic issues (see Figure 3-5). In regard to government services in general, the more religiously devout are less supportive than the less religious. Yet relative to income, religion may lose some of its significance as a vote determinant. Rich churchgoers are much more Republican than poor churchgoers. Among the nonattenders, however, rich and poor alike are solid Democrats. The Democrats' base is thus low-income churchgoers and secular Americans, whereas the Republicans win the votes of middle-class and upper-income churchgoers.[60]

The largest religion gap on economic issues—by a large margin—is on health care. Weekly worshippers are significantly less likely to support universal health insurance than those who occasionally or never attend religious services. While less than two in five of those who regularly attend religious services support universal health insurance, more than half of those who occasionally or never do support it. This may reflect how health care has become more of a cultural wedge issue regarding the proper role of the federal government than an economic issue.

Unlike health care, one's view on increasing aid to the poor has no real relationship with religious attendance. The same is true for Social Security: weekly worshippers are not any more likely than other groups to support partial privatization of Social Security. This view may be related to the relative age of worshippers. Older Americans who are receiving Social Security benefits (or are relatively close to receiving benefits) are more likely to attend religious services than younger age cohorts.

The Religion Gap in Domestic and Foreign Policy Issues

One policy on which those who attend religious services weekly are not notably more conservative than those who worship less often is immigration policy (see Figure 3-6). That those who are more religious are not more supportive of reducing immigration may be due to the fact that many denominations—most noticeably the Catholic Church—are advocates of an inclusive attitude toward immigrants. Also, many recent immigrants to the United States who are supportive of increased immigration, such as Mexican Americans, tend to be relatively religious.

Religiosity does not appear to have much of an impact on attitudes toward gun control. Those who occasionally attend religious services are only somewhat more supportive of increasing the difficulty of buying a gun than those who are less religious. The religious attendance differences on environmental policy, however, are stark. Regular worshippers are significantly less likely to favor increased environmental regulation. But interestingly, most Americans agree with the concept of justifying environmental protection by invoking God as the creator, and even many nonbelievers argue for environmental protection on the basis of God's creation.[61] The large religion gap on environmental regulation suggests that the issue—like health care—has become a cultural wedge issue undergirded by ideology.

In regard to defense spending, regular attendees of religious services tend to be more conservative (less supportive of cutting defense spending) than the population as a whole. More exposure to religion thus may make one somewhat more hawkish on defense. This is consistent with findings that religious views appear to frame some opinions about foreign policy

FIGURE 3-6   The Religion Gap: Domestic and Foreign Policy Issues

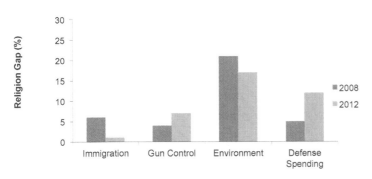

Definitions: Religion gap = largest differential among those who attend religious services weekly, occasionally, and never. Immigration = immigration levels should be reduced. Gun control = buying a gun should be made more difficult. Environment = favor increased regulation to protect the environment. Defense spending = defense spending should be reduced.
Source: ANES 2008 and 2012 datasets.

and explain why Americans advocate a more assertive foreign policy than peoples in other democracies. For example, the concept of a "just war" has many more adherents in the relatively religious United States than in the relatively secular Europe. More than three-fourths of all Americans believe that under some conditions war is justified; only one-fourth of Europeans agree. Also, Americans' attitudes toward Israel are heavily influenced by religion, with one in three Americans who sympathize with Israel saying that their sympathy for the Jewish state comes from their religious beliefs.[62]

Religion and the Cultural Divide

The religious polarization among the parties in contemporary American politics is associated with a growing partisan polarization on cultural issues such as abortion, women's rights, and gay rights. The religious and cultural polarization of party activists is the result of an inability of the parties to foster solutions to cultural policy problems.[63] There is increasingly a polarization of American public culture into distinct moral and religious camps, with one camp adhering to an absolute standard of right and wrong and the other camp embracing a humanistic ethic drawn from personal experience, reason, and science.[64] Disagreements about the appropriate role of religion in American politics are in fact the result of disagreements about the general nature of democratic politics.[65]

Because the Democrats have generally supported a more rigorous interpretation of the Establishment Clause of the First Amendment, which forbids the formation of a state religion, they have been open to attack as "antireligious," even if this is an overly simplistic characterization. But the rising influence of evangelical Protestants, mobilized by abortion, gay marriage, and other social issues, has made explicitly religious political activity an important component of contemporary American political culture.[66]

Opposition to religion in politics, however, is as old as the country itself. In the 1780s Baptists in Virginia were strong supporters of Thomas Jefferson's campaign against financial aid to any church because they feared that such aid would disadvantage their own lay preachers. In the 1840s Congress heeded the call of New England clergymen to honor the Sabbath by ending Sunday mail deliveries, but Jacksonian Democrats quickly reinstated Sunday mail delivery to demonstrate the government's impartiality toward competing religious doctrines.[67] This tradition of separating church and state was still in place as late as the 1960s. In 1968, 53 percent said that "churches should keep out of politics" and 40 percent asserted that "churches should express views." By 2005 this relationship had reversed, with only 44 percent claiming that churches should keep out of politics and 51 percent responding that churches should express views.[68]

The secular instincts of American political institutions are thus increasingly coming under attack. To opponents of secularism, public institutions politically marginalize religious citizens except when they agree with secularism. Justification for government support of a particular public policy seems to depend on whether that policy is defensible on nonreligious grounds. Religious citizens, in this view, are constitutionally permitted to promote a policy only if they can show that their ideas are consistent with secular convictions. Secular democracy is thus perceived by many to be dangerous for the religiously devout because it prevents them from acting in the public sphere when their views spring from their faith.[69] Evangelicals, in fact, appear to respond to perceived "religious threat." The more secularists in their community, the more likely white evangelicals are to vote Republican. Secularists, however, do not appear to respond to the presence of evangelicals in their community.[70]

The dramatic rise in the relationship between religiosity and the vote in the 1990s corresponded with the emergence of Bill Clinton in presidential politics.[71] He created an odd legacy in American politics by bringing the country together on policy and tearing the country apart over values,[72] which suggests that American politics became less about economic interests and more about lifestyle during his years in office. Under the presidency of George W. Bush, this polarization continued as the Republican Party increasingly became an extension of the religious right.[73] The different legacies of Clinton and Bush in regard to the religion gap in American politics are also reflected in the religious preferences of party activists. The elites of the Democratic and Republican parties differ considerably from one another in terms of the place of religion in politics.[74]

This is not to imply, however, that the parties are monolithic in their views of the role of religion in politics. The Republicans in particular are divided between religionists and secularists. In terms of voting behavior and issues preferences, a "religious" conservative Republican is qualitatively distinct from a "secular" conservative Republican.[75] One of the most striking examples of the unstable coalition of economic conservatives and populists in the contemporary Republican Party is in regard to stem cell research, which religious conservatives strongly oppose but many economic conservatives support.[76]

Religion is an important factor in understanding the political differences between rich and poor. Churchgoers are much more Republican than nonchurchgoers. This difference, however, is much larger in wealthier states. Because the most religious states are relatively poor, income is an important factor in attitudes toward moral behavior. This complicates the already unclear relationship between religious values and behavior. Married couples in Massachusetts (a relatively wealthy state), for example, get divorced at less than half the rate of those in Arkansas (a relatively poor state), and the divorce rate among born-again Christians is about the same as among married Americans in general.[77]

Higher levels of religiosity do not necessarily have to lead to an increased likelihood of cultural conservatism. On the death penalty, in fact, the more religiously devout are actually more liberal than the general population (see Figure 3-7). That the more religious are less supportive of the death penalty has defined the politics of the death penalty for years.[78] This is especially true among devout Catholics: Catholics who esteemed Pope John Paul II, for example, were found to be more negative in their evaluation of the death penalty.[79] Moreover, the proportion of Catholics in a state has been found to be a strong predictor of the rate at which that state applied capital punishment.[80] It used to be that the death penalty was a major cultural issue that divided on religious lines. Today, however, the death penalty has become much less of a prominent fissure in America's culture wars. Instead, gay marriage and abortion tend to be the focal points of religiously based morality politics. The result is greater political polarization on the basis of social issues.

Certainly, there are large differences on perceptions of moral standards depending on one's religiosity. The religiously devout are significantly less likely to believe that one should be more tolerant of people with different moral standards than the less religious are. In 2012 while less than two-fifths of those who attended religious services weekly took the position that one should be more tolerant, about two-thirds of those who never attended religious services took this position. The differences on moral standards foreshadow the relationship between religiosity and the issues of gay marriage and abortion.

Gay Marriage

Though rarely a topic debated on the political stage before 2000, in the first decade of the twenty-first century gay marriage emerged as a polarizing political issue. There is unquestionably an extremely strong relationship between religious attendance and support for gay marriage. In both 2008 and 2012, a majority of those who never attended religious services supported

FIGURE 3-7   The Religion Gap: Values and Social Issues

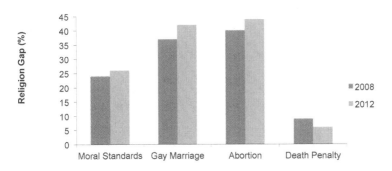

Religion gap = Largest differential among those who attend religious services weekly, occasionally, and never. Moral standards = should be more tolerant of people with different moral standards. Gay marriage = agree that gays should be allowed to marry. Abortion = abortion should never be permitted/permitted only in cases of rape and incest. Death penalty = favor death penalty.
Source: ANES 2008 and 2012 datasets.

gay marriage and less than one-sixth of those who worshipped weekly did. The religion gap on gay marriage is more of a chasm than a gap!

The religious subtext of the controversy over gay marriage may have even been decisive in Bush's narrow reelection in 2004 by motivating religious voters to cast their votes in greater numbers. If John Kerry had won Ohio, he would have won enough Electoral College votes to claim the presidency. Ohio, however, was one of eleven states where a state measure to ban same-sex marriage was on the ballot. Though every state that had such a measure saw it passed, outside of Ohio the issue did not seem to mobilize substantially more people to vote for Bush. In states with gay marriage initiatives on the ballot, there was an overall shift away from Bush.[81] Even though evangelicals did not constitute an appreciably larger share of the 2004 national electorate than they had in 2000, the Ohio ballot initiative helped Bush to pick up evangelical votes.[82] Ohio saw a shift to the right among voters between 2000 and 2004, and the scale of the rural vote suggests that the issue may have given both the state and the presidency to Bush.[83]

Gays are far more likely to support the Democratic Party than heterosexuals are. In 2012, for example, exit polls found that Obama won 76 percent of the vote of the 5 percent of the electorate who identified as gay, lesbian, or bisexual. This margin was actually large enough to swing the overall popular vote to Obama in 2012 as heterosexuals split their vote evenly. In regard to gay marriage, most gays are less concerned about having legally recognized marriages than about winning health care and other employee benefits for their spouses. It is the goal of acquiring spousal benefits, not the right to marry, that influences the degree to which gays support the Democratic Party. The sexual identity gap is thus generated more from gay concerns about acquiring tangible economic benefits than from an interest in pursuing civil rights.[84]

Certainly, there has been a marked change in American public opinion regarding gay marriage over the past generation. Attitudes on gay marriage have significantly liberalized over time: 71 percent had opposed gay marriage in 1988, but by 2007 this figure dropped to 52 percent.[85] This change came largely among Democrats and Independent voters. Polls of Californians in 1977 and 2009 found that Independents went from being opposed to gay marriage in 1977 by 55 percent to being supportive of it in 2009 by 57 percent and Democrats went from opposing the idea in 1977 by 63 percent to supporting it in 2009 by 64 percent. Republicans in California, in contrast, actually grew more strongly opposed to same-sex marriage, with 65 percent opposing it in 1977 and 68 percent opposing it in 2009.[86]

Abortion

Abortion, like gay marriage, is an issue that polarizes not only on the basis of partisanship but also on the basis of religiosity. Attitudes on abortion are strongly correlated with depth of religious belief as measured by religious attendance. In 2012 while nearly 70 percent of those who attended religious services weekly believed that abortion should never be permitted or permitted only during cases of rape or incest, only about 25 percent of Americans who attended religious services occasionally or never held this belief. Of all the gaps analyzed in this book, the religion gap on abortion is the largest.

Religious attendance has become a much better predictor of attitudes on abortion than religious denomination. American Catholics, for example, are no more likely to hold antiabortion views than the rest of the population.

As many Catholics as non-Catholics believe abortion should be legal, and Catholics are no more likely to be "morally opposed" to abortion than other Americans. Among regular church-attending Catholics, however, only 24 percent believed that abortion is morally acceptable, while among nonregular-church-attending Catholics the figure was 52 percent.[87] The political significance of abortion has increased as much among infrequent churchgoers as among those who attend religious services regularly. Thus, although religious convictions have played an important role in the rise of abortion as a political issue, the corresponding mobilization among secular voters has been every bit as powerful.[88]

It has been argued that the American public is not as divided on the specifics of abortion as is often stereotyped: Americans, for the most part, tend to believe that abortion should be legal but that it is reasonable to have constraints on abortion and regulate it in various ways.[89] Also, contrary to the popular belief that women who obtain abortions are not religious, most women who have had abortions identify themselves as religious.[90] Abortion, however, has unquestionably become a much more important consideration in voting behavior since the 1980s as Democratic and Republican elites have increasingly adopted prochoice and prolife positions, respectively. As the partisan elites have become more polarized, so have rank-and-file party members. In California, for example, 70 percent approved of the right of a woman to seek an abortion in 2006, a 19-percentage point jump from 1975. The change in attitudes on abortion, however, was markedly different on the basis of partisanship. While Democratic support of the right to have an abortion rose from 52 percent in 1975 to 82 percent in 2006 and the support of Independents increased from 59 percent to 73 percent, Republican support grew only from 50 percent to 55 percent.[91]

The Changing Dynamic of the Religion Gap

The religion gap offers important information about the political role of religion in the United States. The religion gap in part reflects the continuing political significance of religious affiliation. Religious communities have long been the most important means of linking religion to politics. At the same time, the religion gap reflects the political significance of religiosity. As I have demonstrated, regular worshippers are more likely to hold certain sorts of religious beliefs and those who worship less often are more likely to hold contrary beliefs.

This chapter has measured religiosity in terms of frequency of participation in religious services. But belief may not correspond with religious service attendance. And it is also the case that the religious-secular divide in the United States is far from absolute. African Americans, a group with one of the highest rates of religiosity, are overwhelmingly Democratic. Religious Jews also disproportionately identify with the Democratic Party.[92] Overall, however, religious attendance—as this chapter has demonstrated—is an extremely important indicator of many political and policy preferences.

An Increase in the Religion Gap?

Among nearly every religious group, Obama in 2008 received equal or high levels of support compared to John Kerry in 2004, thus narrowing the religion gap. Obama targeted religious voters more than previous Democratic candidates had, actively courting them. Obama's performance led to some speculation that there might be a smaller religion gap in future elections. After he was sworn into office, however, Obama consistently had much higher job approval ratings among those who seldom or never went to church than he did among those who attended church weekly,[93] and in 2012 Obama was not able to repeat his 2008 performance among religious voters.

If anything, the religion gap appears to have magnified during the Obama presidency. This is consistent with what has transpired since the Clinton presidency, as religion increasingly plays a significant role in evaluations of the president's job performance. Orthodox religious belief was related to a decrease in Bill Clinton's approval ratings in 1996 and to an increase in George H. W. Bush's approval ratings in 1992 and George W. Bush's in 2004. Not only do presidents appeal to specific religious constituencies for electoral and policy support, but also ordinary Americans appear to respond to presidents differently on the basis of religious beliefs.[94]

Ideology and partisanship, however, may be able to influence religious communities by boosting movement within and perhaps eventually across these communities.[95]

In the nineteenth century a number of theorists (Auguste Comte, Karl Marx, Max Weber, and Sigmund Freud, among others) began to argue that religion would gradually fade in importance and cease to be significant with the advent of industrial society. The death of religion was considered inevitable by many social scientists. But contrary to this thesis, religion has not disappeared, nor does it seem likely to do so.[96]

The Secularization of the United States

Religion may not have disappeared, but the United States as a whole is clearly becoming more secular as the number of Americans who identify themselves as religious and attend religious services declines. The number of Americans who claim they are unaffiliated with a particular faith today—about one in six Americans—is more than double the number who say they were not affiliated with a particular religion as children. There was a rise in church membership from the 1930s to about 1960, followed by a plateau and then a gradual drop in church attendance from the 1960s to the 1990s. Since the 1990s secular trends have accelerated.[97] As a result, virtually all the postwar increase in religious participation has now been erased.[98]

The secularization of the United States is largely due to generation replacement. Younger Americans are considerably less religious than older-age cohorts, which reflects the declining status and authority of traditional church institutions, the individualism of the quest for spirituality, and the rise of New Age movements.[99] Younger Americans are not only less likely to attend religious services, but they are also less likely to claim any religious affiliation: one in four of those born after the 1970s are unaffiliated with any religion, far more than the share of older adults when they were under 30.[100] The current trend of younger Americans being less religious is, therefore, more than simply a product of where they are in their life cycle. Historically, younger people were not necessarily less religious than the population as a whole. In fact, religious attendance tends to be rather steady through a person's life. For the baby-boom generation, for example, 13 percent in the late 2000s said they had no religious affiliation, the same rate as in the late 1970s. This indicates that Americans' religious affiliation tends to be steady throughout adult life, suggesting that younger Americans' current secular tendencies will define this generation through the course of their lives.[101] Thus, as an older generation of relatively religious Americans is replaced by a younger cohort of relatively secular Americans, the number of Americans who attend religious services can be expected to continue falling.

Despite the overall popularity of religion in the United States, important social and regional disparities exist. Secularists are far more likely to live in urban cities and on the Pacific Coast or in the Northeast, to have a college degree, to be single, and to be male. Evangelicals are far more likely to live in small towns or rural areas, especially in the South and Midwest, to be married, and to be female.[102] Notably, the religious attendance gap between the regions is widening. Although every state has seen an increase in those identifying with no religion, the largest increases have been in the Northeast and the West, which were relatively secular in the first place. The South has seen the least growth in nonreligious individuals since the 1990s. There is thus an increasingly geographic component to the religion gap in the United States, with red America being more religious than blue America.

The Significance of the Religion Gap

Importantly, as the country has become more secular, those who regularly worship have become more conservative politically. This may be a political reaction by the religious against what they perceive to be an increasingly secular government and political establishment. Today those who attend religious services weekly or more vote more Republican than ever relative to those who attend religious services occasionally or less. As Figure 3-8 shows, this has worked to the Republicans' advantage because the more religiously devout have consistently had higher levels of voter turnout. In every presidential election since 1980, those who weekly attended religious

Figure 3-8   Voter Turnout Rates in Presidential Elections by
Religious Attendance

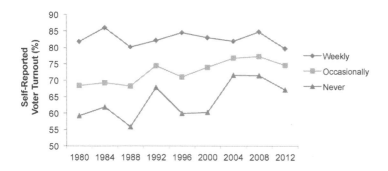

Source: ANES, 1980–2012.

services voted at rates at least 10 points higher than those who did not attend religious services. The problem for Republicans, however, is that their religious base of voters appears to be steadily shrinking.

The increasingly religious nature of the Republican Party has the potential to radically alter American politics. Strategically, the best Democratic response to the increasing power of social conservatives in the Republican Party may be to seek the support of social liberals who are increasingly disaffected by the Republican Party. The Democratic Party can be expected to move to the right on economic issues while staying liberal on social issues.[103] Regardless, as the United States becomes a more secular nation, current trends suggest that this will bode well for the Democrats.

Notes

1. Christopher P. Gilbert, *The Impact of Churches on Political Behavior* (Westport, CT: Praeger, 1993).

2. David E. Campbell, "The 2004 Election: A Matter of Faith?," in *A Matter of Faith*, ed. David E. Campbell (Washington, DC: Brookings Institution Press, 2007), 1–14.

3. "The American–Western European Values Gap: American Exceptionalism Subsides," Pew Research Center, November 17, 2011.

4. Michael Luo, "God '08: Whose, and How Much, Will Voters Accept?," *New York Times*, July 22, 2007; data from the Pew Research Center.

5. Jonathan Tilove, "New Congress Brings with It Religious Firsts," *Current* 491 (2007): 7–8.

6. Luo, "God '08"; data from the Pew Research Center.

7. Geoffrey C. Layman and Edward G. Carmines, "Cultural Conflict in American Politics: Religious Traditionalism, Postmaterialism, and U.S. Political Behavior," *Journal of Politics* 59 (1997): 751–777.

8. Laura Olson and John C. Green, "The Religion Gap," *PS: Political Science and Politics* 39 (2006): 455–459.

9. James Guth, Lyman A. Kellstedt, John C. Green, and Corwin E. Smidt, "America Fifty/ Fifty," *First Things: The Journal of Religion, Culture, and Public Life* 116 (2001): 19–26.

10. Robert D. Putnam, *Bowling Alone* (New York: Simon and Schuster, 2000), 75–76.

11. Ted G. Jelen, "Religious Priorities and Attitudes Toward Church and State," *Review of Religious Research* 42 (2000): 87–95.

12. Paul Djupe and Christopher Gilbert, *The Political Influence of Churches* (New York: Cambridge University Press, 2008).

13. Michael S. Lewis-Beck, William G. Jacoby, Helmut Norpoth, and Herbert F. Weisberg, *The American Voter Revisited* (Ann Arbor: University of Michigan Press, 2008), 328–331.

14. Geoffrey C. Layman, "Religion and Political Behavior in the United States," *Public Opinion Quarterly* 61 (1997): 288–316.

15. Geoffrey C. Layman, "'Culture Wars' in the American Party System," *American Politics Quarterly* 27 (1999): 89–121.

16. Stanley B. Greenberg, *The Two Americas* (New York: Thomas Dunne Books, 2005).

17. Corwin Smidt, "Evangelicals and the 1984 Election," *American Politics Quarterly* 15 (1987): 419–445.

18. Scott Keeter, "Evangelicals and Moral Values," in *A Matter of Faith,* 80–92.

19. David E. Campbell, "Religious 'Threat' in Contemporary Presidential Elections," *Journal of Politics* 68 (2006): 104–115.

20. Clem Brooks, "Religious Influence and the Politics of Family Decline Concern: Trends, Sources, and U.S. Political Behavior," *American Sociological Review* 67 (2002): 191–211.

21. David E. Campbell and J. Quin Monson, "The Case of Bush's Reelection: Did Gay Marriage Do It?," in *A Matter of Faith,* 120–141.

22. Brian Robert Calfano and Paul A. Djupe, "God Talk," *Political Research Quarterly* 62 (2009): 329–339. Among the distinct themes the Republicans have historically used to cue evangelicals include "We have this land, and we're told to be stewards of it, and each other," which Calfano and Djupe refer to as a "land statement."

23. Hugh Heclo, "Is America a Christian Nation?," *Political Science Quarterly* 122 (2007): 59–87.

24. Martin E. Marty, "Righteous Empire: The 'Faith Gap' and American Politics," *New Perspectives Quarterly* 22 (2005): 24–27.

25. Monika L. McDermott, "Religious Stereotyping and Voter Support for Evangelical Candidates," *Political Research Quarterly* 62 (2009): 340–354.

26. Lewis-Beck et al., *American Voter Revisited,* 327–328.

27. Chuck Todd and Sheldon Gawiser, *How Barack Obama Won* (New York: Vintage Books, 2009), 252.

28. Olson and Green, "The Religion Gap," 455–459.

29. D. Paul Sullins, "American Catholics and Same-Sex 'Marriage,'" *Catholic Social Science Review* 15 (2010): 97–123.

30. Campbell, "Religious 'Threat,'" 104–115.

31. Paul Perl and Mary E. Benyna, "Perceptions of Anti-Catholic Bias and Political Party Identification Among U.S. Catholics," *Journal for the Scientific Study of Religion* 41 (2002): 653–668.

32. Louis Bolce and Gerald De Maio, "Our Secularist Democratic Party," *Public Interest* 149 (2002): 3–20.

33. Layman, "'Culture Wars,'" 89–121.

34. J. Mathew Wilson, "The Changing Catholic Voter: Comparing Responses to John Kennedy in 1960 and John Kerry in 2004," in *A Matter of Faith,* 163–179.

35. Campbell, "The 2004 Election," 8–9.

36. Todd Breyfogle, "Some Paradoxes of Religion in the 2000 Presidential Election," *Reviews in Religion and Theory* 18 (2001): 543–548.

37. Bolce and De Maio, "Our Secularist Democratic Party," 3–20.

38. National exit polls; data assembled by the *Washington Post.*

39. Republican and Democratic primary exit polls in Utah, February 5, 2008.

40. Olson and Green, "The Religion Gap," 455–459.

41. Laura R. Olson and Adam L. Warber, "Belonging, Behaving, and Believing: Assessing the Role of Religion on Presidential Approval," *Political Research Quarterly* 61 (2008): 192–204.

42. Layman, "'Culture Wars,'" 89–121.

43. For the purposes of this study, I classify religious attendance using ANES data (variables V083185 and V083186) as follows: (1) weekly = those who attend church weekly + those who attend church more than weekly; (2) occasionally = those who attend church a few times a year + those who attend church once or twice a month + those who attend church almost every week; and (3) never = those who answered "no" to ever attending church.

44. Morris Fiorina, *Culture War?: The Myth of a Polarized America* (New York: Pearson Longman, 2005).

45. Layman, "Religion and Political Behavior," 288–316.

46. Olson and Green, "The Religion Gap," 455–459.

47. Alan I. Abramowitz, *The Disappearing Center* (New Haven, CT: Yale University Press, 2010), 78–82.

48. Peter Steinfels, "In Politics, the 'God Gap' Overshadows Other Differences," *New York Times,* December 9, 2006.

49. Geoffrey Layman, *The Great Divide: Religious and Cultural Conflict in American Party Politics* (New York: Columbia University Press, 2001).

50. Olson and Green, "The Religion Gap," 455–459.

51. James Davision Hunter, *Culture Wars: The Struggle to Define America* (New York: Basic Books, 1992).

52. Bolce and De Maio, "Our Secularist Democratic Party," 3–20.

53. Guth et al., "America Fifty/Fifty," 19–26.

54. Bolce and De Maio, "Our Secularist Democratic Party," 3–20.

55. Todd and Gawiser, *How Barack Obama Won,* 252.

56. "How Religious Is Your State?," Pew Research Center, December 21, 2009.

57. According to author calculations of responses to questions V083185, V083186, and V085165 in the ANES 2008 dataset, 52 percent of those who attended religious services weekly thought we "should worry less about equality," a figure 10 percentage points higher than those who attended religious services occasionally or never.

58. Marylee C. Taylor and Stephen Merino, "Assessing the Racial Views of White Conservative Protestants," *Public Opinion Quarterly* 75 (2011): 761–778.

59. Pippa Norris and Ronald Inglehart, "God, Guns, and Gays," *Public Policy Research* 12 (2006): 224–233.

60. Andrew Gelman, *Red State, Blue State, Rich State, Poor State* (Princeton, NJ: Princeton University Press, 2008), 89.

61. Willet Kempton, James S. Boster, and Jennifer A. Hartley, *Environmental Values in American Culture* (Cambridge, MA: MIT Press, 1995), 91–92.

62. Andrew Kohut and Bruce Stokes, *America Against the World* (New York: Henry Holt, 2006), 114–115.

63. Layman, "'Culture Wars,'" 89–121.

64. Hunter, *Culture Wars*.

65. Ted G. Jelen, "Religion and the American Political Culture: Alternative Models of Citizenship and Discipleship," *Sociology of Religion* 56 (1995): 271–284.

66. Ted G. Jelen, "Religious Priorities and Attitudes Toward Church and State," *Review of Religious Research* 42 (2000): 87–95.

67. Jeremy Rabkin, "The Culture War That Isn't," *Policy Review* 96 (1999): 3–19.

68. Kohut and Stokes, *America Against the World*, 113.

69. Gary D. Glenn and John Stack, "Is American Democracy Safe for Catholicism?," *Review of Politics* 62 (2000): 43–47.

70. Campbell, "Religious 'Threat,'" 104–115.

71. Fiorina, *Culture War?*

72. William Schneider, "American Religion and Political Polarities," *American Sociologist* 34 (2003): 81–84. For example, whereas Bill Clinton was seen as a political centrist who helped to reduce welfare spending, among other accomplishments, his impeachment in 1998 over the Monica Lewinsky scandal displayed just how polarizing his personal behavior was.

73. Henry A. Giroux, "The Passion of the Right: Religious Fundamentalism and the Crisis of Democracy," *Cultural Studies/Critical Methodologies* 5 (2005): 309–317.

74. John C. Green and John S. Jackson, "Faithful Divides: Party Elites and Religion," in *A Matter of Faith*, 37–62.

75. Jonathan Knuckley, "Religious Conservatives, the Republican Party, and Evolving Party Coalitions in the United States," *Party Politics* 5 (1999): 485–496.

76. Gary Miller and Norman Schofield, "The Transformation of the Republican and Democratic Party Coalitions in the U.S.," *Perspectives on Politics* 6 (2008): 433–450.

77. Gelman, *Red State, Blue State*, 78.

78. Harold G. Grasmick, John K. Cochran, Robert J. Bursik Jr., and M'Lou Kimpel, "Religion, Punitive Justice, and Support for the Death Penalty," *Justice Quarterly* 10 (1993): 289–313; James D. Unnever and Francis T. Cullen, "Christian Fundamentalism and Support for Capital Punishment," *Journal of Research in Crime and Delinquency* 43 (2006): 169–197.

79. Kenneth Mulligan, "Pope John Paul II and Catholic Opinion Toward the Death Penalty and Abortion," *Social Science Quarterly* 87 (2006): 739–753.

80. Barbara Norrander, "The Multi-Layered Impact of Public Opinion on Capital Punishment Implementation in the American States," *Political Research Quarterly* 53 (2000): 771–793.

81. Stephen Ansolabehere and Charles Stewart, "Truth in Numbers: Moral Values and the Gay-Marriage Backlash Did Not Help Bush," *Boston Review* 30 (2005): 40.

82. Adolph Reed, "The 2004 Election in Perspective: The Myth of 'Cultural Divide' and the Triumph of Neoliberal Ideology," *American Quarterly* 57 (2005): 1–15; Campbell and Monson, "The Case of Bush's Reelection," 120–141.

83. Edward Ashbee, "The 2004 Presidential Election, 'Moral Values,' and the Democrats' Dilemma," *Political Quarterly* 76 (2005): 209–217.

84. Brian Schanffner and Nenad Senic, "Rights or Benefits? Explaining the Sexual Identity Gap in American Political Behavior," *Political Research Quarterly* 59 (2006): 123–132.

85. Dawn Michelle Baunach, "Decomposing Trends in Attitudes Toward Gay Marriage, 1988–2006," *Social Science Quarterly* 92 (2011): 346–363.

86. Mark DiCamillo and Marvin Field, "The Changing California Electorate (Part 2): Voters, Especially Democrats, Have Become More Socially Tolerant on a Number of Issues over the Past Three Decades," Field Poll, August 5, 2009.

87. Frank Newport, "Catholics Similar to Mainstream on Abortion, Stem Cells," Gallup, March 30, 2009.

88. Larry Bartels, *Unequal Democracy* (New York: Russell Sage, 2008), 90–93.

89. Fiorina, *Culture War?*, 63–64.

90. Rachel K. Jones, Jacqueline E. Darroch, and Stanley K. Henshaw, "Patterns in the Socioeconomic Characteristics of Women Obtaining Abortions in 2000–2001," *Perspectives of Sexual and Reproductive Health* 34 (2002): 294–303.

91. DiCamillo and Field, "The Changing California Electorate."

92. David E. Campbell, "The Young and the Realigning," *Public Opinion Quarterly* 66 (2002): 209–234.

93. Gallup Presidential Job Approval Center, www.gallup.com.

94. Olson and Warber, "Belonging, Behaving, and Believing."

95. Statos Patrikios, "American Republican Religion? Disentangling the Causal Link Between Religion and Politics in the US," *Political Behavior* 30 (2008): 367–389.

96. Norris and Inglehart, "God, Guns, and Gays," 224–233.

97. Greenberg, *Two Americas,* 128–129.

98. Putnam, *Bowling Alone,* chap. 4.

99. Wade Clark Rook, *Spiritual Marketplace: Baby Boomers and the Remaking of American Religion* (Princeton, NJ: Princeton University Press, 2001).

100. "The Millennials: Confident. Connected. Open to Change," Pew Research Center, February 24, 2010.

101. "Democrats' Edge Among Millennials Slips," Pew Research Center, February 18, 2010.

102. Norris and Inglehart, "God, Guns, and Gays," 224–233.

103. Miller and Schofield, "The Transformation," 433–450.

4

The Gender Gap

Gender and American Political Behavior

Differences in political behavior between men and women are pervasive in American politics and exist apart from specific elections. Such differences are a product of the interaction of societal conditions and politics.[1] There is a stable gender gap in vote choice of roughly 8 to 10 percentage points even after a variety of sociodemographic and religious characteristics have been controlled.[2]

Of all the gaps I will analyze in this book, the gender gap has received the greatest attention from political scientists and journalists since its initial appearance in the 1970s.[3] The gender gap has always been portrayed as a two-sided coin, with Democrats doing better with women and Republicans with men. Early studies of the gender gap tended to focus on women as the impetus of the gap. More recent studies, however, tend to point to men's changing politics as the long-term structural foundation of the gender gap. From the 1950s to the 1980s, both men and women became more Republican. It was the disproportionately large movement among men toward the Republican Party, however, that created the gender gap.[4] Thus, it was not—despite a common perception to the contrary—the result of growing affection for the Democratic Party among women. Instead, it developed because support for the Democratic Party declined less dramatically among women than men.

Women, however, have unquestionably become an important part of the Democratic Party's base. In Senate and gubernatorial elections, for example, the larger the Democratic candidate's advantage over the Republican opponent, the larger the gender gap, which illustrates the importance of women voters to decisive Democratic victories.[5] Women are not only significantly more likely than men to identify as Democrats, but also this gap is evident across all ages and within all racial, ethnic, and marital-status segments of society.[6]

A biological explanation for gender political differences suggests that women prefer the Democratic Party because it is the compassionate and nurturing "mommy" party, whereas men prefer the Republican Party because it is the strict, disciplined "daddy" party.[7] Regardless, Americans have increasingly come to view the parties in terms of masculinity and femininity.[8] Such ideas about the two political parties are related to ideas about the two genders, both in the images citizens consciously hold of the parties and in the implicit level of unconscious cognitive connections between gender and party stereotypes. Women have also consistently been less likely than men to identify themselves as political Independents since the 1950s. Women tend to opt for weak partisanship, whereas men choose the leaning-Independent category. This may be due to men placing a greater value on separateness and women placing a greater value on connections with others.[9]

The political differences between men and women may be the result of biological differences or, contrarily, may be the result of socialization. It, in fact, has been found to exert an impact on voter preferences above and beyond biological differences.[10] The gender gap in policy and partisanship has been found to be established before children reach adulthood, suggesting that the persistent gender gap in adult views about politics is either biological or rooted in gender differences during childhood socialization.[11] This is supported by the finding that gender differences observed at the end of college are largely unrelated to the college experience itself. Rather, the source of gender differences extends back to precollege years, when young women and men develop different values, aspirations, and patterns of behavior.[12]

The fact that women had virtually the same political attitudes as men for two generations after obtaining enfranchisement also seems to undermine the biological argument. When the right to vote was extended to women with the ratification of the Nineteenth Amendment in 1920, there was considerable speculation about the possibility that a distinct women's vote would emerge. Many suffragists argued that women would make the world a better place with their vote because their experience as mothers and caregivers would give them a distinct desire to end wars, poverty, and homelessness. This new bloc of female voters was thought to have the potential to immediately produce electoral change, to the consternation of many.[13]

It took a couple of generations, however, for that distinctive vote to emerge. Women at first did not turn out at the polls at the same rate as men, and when women did vote, their vote generally did not vary much from that of men. Early on women tended to slightly favor the Republicans. The current partisan dynamics of the gender gap—with women more aligned with the Democratic Party and men more aligned with the Republican Party—did not emerge for the first time until 1964 with the election of Lyndon Johnson over Barry Goldwater.[14]

The 1960s and 1970s produced social change that eventually led to the emergence of the gender gap. Women during this period became less dependent on men and more aware that they had their own political interests and concerns. Women's growing financial independence from men, as they became more educated and entered the job force at unprecedented levels, added to their sense that their political interests might be different from those of men.[15]

It was not until 1980, however, that a persistent gender gap emerged. The initial explanations for this gap focused on how Ronald Reagan's opposition to abortion and the Equal Rights Amendment (ERA)—an attempt to make equality of the sexes a constitutional requirement—led women to be less likely than men to vote for him.[16] According to this train of thought, the social and psychological independence of women from men begun in the 1960s combined with Reagan's strong policy positions during the 1980 presidential campaign led to a permanent change in women's voting patterns.[17]

Though Reagan tried to regain women's support for the Republican Party by nominating Sandra Day O'Conner to be the first woman on the Supreme Court and emphasizing growing job opportunities for women, his opposition to the ERA and other measures to promote female equality contributed to his substantially lower support among women than among men throughout his presidency.[18]

The 17-point gender gap in the 1980 election proved to be a harbinger of what was to come, as women have consistently been more likely than men to support the Democratic nominee for president (see Figure 4-1). Since 1980 the gender gap has ranged from 5 percentage points (Bill Clinton's initial election in 1992) to 22 percentage points (Al Gore's loss to George W. Bush in 2000). In the nine presidential elections from 1980 to 2012, women gave a plurality of their vote to the Democrat six times, while men were more supportive of the Republican in seven elections. Over the course of these nine elections, women supported Democratic presidential nominees more than men did by an average of 15 percentage points.

The Gender Gap in the 2008 and 2012 Elections

In 2008 Barack Obama won the female vote by 13 percentage points while winning a bare plurality of the male vote. He maintained about the same advantage among women (11 points) in 2012 but lost quite a bit ground among men: he lost the male vote by 7 points in his reelection bid. In 2008 Obama was only the second Democratic nominee since 1980 (along with Bill Clinton in 1992) to win a plurality of the male vote. Obama's relative strength among women in both 2008 and 2012 was across all racial/ethnic groups: he did 9 points better among white women than among white men in 2008 and 7 points better in 2012, 7 points better among Hispanic women than among Hispanic men in 2008 and 11 points better in 2012, and 3 points better among African American women than African American men in 2008 and 9 points better in 2012.

Obama's strength among female voters can be seen in Figure 4-2, which represents how Electoral College maps of the 2008 and 2012 elections would

FIGURE 4-1   Partisan Vote for President by Gender

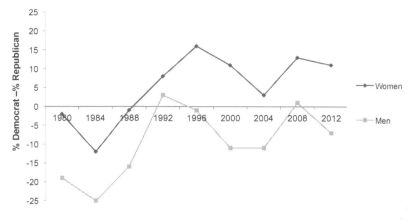

Source: Exit polls, 1980–2012.

have looked if only women had voted. Along with all the twenty-eight states that Obama actually won in 2008, Obama would have won a plurality of female votes in Missouri, Montana, and Georgia. In 2012 Obama would have won the female vote in North Carolina and Georgia as well as in the twenty-six states he did carry. Altogether, the states in which Obama won the women's vote would have consisted of 393 Electoral College votes in 2008 and 363 in 2012, considerably more than the 270 required to win the election.

If only men had voted, Obama would have lost three states that he actually won in 2008 (Colorado, Indiana, and North Carolina) and an astonishing nine (Florida, Iowa, Minnesota, Nevada, New Hampshire, Ohio, Pennsylvania, Virginia, and Wisconsin) that he carried in 2012 (see Figure 4-3). Though Obama would still have won the election in the Electoral College in an electorate composed of only men in 2008, carrying 329 Electoral College votes, he would have lost rather decisively in 2012, as his Electoral College total would have been only 216.

After winning the Republican nomination, John McCain had high hopes of cutting into the Democrat's traditional strength among women voters because of a perception that Obama might have alienated many Democratic-leaning women during his nomination contest with Hillary Clinton. This

FIGURE 4-2   Electoral College Maps of 2008 and 2012 Presidential Votes: Women's Vote

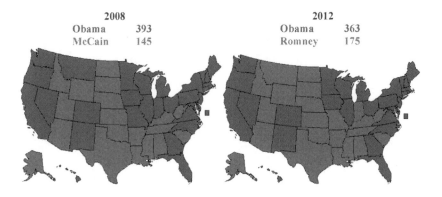

Source: Exit polls, 2008–2012.

FIGURE 4-3   Electoral College Maps of 2008 and 2012 Presidential Votes: Men's Vote

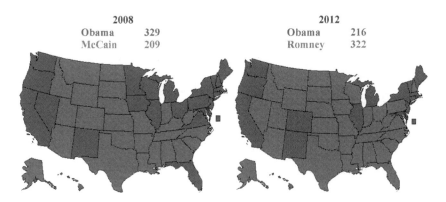

Source: Exit polls, 2008–2012.

idea was widely held to be one of the reasons that McCain picked Sarah Palin to be his running mate. Hillary Clinton, attempting to become the first woman to win a major party's presidential nomination, was expected to do well among women voters during the Democratic primaries. She did win the women's vote, but not by as much as expected. In the thirty-three states that had presidential primaries on or after February 5, Clinton won 53 percent of the female vote and 46 percent of the male vote. The gender gap in the Democratic primaries might help explain the coalitions in support of Obama and Clinton, but it ranks behind race, age, education, religion, and income in terms of the size of the gap in the primaries.[19]

Gender and Public Policy Preferences

Most of the gender gap research points to male-female differences in policy positions as the primary explanation for gender differences in political behavior. Men and women attach different levels of priority to certain political issues and think differently about policy and problem solving.[20] Women's support for Democratic candidates is consistent with their ideological and public policy preferences. As Figure 4-4 displays, men tend to view themselves as being ideologically more conservative—the mean ideological score for men is to the right of that for women. This ideological orientation among the genders is reflected in a number of public policy issues. Since the 1970s both men and women have increasingly been willing to adopt an ideological identification. Men's increased conservatism is a reflection of the fact that they have become more consistently conservative as the class basis of ideological identification has declined. Women's increased liberalism comes primarily from changing demographics: well-educated and single women have always been more liberal than their less educated and married counterparts, and over time well-educated and single women have become more numerous in the population. Consequently, the gender gap in ideology is as much one of divisions among women as differences across the genders.[21] As women have moved to the ideological left of men, the partisanship of the gender gap has had greater policy consequences. In the House of Representatives, for example, a sizable gender gap favoring men exists in districts represented by Republicans while a considerable gap favoring women exists in districts represented by Democrats. Interestingly, although a Democratic majority in the House improves women's policy representation, having a female representative does not.[22]

One ideological difference lies in how men and women view equality: men are less concerned with it than women.[23] Women's relative support

FIGURE 4-4   Gender and Ideology

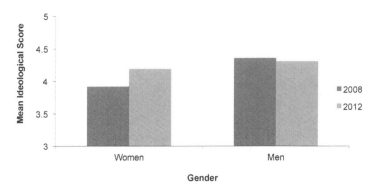

Definition: Self-Identification Scale from 1 to 7, with 1 = most liberal and 7 = most conservative.
Source: ANES 2008 and 2012 datasets.

for equality has its roots in the women's rights movement of the 1960s and 1970s, an era in which women were able to push the ERA into the national spotlight. In the early 1970s both parties were in support of the ERA and began including women's equality issues in their platforms. By the end of the 1970s, however, the Republicans dropped their support of the ERA as the Democrats remained strongly behind it. This clearly differentiated the parties' philosophy toward gender equality. Since the 1970s white men in particular have become increasingly resistant to the liberal cultural agenda of the Democratic Party, which has made them more likely to identify themselves as conservative. Social policies that advocate for greater female equality, particularly in the workplace and in the family, pose substantial challenges to a traditional social order in which white men have been relatively privileged.[24] At the same time, the state molds gender inequality by influencing women's class positions and regulating class inequality.[25] As a result, men in the United States tend to be ideologically more individualistic and libertarian, while American women are more egalitarian.

The Gender Gap in Economic Issues

On economic issues men tend to be more conservative than women, though not necessarily by large margins (see Figure 4-5). On questions regarding government services, health care, aid to the poor, and privatization of Social

FIGURE 4-5   The Gender Gap: Economic Issues

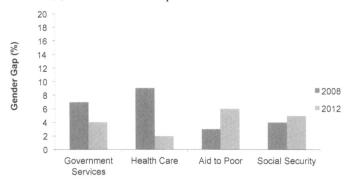

Definitions: Gender gap = difference between men and women. Government services = government should provide more services. Health care = favor universal health insurance. Aid to poor = aid to the poor should be increased. Social Security = favor Social Security invested in stocks and bonds. Source: ANES 2008 and 2012 datasets.

Security, men are somewhat more likely to support a smaller government role. Male partisanship, therefore, is connected to opinions about the social welfare state. The influence of economic issues in shaping ideological identities may have declined since the 1970s, but economic issues retain a relatively strong influence on men's identities.[26] Female partisanship is less tied to social welfare beliefs and more to cultural attitudes.[27]

One reason that men are more conservative on economic issues is the substantial income gap between the sexes. College-educated men in their mid-twenties already earn on average about $7,000 more per year than do college-educated women.[28] This income gap is still considerable ($4,400) when women and men have similar educational credentials. Although women's gains in education have been central to a narrowing of the gender gap in income, gender differences in fields of study continue to disadvantage women. Gender differences in work-related factors, in fact, are more important than are educational differences for understanding the contemporary income gap between men and women. As a result of this income difference, women are more likely to attach greater weight to economic issues and social spending.[29]

Women's stronger support of government social welfare spending is the most common explanation for the gender gap over time.[30] This stronger support and the preeminence of opinions about social welfare in the partisan calculus of men and women largely explain the persistence of the gender gap.[31] This difference in support for social welfare programs is partly due to women having a predisposition to display empathy toward distressed others in society.[32] But it is also the result of income inequality: social welfare programs largely benefit the poor, who are disproportionately female. Because women earn less than men, it is in their economic self-interest to support welfare and financial assistance programs sponsored by the government. Women, for example, are more likely not to have health insurance, which helps to explain why they are more supportive of universal health insurance. The same relationship can be seen with Social Security: women are less likely to support putting Social Security in stocks and bonds because they are considerably more reliant on Social Security as their major source of income after they retire.

The greater reliance of women on social welfare programs explains why the gender gap has tended to grow in economic downturns when the percentage of economically vulnerable single women increases. As a result, women in general have been found to be more pessimistic about the state of the economy than men. Not only are women more economically vulnerable than men and thus greater beneficiaries of welfare programs, but also the types of jobs women hold tend to be more reliant on government funds and subsidies.[33]

Changes in the labor force and the changing demographics of American households also explain women's relative liberal leanings on economic issues.[34] Women have developed into a distinct voting bloc with the expansion of the female labor force.[35] The percentage of women who describe themselves as housewives has dropped sharply since a majority of women entered the labor force. As a result, working women now make up 30 percent of the total electorate. As women entered the workforce, they became more exposed to gender inequalities in the workplace, such as unequal pay. Additionally, women got more exposure to politics as workers than they had ever received as homemakers.[36] And women were increasingly likely to be unmarried and single. With the increase in single females since the 1960s, females have become a notably larger share of the lowest-income quintile and a smaller share of the top quintile.[37] Employment and economics, therefore, have had a significant effect in creating and maintaining the gender gap.[38]

The Gender Gap in Domestic and Foreign Policy Issues

On domestic and foreign policy, unlike economic issues, women are not consistently more liberal than men (see Figure 4-6). The gender differences on immigration policy and environmental regulation are minimal, and women's views on the environment in 2008 and immigration policy in 2012 were actually slightly more conservative than those of men. One issue on which men and women do have enormously different viewpoints, however, is gun control: women are considerably more likely to believe that buying a gun should be made more difficult. That men are considerably more likely to oppose gun control is partially explained by the fact that 75 percent of gun owners are men, as are 87 percent of hunters. The gender gap on gun control is undoubtedly cultural in nature. There is a male "rite of passage" connection between guns and maturity, a value rarely found in the socialization of females.[39]

FIGURE 4-6   The Gender Gap: Domestic and Foreign Policy Issues

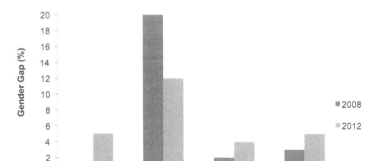

Definitions: Gender gap = difference between men and women. Immigration = immigration levels should be reduced. Gun control = buying a gun should be made more difficult. Environment = favor increased regulation to protect the environment. Defense spending = defense spending should be reduced.
Source: ANES 2008 and 2012 datasets.

As is the case with immigration and the environment, on defense spending men and women do not have consistent ideological differences: men were slightly less likely to favor reducing defense spending in 2008, but women were somewhat more reluctant to support paring defense spending in 2012. This lack of a notable gender gap on defense spending is new: women historically tended to be more likely than men to support reduced military spending.[40] Men's greater reluctance to cut military spending in the past corresponded with their more hawkish tendencies on war-related concerns.[41] Historically, men were considerably more hawkish than women on the use of military force, and this was certainly the case with both the Gulf War and the Iraq War.[42] An exception occurred after the terrorist attacks of September 11, 2001, when for a brief period the gender gap on security issues disappeared. The changed security situation after 9/11 exerted cross-pressures on security issues that created a precipitous drop in the gender gap in the 2002 congressional elections,[43] which was a considerable help to Republican congressional candidates. These cross-pressures generally faded away by the 2004 elections, and the normal dynamics of the gender gap reasserted themselves.[44]

The Gender Gap in Values and Social Issues

Though there is unquestionably a large economic component to the gender gap, the divergence in men's and women's political attitudes has also been portrayed as a consequence of the culture wars that have divided Americans since the 1970s. When the gender gap emerged in 1980, women's rights issues were seen as instrumental in pushing women to the political left of men. To the extent that cultural issues are influencing the partisan balance in the United States today, men and women have largely been seen as responding differently to the cultural agenda. Female college students, for example, are more likely than male students to move to the left during the course of their college careers.[45] This supports the idea that women are reacting politically to noneconomic issues. Also, women who strongly support role equity and feel positive toward the women's movement have been much more likely to vote Democratic since 1980. In 1988, for example, 74 percent of those women who considered themselves feminist voted for Michael Dukakis, the Democratic nominee for president, whereas nonfeminist women gave him only 36 percent of their vote.[46]

Salient cultural issues influence the partisan choices for both men and women, but in somewhat different ways. For women, issues—female equality, abortion—have become increasingly important determinants of party identification. For men, the influence of cultural conflict on partisanship is less direct.[47]

Women have different attitudes from men on social issues, though these differences vary considerably from issue to issue and are not necessarily consistent with stereotypes (see Figure 4-7). Women tend to be more tolerant on moral standards, more supportive of gay marriage, and less likely to support the death penalty. Yet, on abortion—despite widespread notions to the contrary—women's attitudes are not much different from those of men.

Women's greater tolerance on moral standards and their greater support for gay marriage are related. Men have consistently been less likely to embrace gay rights than women have.[48] A similar relationship exists with the death penalty: men are much more likely to support the death penalty than women. The effect of gender on capital punishment support is robust even

FIGURE 4-7   The Gender Gap: Values and Social Issues

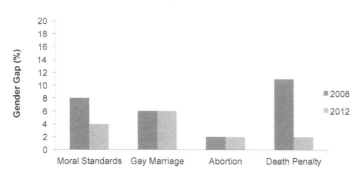

Definitions: Gender gap = difference between men and women. Moral standards = should be more tolerant of people with different moral standards. Gay marriage = agree that gays should be allowed to marry. Abortion = abortion should never be permitted/permitted only in cases of rape and incest. Death penalty = favor death penalty.
Source: ANES 2008 and 2012 datasets.

when a multitude of other explanations are controlled.[49] Part of the reason for the gender gap on the death penalty is that men tend to emphasize retribution and women to focus on forgiveness and compassion. Men are also more likely to believe that the death penalty is applied fairly than women are.[50]

Symbolically, the issue of abortion has had a huge influence on the perceptions of the gender gap. After the Supreme Court's 1973 ruling in *Roe v. Wade* legalizing abortion, the national Republican Party, which prior to *Roe* had not had differed much from the Democratic Party on the matter, took a strong stance against abortion just as the national Democratic Party began actively supporting abortion rights. This change in the parties' positions on abortion fueled the idea that women had a clear vision of which party symbolically supported women's rights, which ostensibly helped birth the gender gap in 1980.

Part of the conviction that women are more concerned about abortion rights than men stems undoubtedly from the fact that women, not men, have abortions. But the demographics of women who have abortions are far from being representational of the American female population. Women who have abortions tend to be younger, less often white, more likely to live in urban areas, and more likely to be unmarried. The most important characteristic of those who have abortions, however, is economic: those who have abortions are substantially poorer than the average American female. Women with incomes below 200 percent of the poverty line make up about 30 percent of all women of reproductive age but account for nearly twice that proportion of abortions.[51]

This important economic component of abortion indicates the complexity of the issue. It has been argued, in fact, that abortion is extremely overrated as an issue of vote choice for most Americans. Public opinion on abortion, according to this school of thought, is not as divided as the public thinks.[52] Certainly, that men's and women's views on abortion are quite similar seems to imply that the issue is overrated as a primary determinant in the political differences between men and women.

Gender differences on cultural issues seem to be contradicted by levels of religiosity. Religious devotion has been found to play an equal role in influencing the political choices of both men and women.[53] Women, however, are on average more religious than men. Women are not only more likely than men to regularly attend religious services, but they are also considerably less likely than men to indicate that they never attend religious services. Religiosity is strongly associated with women's voting behavior, especially among whites. Religiosity exerts a consistently conservative influence on white women's voting behavior. As a result, religious white women tend to support the Republican Party while secular white women lean toward the Democratic Party. Religious women support the Republican Party because they think the party shares their values.[54]

Overall, however, gender differences in opinion on nonreligious issues sustain the partisan gap. Men are more conservative on questions of social welfare, and they carry considerably more weight in shaping men's partisan choices than do other issues. Religious devotion, therefore, affects partisan choices but does not override the powerful effects of gender.[55]

In light of women's greater levels of religiosity, the growing political focus on such issues as abortion and gay marriage creates greater cross-pressures on religious women. Yet there is no evidence that religiosity had any impact on the gender gap in voting in recent elections.[56] The gender gap's emergence derives not from the culture war on issues such as abortion, but rather from the association of the Democratic Party with an activist government that supports the vulnerable and disadvantaged as well as with a less belligerent foreign and defense policy. If women disagree about feminism, abortion, and family values, it becomes difficult to talk about a "women's vote" based on these issues. There is no single "women's message" in US politics. Despite widespread beliefs to the contrary, economic, not social, issues undergird the prevalence of the gender gap.

The Marriage Gap

An important component of the economic gender gap is the varying importance each sex assigns to marriage. Economically, the institution of marriage is much more important to women that it is to men. Consequently, marital status has increasingly become a strong gauge of one's political preferences. Whether one is married, single, or divorced provides key insight into the differing circumstances that are likely to shape one's political worldview. Married Americans have become much more likely to support Republican candidates than unmarried Americans have since 1980. The political rift on the basis of marital status lies in the differing circumstances and economic realities of those who are married relative to those who are unmarried. Married voters are more likely to have a greater concern for values or issues of individual morality, whereas unmarried voters are more likely to have a greater concern for safeguarding their economic vulnerabilities. Such priorities lead the unmarried to support a more active government that is supportive of social programs that benefit poorer Americans.

As is the case with the gender gap, prior to 1980 the marriage gap was relatively miniscule. Since 1980, however, there has been a strong relationship between marital status and support for a particular political party in presidential elections (see Figure 4-8). Married voters have strongly favored the Republican nominee, with the exceptions of 1992 and 1996 when they narrowly supported Bill Clinton. Those who had never been married have voted more Democratic than Republican for president in every single presidential election since 1980, sometimes by extremely large margins: Clinton (twice), Gore, and Obama all won more than 60 percent of the never-married vote. Divorced and separated voters tend to fall between the partisan extremes of the married and the never married. Since 1984, when the divorced and separated supported Ronald Reagan for president, this marital-status group has consistently offered more support to Democratic presidential candidates, though never to the extent of the never married.

The marriage gap appears to be widening rather than diminishing. In 2012 among the three-fifths of the electorate that was married, Mitt Romney beat Barack Obama by 14 percentage points. Of the unmarried, however, Obama won by 27 percentage points. This large Obama margin reflected a large gender gap in regard to marital status. Of the married, women were 8 points more likely to support Obama in 2012 than men were. Among unmarried men, Obama won 56 percent of their vote. He did even better

FIGURE 4-8   Partisan Vote for President by Marital Status

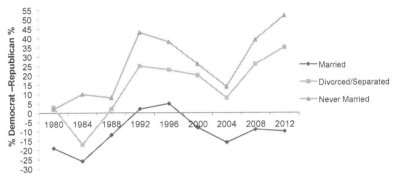

Source: ANES, 1980–2012.

among unmarried women: they gave him 67 percent of their vote. Obama's successful reelection campaign unquestionably rested in a large part on his overwhelming success among single females.

The Marriage Gap in Economic Issues

Because the married are generally wealthier, they tend to be Republican leaning, so the difference between the political behavior of married couples and of single individuals is a consequence of their differing economic circumstances.[57] The married have lower poverty rates and higher income security than the unmarried. And those who earn a higher income are more likely to get married in the first place.

Married couples, unlike singles, benefit from the possibility of having two sources of income. Married people are also likely to have a greater concern for issues that affect family life and more "permanent" structures in society. Examples of such concerns include quality-of-life issues (environmental conditions, safety, clean air and water, etc.), education, violence and sex in the media, and child care. Unmarried people have more reason to be concerned about economic security, health care, and insurance coverage. Such priorities lead unmarried Americans to support a strong, active government with efficacious social programs.[58]

Because the married tend to be more economically secure than the unmarried, not only do they lean Republican on economic grounds (to protect their own economic interests), but also they have the luxury of voting based on their preferences for family-based and value-rooted issues, which the poorer unmarried might not be able to afford to do. Measured by religious attendance, the unmarried are relatively less religious than the married. The married are also more conservative on value issues such as abortion and same-sex marriage.[59] Being part of a "traditional" family structure, therefore, appears to make married people less inclined to be accepting of non-traditional family structures

The Marriage Gap in Cultural Issues

The rift between married and unmarried Americans on moral and cultural issues stems from their divergence on other important factors that shape political behavior. That singles are younger, less religious, less attached to a community, and more mobile than married Americans inspires their support of more progressive politics. The cultural and moral realities that shape married and single Americans thus influence the political differences that foster the marriage gap. People in blue states, for example, marry later, are more likely to live together without marriage, and are less likely to become teenage mothers than people in red states.[60]

The percentage of unmarrieds has grown dramatically since the 1960s. The growth of the unmarried population is outpacing the growth of the married population by 2.5 to 1. If the current growth trend continues, the unmarried population will become a majority in the 2020s.[61] The changing demographics of marriage may influence future politics and potentially help out the Democrats. As the number of singles increases, a segment of the Democratic base gets larger.

Along with marriage, parenthood overlaps with the gender gap and has a significant impact on several policy issues, including education, government spending and service, health care, and gay marriage. The parenthood gap thus reinforces the gender gap. On several issues that historically had a significant gender gap, including government spending, health care, child care, and other social welfare programs, it appears that having and raising children contribute to the gender gap by pushing women in a liberal direction. Men with children, in contrast, actually tend to be more conservative than childless men.[62] Having children, in other words, leads to a widening of the gender gap.[63] Interestingly, a gender gap also exists in regard to the gender of one's child: having daughters makes people more likely to vote Democratic, whereas having sons leads people to vote Republican.[64]

The Significance of the Gender Gap

The extent of research aside, the gender gap is not as pronounced as other demographic gaps. Even though overall women lean toward the Democrats and men toward the Republicans, there is considerable diversity among female and male voters.[65] This is not to say, however, that the gender gap is inconsequential. Part of its political significance lies in a difference in participation rates between men and women. In the six decades after women gained the right to vote nationally, voter turnout among men was consistently higher than among women and not by small margins: surveys found that women turned out at rates of about 10 percent less than men throughout the 1950s and early 1960s.[66] The gender gap in turnout, however, was almost completely a result of women's lower participation rates in the South. The subsequent decline of the turnout gender gap came from converging rates of political engagement and employment for women and men in the South.[67] As Figure 4-9 shows, since 1980 the turnout of women has been

FIGURE 4-9   Voter Turnout Rates in Presidential Elections by Gender

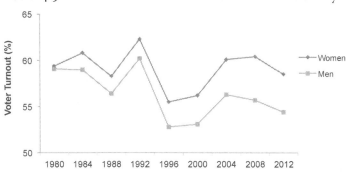

Source: US Census Bureau.

higher than that of men and the rate by which women have gone to the polls more than men has been increasing, reaching a record high difference (for presidential elections) of nearly 5 percentage points in 2008, a figure that was only slightly smaller in 2012

Women are more likely to vote even though both men and women perceive women to be less knowledgeable about politics than men.[68] Importantly, however, this is not the case among younger voters.[69] Among adolescents, in fact, females appear to be more interested in politics. A study of fourteen-year-old girls and boys found that girls in this age group indicated more interest in political and social-movement-related participation.[70]

In terms of political participation, the impact of education is greater for women than men.[71] In 1960 women made up 35 percent of college graduates. By 1980 bachelor degree recipients were equally matched by sex. Today women are awarded 60 percent of all bachelor's degrees, and these numbers are projected to become even more pronounced in the future. As women become more educated, their political participation rates will likely continue to increase relative to men's.[72]

That women are more likely to vote demonstrates their potential political power as a voting bloc. That women have been inclined to disproportionately support Democratic candidates suggests that the gender gap is working to the Democrats' advantage. Certainly, Democratic candidates have been assiduously courting female voters. Yet when Democratic nominees (Bill Clinton, Barack Obama) won the presidency, it was because they did relatively better among men. Democrats, therefore, cannot rely simply on their appeal to women voters: they need to improve their standing among men as well as carry the women vote. At the presidential level it has been suggested that the masculinization of the Republican Party and the feminization of the Democratic Party have worked to the Republicans' advantage.[73] For Democratic presidential candidates to be successful, they need to reduce the gender gap.

For Republicans, the gender gap symbolizes a weakness for them among potential women voters, which is reinforced by the fact that women in political office are disproportionately Democrats. Of those elected to serve in the

113th Congress (2013–2015), for example, three-fourths of the women were Democrats.[74] There are relatively few differences in the attitudes that women and men hold about women candidates, however, and those differences that do exist tend to be in how women and men evaluate Democratic, but not Republican, women candidates. This signals that a candidate's party matters alongside a candidate's sex. Thus, it may be that women voters are simply choosing candidates of their party, many of who happen to be women.[75]

The gender gap's emergence in 1980 resulted in part from the women's movement's energetic efforts to change the view of women in American society and establish a voting bloc to bring about political change. But it also derived from the differing views men and women held on economic issues, the shift of women into the workforce and women's view of their own economic independence, and the significant increases in divorce rates and the amount of women choosing to remain single.

The future of the gender gap has important consequences for the Democratic and Republican parties. It exposes the weakness of both parties' support and suggests that both parties' appeal is limited. For the Democrats, the significant loss of male voters beginning in 1980 implies that increasing attention to "compassion" issues and greater support of a more dovish foreign policy have eroded their political base. For Republicans, their weakness among female voters suggests that their libertarian views on economics but not on social issues limits the ability of their political base to grow.

The 18-point gender gap in 2012 unquestionably reflected an important characteristic of American politics. Yet the gender gap has declined from its apex in 2000, when the gap was 22 points. A sustained contraction of the gender gap is probably more beneficial to the Democrats than the Republicans. As articulated previously, the gender gap is more the product of men leaving the Democratic Party than of the Democrats attracting new female voters. In the more than three decades since the gender gap emerged as a regular feature in American elections, the Republicans have done considerably better than they had previously at all levels of government. When the Democrats have made gains, such as with the elections of Bill Clinton in 1992 and Barack Obama in 2008, their ability to reduce the gender gap was one cause: the smallest gender gaps in presidential elections since 1980 were in 1992 and 2008.

Demographic trends, however, suggest that the gender gap can be expected to remain a significant characteristic of American politics. Hispanic women, for example, have been found to be more liberal and more pro-Democratic than Hispanic men.[76] Thus, the growing Hispanic population may reinforce the gender gap. Also, a strong gender gap has emerged among younger Americans. Young white men and young white women appear to be heading in different political directions, with young white men much more likely than young white women to identify with the Republicans.[77] In 2008 and 2012 the gender gap among voters under 30 years was larger than that of those 30 and older, suggesting a potential widening of the gender gap with generation replacement as younger Americans take the place of older Americans in the electorate. The gender gap, therefore, is likely to remain a continual feature of the American political landscape that shapes everything from elite political behavior to election outcomes.

Notes

1. Janet M. Box-Steffensmeier, Suzanne de Boef, and Tse-Min Lin, "The Dynamics of the Partisan Gender Gap," *American Political Science Review* 98 (2004): 515–528.

2. Leonie Huddy, Erin Cassese, and Mary-Kate Lizotte, "Sources of Political Unity and Disunity Among Women," in *Voting the Gender Gap*, ed. Louis Duke Whitaker (Urbana: University of Illinois Press, 2008), 141–169.

3. Alan I. Abramowitz, *The Disappearing Center* (New Haven, CT: Yale University Press, 2010), 77.

4. Karen M. Kaufmann, "The Gender Gap," *PS: Political Science and Politics* 39 (2006): 447–453.

5. Margies Omero, "Using Exit Polls to Explore the Gender Gap in Campaigns for Senate and Governor," in *Voting the Gender Gap*, 108–188.

6. "Women More Likely to Be Democrats, Regardless of Age," Gallup, June 12, 2009.

7. Val Plumwood, *Feminism and the Mastery of Nature* (New York: Routledge, 1993).

8. Nicholas J. G. Winter, "Masculine Republicans and Feminine Democrats: Gender and Americans' Explicit and Implicit Images of the Political Parties," *Political Behavior* 32 (2010): 587–618.

9. Barbara Norrander, "The Independence Gap and the Gender Gap," *Public Opinion Quarterly* 61 (1997): 464–472.

10. Peter K. Hatemi et al., "The Different Effects on Gender and Sex on Vote Choice," *Political Research Quarterly* 65 (2012): 76–92.

11. Kim L. Fridkin and Patrick J. Kenny, "Examining the Gender Gap in Children's Attitudes Toward Politics," *Sex Roles* 56 (2007): 133–140.

12. Linda J. Sax and Casandra E. Harper, "Origins of the Gender Gap: Pre-College and College Influences on Differences Between Men and Women," *Research in Higher Education* 48 (2007): 669–690.

13. Susan J. Carroll, "Voting Choices: Meet You at the Gender Gap," in *Gender and Elections: Shaping the Future of American Politics,* ed. Susan J. Carroll and Richard L. Fox (New York: Cambridge University Press, 2006), 74–96.

14. Michael S. Lewis-Beck, William G. Jacoby, Helmut Norpoth, and Herbert F. Weisberg, *The American Voter Revisited* (Ann Arbor: University of Michigan Press, 2008), 325–327.

15. Carroll, "Voting Choices," 74–96.

16. Barbara Norrander, "The Evolution of the Gender Gap," *Public Opinion Quarterly* 63 (1999): 566–576.

17. Susan J. Carroll, "Partisan Dynamics of the Gender Gap Among State Legislators," *Spectrum: The Journal of State Government* 75 (2002): 18–22.

18. Kira Sanbonmatsu, *Where Women Run: Gender and Party in the American States* (Ann Arbor: University of Michigan Press, 2006), 175.

19. Patrick Fisher, "The Gapology of the Obama Vote in the 2008 Democratic Presidential Primaries," *Society* 48 (2011): 502–509.

20. Carol Gilligan, "In a Different Voice: Women's Conceptions of Self and Morality," *Harvard Educational Review* 47 (1977): 481–517.

21. Barbara Norrander and Clyde Wilcox, "The Gender Gap in Ideology," *Political Behavior* 30 (2008): 503–523.

22. John Griffin, Brian Newman, and Christina Wolbrecht, "A Gender Gap in Policy Representation in the U.S. Congress?," *Legislative Studies Quarterly* 37 (2012): 35–66.

23. According to author calculations of responses to questions V081101 and V085165 in the ANES 2008 dataset, 44 percent of women thought we "should worry less about equality" while 46 percent of men agreed with this statement.

24. Karen M. Kaufmann, "Culture Wars, Secular Realignment, and the Gender Gap in Party Identification," *Political Behavior* 24 (2002): 283–306.

25. Handas Mandel and Michael Shalev, "How Welfare States Shape the Gender Pay Gap: A Theoretical and Comparative Analysis," *Social Forces* 87 (2009): 1873–1911.

26. Barbara Norrander and Clyde Wilcox, "The Gender Gap in Ideology," *Political Behavior* 30 (2008): 503–523.

27. Karen M. Kaufmann, "Culture Wars, Secular Realignment, and the Gender Gap in Party Identification," *Political Behavior* 24 (2002): 283–306.

28. Donna Bobbitt-Zeher, "The Gender Income Gap and the Role of Education," *Sociology of Education* 80 (2007): 1–22.

29. Lilliard E. Richardson and Patricia K. Freeman, "Issue Salience and Gender Differences in Congressional Elections, 1994–1998," *Social Science Journal* 40 (2003): 401–417.

30. Karen M. Kaufmann and John R. Petrocik, "The Changing Politics of American Men:

Understanding the Sources of the Gender Gap," *American Journal of Political Science* 43 (1999): 864–887.

31. Karen M. Kaufmann, "The Partisan Paradox: Religious Commitment and the Gender Gap in Party Identification," *Public Opinion Quarterly* 68 (2004): 491–511.

32. Clifford P. McCue, "Dispositional Empathy and the Political Gender Gap," *Women and Politics* 21 (2000): 20–26.

33. Box-Steffensmeier et al., "The Dynamics of the Partisan Gender Gap," 515–528.

34. M. Margaret Conway, Gertrude Steuernagel, and David Ahern, *Women and Political Participation: Cultural Change in the Political Arena*, 2nd ed. (Washington, DC: CQ Press, 2005).

35. Claudia Goldin, *Understanding the Gender Gap: An Economic History of American Women* (New York: Oxford University Press, 1990).

36. Jeff Manza and Clem Brooks, "The Gender Gap in U.S. Presidential Elections: When? Why? Implications?," *American Journal of Sociology* 103 (1998): 1235–1266.

37. Nolan McCarty, Keith T. Poole, and Howard Rosenthal, *Polarized America: The Dance of Ideology and Unequal Riches* (Cambridge, MA: MIT Press, 2006), 89.

38. Susan E. Howell and Christine L. Day, "Complexities of the Gender Gap," *Journal of Politics* 62 (2000): 858–874.

39. Robert J. Spitzer, *The Politics of Gun Control*, 3rd ed. (Washington, DC: CQ Press, 2004), 102.

40. David L. Leal, "American Public Opinion Toward the Military Differences by Race, Gender, and Class?," *Armed Forces and Society* 32 (2005): 123–138.

41. Kaufmann, "The Gender Gap," 447–453.

42. Ibid.; Clyde Wilcox and Lara Hewitt, "The Gender Gap in Attitudes Toward the Gulf War: A Cross-National Perspective," *Journal of Peace Research* 33 (1996): 67–82.

43. Susan Carroll, "Security Moms and Presidential Politics," in *Voting the Gender Gap*, 75–90.

44. Cal Clark and Janet M. Clark, "The Reemergence of the Gender Gap in 2004," in *Voting the Gender Gap*, 50–74.

45. Mack D. Mariani and Gordon J. Hewitt, "Indoctrination U.? Faculty Ideology and Changes in Student Political Orientation," *PS: Political Science and Politics* 41 (2008): 773–780.

46. Elizabeth Adell Cool, "Feminist Consciousness and Candidate Preference Among American Women, 1972–1988," *Political Behavior* 15 (1993): 227–246.

47. Kaufmann, "Culture Wars," 283–306.

48. "Most Still Oppose Gay Marriage, but Support for Civil Unions Continues to Rise," Pew Research Center, October 9, 2009.

49. John K. Cochran and Beth A. Sanders, "The Gender Gap in Death Penalty Support: An Exploratory Study," *Journal of Criminal Justice* 37 (2009): 525–533.

50. James D. Unnever and Francis T. Cullen, "Christian Fundamentalism and Support for Capital Punishment," *Journal of Research in Crime and Delinquency* 43 (2006): 169–197.

51. Rachel K. Jones, Jacqueline E. Darroch, and Stanley K. Henshaw, "Patterns in the Socioeconomic Characteristics of Women Obtaining Abortions in 2000–2001," *Perspectives of Sexual and Reproductive Health* 34 (2002): 294–303.

52. Morris Fiorina, *Culture War? The Myth of a Polarized America* (New York: Pearson Longman, 2005).

53. Kaufmann, "The Partisan Paradox," 491–511.

54. Anna Greenberg, "Race, Religiosity, and the Women's Vote," *Women and Politics* 22 (2001): 59–82.

55. Kaufmann, "The Partisan Paradox," 491–511.

56. Clark and Clark, "The Reemergence of the Gender Gap," 50–74.

57. Katherine Q. Seely, "The 2000 Campaign: Women Voters; Marital Status Is Shaping Women's Leanings, Surveys Find," *New York Times*, September 20, 2000.

58. Elizabeth Warren and Ameila Warren Tyagi, *The Two-Income Trap: Why Middle-Class Mothers and Fathers Are Going Broke* (New York: Basic Books, 2003).

59. Calculated from ANES 2008 dataset.

60. Tamar Lewin, "Data on Marriage and Births Reflect the Political Divide," *New York Times*, October 13, 2005.

61. Greenberg Quinlan Rosner, "A New America: Unmarrieds Drive Political and Social Change," October 31, 2007, www.greenberresearch.com.

62. According to National Election Pool exit poll data from the 2012 presidential election, the vote by gender and parental status (children in household under 18) was as follows:

Status	Obama	Romney	% Total
Men with children	45%	53%	16%
Women with children	56%	43%	20%
Men without children	47%	50%	30%
Women without children	54%	45%	34%

63. Laurel Elder and Steven Greene, "Parenthood and the Gender Gap," in *Voting the Gender Gap*, 119–140.

64. Andrew J. Oswald and Nattavudh Powdthavee, "Daughters and Left-Wing Voting," *Review of Economics and Statistics* 92 (2010): 213–227.

65. Greenberg, "Race, Religiosity," 59–82.

66. Janet V. Lewis, *Women and Women's Issues in Congress, 1832–2000* (Huntington, NY: Nova Science, 2001), 3.

67. Andrew S. Fullerton and Michael J. Stern, "Explaining the Persistence and Eventual Decline of the Gender Gap in Voter Registration and Turnout in the American South, 1956–1980," *Social Science History* 34 (2010): 129–169.

68. Jeanette Morehouse and Tracey Osborn, "Gender and the Perception of Knowledge in Political Discussion," *Political Research Quarterly* 63 (2010): 269–279.

69. Mary Christine Banwart, "Gender and Young Voters in 2004: The Influence of Perceived Knowledge and Interest," *American Behavioral Scientist* 50 (2007): 1152–1168.

70. Marc Hooghe and Dietlind Stolle, "Good Girls Go to the Polling Booth, Bad Boys Go Everywhere: Gender Differences in Anticipated Political Participation Among American Fourteen-Year-Olds," *Women and Politics* 26 (2004): 1–23.

71. Lewis-Beck et al., *American Voter Revisited*, 348–354.

72. Andrew Hacker, "How the B.A. Gap Widens the Chasm Between Men and Women," *Chronicle of Higher Education* 49 (2003): B10–B11.

73. Winter, "Masculine Republicans and Feminine Democrats," 587–618.

74. "Record Number of Women Will Serve in Congress; New Hampshire Elects Women to All Top Posts," Center for American Women and Politics at Rutgers University, November 7, 2012.

75. Kathleen A. Dolan, "Women Voters, Women Candidates," in *Voting the Gender Gap*, 91–107.

76. Susan Welch and Lee Sigelman, "A Gender Gap Among Hispanics? A Comparison with Blacks and Anglos," *Western Political Quarterly* 45 (1992): 181–199.

77. Stanley B. Greenberg, *The Two Americas* (New York: Thomas Dunne Books, 2005).

5

The Race Gap

Race and American Political Behavior

The single largest divide—by a good margin—within the contemporary American electorate is the race gap. The political behavior of whites is substantially different from the behavior of minority racial and ethnic groups. African Americans, in particular, are noteworthy for their distinct politics, and the black-white gap is by far the largest gap in American politics. Since Lyndon Johnson's landslide victory in 1964, African Americans have overwhelmingly supported Democratic candidates. Another politically distinct demographic group is Hispanics.[1] Though not nearly as monolithic in their voting behavior as African Americans, Hispanics have also proven to be distinct in their support for the Democratic Party.

The strength of this preference—and the strength of the support from whites for Republicans—can be seen in Figure 5-1. The pattern is in fact quite consistent. In every presidential election since 1980, African Americans overwhelmingly supported the Democratic presidential nominee, whites supported the Republican presidential nominee, and Hispanics fell between the two in their partisan presidential preferences. In the nine presidential elections from 1980 to 2012, African Americans supported Democratic presidential nominees by ranges of an extraordinary 72 (Bill Clinton in 1996) to 91 (Barack Obama in 2008) percentage points, Hispanics supported

FIGURE 5-1   Partisan Vote for President by Race

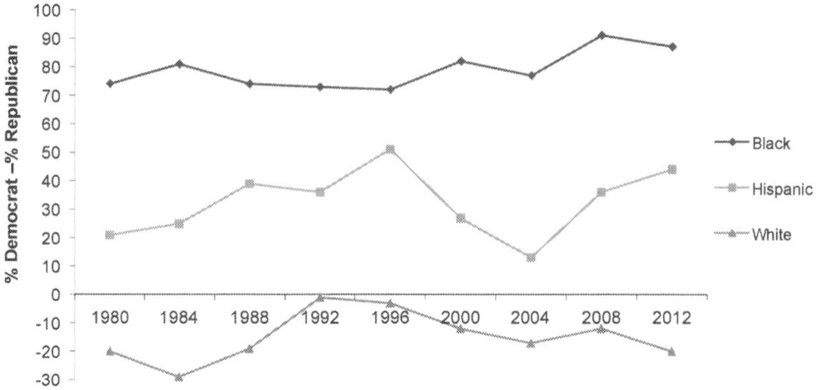

Source: Exit polls, 1980–2012.

Democratic candidates by 13 (John Kerry in 2004) to 51 (Bill Clinton in 1996) points, and whites supported the Republican presidential nominee by 1 (George H. W. Bush in 1992) to 29 points (Ronald Reagan in 1984).

The Political Behavior of African Americans

African Americans' distinctive voting behavior is a consequence of their shared political culture within the United States. The development and continuing strength of uniquely black institutions are important reasons for black political distinctiveness.[2] Many African Americans receive politically relevant information from indigenous black media and churches. African Americans are a very cohesive group, with extremely high levels of identification—so strong, in fact, that sometimes it becomes difficult using survey research to track differences in black public opinion.[3] Many African Americans whose individual economic interests might be better served by the Republican Party continue to support the Democratic Party because they typically prioritize group needs over individual self-interest.

African American support for Democrats, however, is more than merely symbolic; it also is unquestionably issue based. The Democratic Party is perceived by many as the prominority party, and the Republican Party is alleged to be less helpful to minorities.[4] For more than a half century after the

Civil War, blacks who were allowed to participate in politics overwhelmingly supported the Republican Party, the antislavery party of Abraham Lincoln. Blacks did not begin supporting Democratic candidates in large numbers until Franklin Roosevelt's New Deal. As late as 1960 Richard Nixon received more than 20 percent of the African American vote. This changed in 1964 when 94 percent of African Americans voted for Lyndon Johnson in his landslide victory over Republican nominee Barry Goldwater, who ran on a states' rights anti-civil-rights platform.[5] Ever since, the black vote has been overwhelmingly Democratic, becoming even more Democratic in 2008 and 2012 as blacks supported Barack Obama in record numbers.

Today the Democrats are widely perceived as offering more concrete benefits to African Americans as a group. This became readily evident with Lyndon Johnson's support of the 1964 Civil Rights Act, the 1965 Voting Rights Act, and the 1968 Fair Housing Act, as well as a number of Great Society programs designed to help African Americans. Beginning in the 1960s a clear difference arose between the Democratic and Republican parties on civil rights and other racially charged issues such as affirmative action, busing, crime, and welfare.[6] Black citizens have not merely sought out Democrats; Democrats have sought them out in turn. African Americans' preference for Democrats prevails not only in presidential elections, but also in congressional elections: very few Republican Senate and House candidates have received much more than 10 percent of the black vote in any election since 1960.[7] And if the 2008 and 2012 presidential elections are any indication, blacks can be expected to remain overwhelmingly Democratic over the long term. The election of Barack Obama, the nation's first African American president, unquestionably reinforced the loyalty of blacks to the Democratic Party.

The Republican Party has occasionally made attempts to recruit black voters, but with little success. One strategy the Republicans have attempted is targeting the growing African American middle class. This strategy, however, has not been successful due to the vulnerability of the black middle class to changes in the economy and the strength of African American group consciousness.[8] In the 2000 presidential election Republicans painted themselves as a more inclusive party by showcasing prominent African

American members of the party, such as Colin Powell and Condoleezza Rice. This attempt to change the party image, however, appeared only to influence moderate whites.[9]

In contrast to other major social groups in the country, African Americans as partisans remain rooted in group identity rather than in ideology. Many African Americans, however, undoubtedly are attracted to the Democratic Party because blacks as a group are disproportionately of lower socioeconomic status. As Obama has noted, the "concept of a black underclass—separate, apart, alien in its behavior and in its values—has also played a central role in modern American politics."[10] Many race-related issues—affirmative action, welfare, Medicaid, subsidized housing—are now perceived to be questions of redistribution, not specifically or overtly of race. The overwhelming African American identification with the Democrats, however, outweighs any effects arising from changes in the income distribution of blacks.[11]

A similar trend can be seen in regard to religion. African Americans at all income levels are more religiously observant than white Americans. Yet although religiosity pushes both blacks and whites to vote more Republican, religious blacks are still overwhelmingly a Democratic voting group. Of African Americans who self-identified as being very religious, only 10 percent considered themselves Republican leaning, while 78 percent leaned toward the Democrats.[12]

The Political Behavior of Hispanic Americans

Hispanics, though generally strong supporters of Democratic candidates, are not as overwhelmingly Democratic as African Americans. In the 2004 presidential election, for example, George W. Bush received more than two-fifths of the vote among Hispanics in his reelection bid, the largest ever recorded by a Republican presidential candidate. The 2004 presidential election suggested that the Republicans might have turned a corner in making gains in the Hispanic vote. The 2008 elections, however, dispelled this belief as Obama won the Hispanic vote by a 2 to 1 margin, a margin he actually improved upon in 2012. By the end of the Bush presidency, Hispanics turned decisively against the Republican Party. Despite President Bush's support for legislation to give legal status to illegal immigrants, 41 percent of Latinos in 2007 said that Bush's policies had been harmful to them politically; just 16 percent said that Bush's policies had helped them politically.[13]

Hispanics are a diverse group, originating from all over the world. As a result of this difference in national origins and experiences within the United States, Hispanics as a group are less cohesive than African Americans. This has allowed some Republican success in recruiting Latino votes.[14] Whereas Mexican American and Puerto Ricans have been strongly Democratic, Cuban Americans have been enthusiastically Republican. Hispanics in Texas and Florida have been less likely to vote for Democrats than Hispanics in California, Illinois, or New York. Latinos in California and Illinois are also an overwhelmingly urban constituency, whereas the Hispanic population in Texas is much more rural.[15] Also, racial self-identification influences Latinos' vote decisions.[16] In some areas, such as California, Mexicans identify themselves and are identified by others as a racial minority, whereas in other areas, such as Texas, their politics is much less racially oriented.[17]

The political importance of the Hispanic vote has become much more significant with the rapid growth of the Hispanic population in the United States. From 1990 to 2010 the Hispanic population more than doubled from 22 million to 50 million. Hispanics are by far the fastest-growing segment of the American population. Even though Latinos today make up less than one-tenth of Americans aged 65 and older, they are almost one-quarter of Americans under the age of 5.[18] Approximately 12 million Hispanics went to the polls in 2012, an increase of more than 25 percent from 2004. The geographic concentration of Latino voters, particularly in swing states such as Colorado, Nevada, New Mexico, and Florida, substantially increases the likelihood that Hispanic voters will have a significant impact in determining presidential elections.[19]

The Political Behavior of White Americans

White Americans, in contrast, are consistently less likely to support Democratic candidates than African Americans and Hispanics and have moved toward the Republican Party since the 1960s. The last Democratic presidential nominee to have won a majority of the white vote was Lyndon Johnson in 1964. The movement of whites away from the Democrats began in the 1960s as the Democratic Party came to be identified with the civil rights movement. This was especially true in the South. As late as 1960 native-born southern whites were more Democratic in their partisan affiliations than were blacks. By 1968, however, this trend had thoroughly reversed.[20]

The 230 million whites in the United States, of course, are very diverse, and the white vote is far from monolithic. Whites from Polish, Greek, Portuguese, Swedish, Norwegian, and Danish ethnic enclaves, for example, tend to be more Democratic than those from Cajun, Italian, Czech, German, and Dutch ethnic enclaves.[21] Though it is reasonable to assume that those identifying with a European ancestry probably vote in a more uniform manner when they live in an ethnic enclave rather than outside one, large differences among white ethnic enclaves persist nonetheless. White ethnicity often has carried evocations of working-class, typically Catholic conservatism. Each of these characteristics—working-class identity, ethnicity, Catholicism, conservatism, traditionalism—routinely signals or substitutes for the others.[22] At the same time, "unhyphenated Americans"—whites who claim an "American" ancestry, or none at all, are increasingly becoming an important component of the Republican base. Obama did poorly in both 2008 and 2012 in regions where these voters were concentrated, and this anti-Democratic trend can also be seen in the 2010 midterm elections as congressional districts where unhyphenated Americans were concentrated saw Democratic candidates having a significantly reduced vote share and chance of victory.[23]

The political behavior of whites in general, however, tells us much about American political culture as long as we distinguish between policy attitudes or socioeconomic characteristics and party identification or vote choice.[24] The first thing to understand about the race gap in the United States is that it is not uniform across the country. Outside the South, Democrats are generally competitive among white voters. In the South, however, the Democratic share of the white vote has steadily become smaller and smaller since the 1960s as a result of (1) initial southern white opposition to the national

Democratic Party's pro-civil-rights agenda and (2) growing class divisions as affluent whites in the South have become increasingly supportive of the Republican Party because they find its positions more compatible with their interests.[25] But the problem with the class division argument as an explanation for the Republican Party's dominance in the South is that overall the South is much poorer than the rest of the country and poor whites in the South are much more likely to vote Republican than poor whites elsewhere.

The impact of a person's ideology on vote choice grew in magnitude from the 1970s to the 1990s, but these changes were not felt uniformly throughout the electorate—southern whites exhibited the greatest changes. In the case of southern white males, racial issues appeared to be more closely related to their party identification.[26] Today the racial divide in some parts of the South is so great that the Republican Party has come to be viewed as the white political party and the Democratic Party as the black political party.[27]

Racial environment, defined by the percentage of blacks in a county, has a strong and consistent effect on racial-political attitudes in the South. Whites from the heavily black areas of the South are the most conservative in the region.[28] There is evidence, therefore, to suggest that white voting behavior is strongly influenced by racial and ethnic diversity in a community.[29] For example, whites in communities with higher percentages of African Americans have been found to be more likely to vote for candidates who designate themselves as "racially conservative." This can be explained by the "racial threat hypothesis," which holds that voters will be politically motivated by the presence of a large proximate racial group.[30] This is also consistent with the "group conflict hypothesis," which holds that physical proximity of different groups to each other leads to conflict.[31] A number of scholars have argued that a new, more subtle racism has supplanted the previous overt racism. However, an analysis of college students in the state of Mississippi—the state with the largest percentage of African Americans—reveals that overt racism provides the strongest explanation for white support for the Mississippi state flag, which bears the Confederate flag's image.[32]

As late as the 1950s virtually all votes cast in the South came from white men and women. The mobilization of black voters beginning in the 1960s fundamentally altered the electoral strategy of southern Democrats. The exact size of the white and black targets for Democratic candidates to win varies from state to state in the South, but the typical minimum targets Democrats need to win have been about 90 percent of the black vote combined with about 40 percent of the white vote.[33] However, Democratic candidates have found achieving this minimum target increasingly difficult.

The Race Gap in the 2008 and 2012 Elections

The race gap in the 2008 and 2012 presidential elections fit the pattern seen since the civil rights movement of the 1960s: the Democrat presidential nominee overwhelmingly won the black vote while also winning the Hispanic vote, and the Republican presidential nominee won a majority of the white vote. Obama won only 43 percent of the white vote in 2008 and 39 percent in 2012 (whites were about three-fourths of the electorate), but won 67 percent of the Hispanic vote in 2008 and 71 percent in 2012 (Hispanics constituted approximately one-tenth of the electorate) and 95 percent of the black vote in 2008 and 93 percent in 2012 (blacks made up about one-eighth of the electorate). The minority vote was thus critical to both Obama victories: minority voters made the difference in Obama's victory margin in nine states in 2008 and fourteen states in 2012, including Florida, Ohio, and Pennsylvania in both years.

Obama's share of the white vote was very similar to that of the previous two Democratic nominees, Al Gore and John Kerry. The key to Obama's victory was not only that he overwhelmingly won the minority vote, but also that the nonwhite electorate was considerably larger than it had been. Especially noteworthy is the fact that the longstanding gap between blacks and whites in voter participation evaporated in 2008 and 2012.

Because Obama won the vote of minority groups by such an overwhelming margin, the key aspect of the race gap in 2008 and 2012 was Obama's ability to win enough white voters to win the election. Figure 5-2 represents an Electoral College map of the white vote in 2008 and 2012. In a universe of just white voters, John McCain and Mitt Romney would have won their

FIGURE 5-2   Electoral College Maps of 2008 and 2012 Presidential Votes:
White Americans

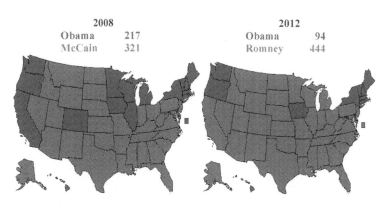

2008			2012	
Obama	217		Obama	94
McCain	321		Romney	444

Source: Exit polls, 2008–2012.

respective election. But Obama, seeking to become the first nonwhite to be elected president, was still able to win a majority of the white vote in eighteen states (worth 217 Electoral College votes) in 2008, though this figure went down to twelve states (worth 94 Electoral College votes) in 2012. At one extreme, in the state of Vermont white voters gave Obama more than two-thirds of their vote in both 2008 and 2012. At the other extreme, he won only one-tenth of the white vote in Alabama in 2008 and Mississippi in 2012. There is no denying that there was an extremely strong relationship in both of Obama's elections between race and a person's vote for president in the Deep South.

As Obama's poor showing among white voters in the Deep South seems to indicate, there was a notable relationship between the percentage of the vote that Obama received among white voters in a state and the percentage of whites in the overall population (see Figure 5-3). Simply put, the larger the African American population in a state, the lesser the percentage of the white vote for Obama. In 2008 of the six states where African Americans were more than one-fourth of the population, Obama won 26 percent or less of the white vote in five (the exception being Maryland, where Obama won 47 percent of the white vote). In the two states—Maine and

FIGURE 5-3   White Vote for Obama in 2008 in Relation to African American Population by State

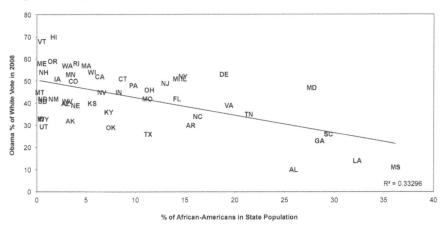

Source: 2008 National Election Pool exit polls.

Vermont—where whites made up 95 percent or more of the population, Obama easily carried the white vote. Nevertheless, there is no denying that racial prejudice still has a significant influence on Americans' behavior at the ballot box. In fact, the influence of racial attitudes on voting in 2008, triggered by Barack Obama on the ballot, was on par with the influence of partisanship and ideology.[34]

Obama's poor showing among whites in the South has deep historical roots. The divisions of the Civil War were still remarkably evident in Obama's elections. In every state that was part of the Confederacy, the Republican presidential nominee in 2008 and 2012 won a larger share of the white vote than Obama did nationwide. In 2008 Obama won every state that Lincoln had carried in 1860 and all but one (Indiana) in 2012. Obama's share of the white vote in a state in his initial election, in fact, is strongly correlated with Lincoln's share of the state vote in 1860 (see Figure 5-4). In states where Lincoln had done well in 1860, Obama tended to win relatively easily; in states where Lincoln had done poorly (he was not even on the ballot in most of the South and thus received no votes in many states), Obama generally fared poorly. The strength of the relationship between Lincoln's and Obama's vote can be demonstrated by the fact that Lincoln's best state

FIGURE 5-4   White Vote for Obama in 2008 and Vote for Lincoln in 1860 by State

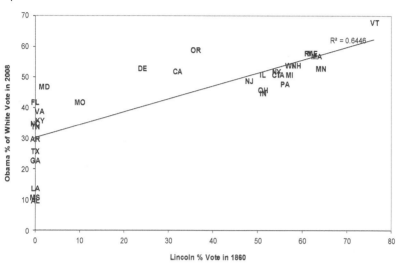

Source: 2008 National Election Pool exit polls; David Leip, "Atlas of U.S. Presidential Elections," http://uselectionatlas.org.

in 1860 was Vermont, which so happened to be Obama's best state in the contiguous United States.

Besides handily winning the African American vote, Obama did very well among Hispanics. Obama won eight of the ten states with the highest proportion of Hispanics in 2008 and 2012 (losing only Texas and Arizona). Hispanic voters shifted in significant numbers away from the Republicans to vote for Barack Obama. His ability in 2008 and 2012 to win Colorado, Nevada, and New Mexico—states that had voted for Bush in 2004—was largely due to his strong support among Latinos in these states. Obama's support among Hispanics, however, was much more context specific than was the case with African Americans, who tended to support Obama overwhelmingly regardless of where they lived. After Latinos reached roughly 40 percent of a county's population, Obama's share of the vote actually went down.[35] Obama's most impressive gains among Hispanics took place in Florida, where he was the first Democratic presidential nominee to carry the Hispanic vote since exit polls first were conducted in that state. South Florida's large Cuban American population has remained Republican leaning, and given the slow process of immigrant political incorporation, they are expected to remain so in the foreseeable future.[36] Obama's strength among Latinos in Florida was mainly a result of a growing group of Puerto Rican voters in central Florida who tend to be strongly Democratic.

Nationally, Hispanics made up 10 percent of total voters in 2012, up from 8 percent in 2004. Some states, however, increased their Latino vote shares by much larger margins. In Colorado Latinos went from 8 percent of the electorate in 2004 to 14 percent in 2012, and in New Mexico Latinos went from 32 percent of the electorate to 37 percent. Among Hispanic voters nationwide Obama won a greater share in 2012 than in 2008. Perhaps more important for his reelection effort, however, was his success in increasing the share of Hispanic voters among the total voting population in battleground states, including Colorado and Nevada. This was especially evident in Nevada, where Hispanics went from being 15 percent of the electorate in 2008 to 19 percent of the electorate in 2012. Because Obama did so well among Hispanics, this increased voter turnout helped him considerably in both 2008 and 2012. Conversely, the relatively small Hispanic populations in the South worked to Obama's disadvantage. Although the Latino population in the South has increased significantly since 2000, the proportion of Latinos living in southern states remains relatively low in comparison to the general population.[37]

Interestingly, Obama's strong performance among Hispanics was by no means a given. Early in his first presidential campaign the general perception was that he did not appeal to Hispanic voters (in part because he was African American), and he struggled with this group during the nomination stage. In fact, even though he won two-thirds of their support against John McCain in the 2008 general election, Obama actually lost three-fifths of Latino votes to Hillary Clinton in the 2008 Democratic primaries. Latinos were critical in determining the outcome of the primary or caucus in a number of important states (such as California), significantly helping Clinton's campaign. Clinton's strong support among Hispanics, however, proved to be more a consequence of the nature of the two campaigns and the name recognition of the respective candidates than the result of any underlying social biases Latinos might have possessed and their long-term willingness to vote for an African American candidate.[38]

Given that Barack Obama was attempting to become the first African American to be elected president, many perceived race to be a significant factor in the 2008 campaign. Yet of those who voted, 80 percent said that race was not a factor in their vote; only 2 percent said that race was the single most important factor. Among the latter group, Obama won 58 percent of the vote; among the former, he won 51 percent of the vote. White voters who acknowledged that race was important voted for McCain by a 2 to 1 margin, meaning that one-third of white voters who said Obama's race was the single most important factor actually voted for Obama.[39]

Those who voted for Obama were much more optimistic about the future of race relations in the country. According to exit polls, of the nearly one-half of the voters who thought that race relations would get better in the next few years, 70 percent voted for Obama. Of the one-sixth who thought that race relations would get worse in the next few years, 70 percent voted for McCain.

Obama's credible aspirations for the presidency rested on his articulation of himself as occupying postracial and postpartisan spaces. Obama's campaign promised leadership that would transcend race and be independent of his ties to the black community. Obama's biracial heritage, Ivy League pedigree, and international, rather than southern, roots distanced him from the stereotypical views that some Americans had of blacks. That Obama presented none of the popular stereotypes of black masculinity—anger, aggression, danger, criminality—made him more palatable to white voters.[40]

Yet there is also evidence to suggest that negative stereotypes about blacks significantly eroded white support for Barack Obama. Racial stereotypes did not predict support for previous Democratic presidential candidates or other prominent Democrats, indicating that white voters punished Obama for his race rather than for his party affiliation. Interestingly, prejudice had a particularly large impact on the decisions of Independent voters and a substantial impact on Democrat voters, but very little influence on Republican voters.[41] Racial prejudice was especially a factor in limiting support for Obama among white voters in the South and in the border states.[42]

Thus, even though Obama ended up gaining the votes of enough whites to win by a relatively solid margin in 2008, it is possible that race prevented Obama from winning a landslide victory. In a truly race-blind society, Obama might have won by a considerably larger margin. The white vote for Democratic presidential candidates barely increased from 2004 to 2008, even in the face of economic and political woes, the worst since the end of World War II. Those who believed that blacks were worse off because of the continuing effects of racism were more likely to have voted for Obama, thus offsetting those who voted against him because he was perceived as favoring African Americans. However, those who were more sympathetic toward blacks were no more likely to convert their economic discontent into an Obama vote. Simply put, racial esteem in 2008 did not cancel out racial prejudice.[43] Similarly, it appears that race may have also cost Obama in his reelection bid in 2012: one study found that Obama lost more than 3 percent of the vote from racially intolerant voters who otherwise would have been expected to support him.[44]

Unlike the general election, however, Obama's race probably benefited him in the 2008 Democratic primaries and caucuses. From a demographic-support perspective, the key to Obama's ability to win the Democratic nomination was his tremendous support from African American voters. Of the thirty-three states that had Democratic primaries, Obama's average vote among African Americans was 83 percent and among whites it was only 40 percent, the same as Obama's percentage among Hispanics.[45] By winning more than four out of five black primary votes, Obama's margins were close to what Democrats typically win among African Americans against Republicans in general elections.

In many respects Obama's coalition of support for the 2008 Democratic nomination resembled that of previous nonestablishment reformers who ran competitive races for the Democratic presidential nomination, including Gary Hart in 1984, Paul Tsongas in 1992, and Bill Bradley in 2000. All these candidates, however, were ultimately unsuccessful in their quest for the nomination. The important difference between these previous outsider candidates and Obama was Obama's ability to overwhelmingly win the black vote.[46] Essentially, Obama was able to duplicate previous nonestablishment candidates' ability to win younger, well-educated, secular, wealthier, and liberal voters. But previous outsider candidates were unable to peel off much black support from the more establishment candidate. It was thus Obama's ability to add the overwhelming support of African Americans, along with the groups that had supported outsider candidates in the past, that helped put him over the top.

Race and Public Policy Preferences

Americans' ideological leanings are heavily influenced by race. Conservatives are more likely to be racially prejudiced, but racial prejudice actually plays a larger role in shaping the thinking of liberals than of conservatives on matters of race.[47] The levels of support the Democratic and Republican parties get from different racial groups is consistent on ideological lines. The declining support for the Democratic Party among southern whites, northern white working-class voters, and northern ethnic voters beginning in the 1960s was the result of an ideological realignment in the electorate.

Whites are considerably more likely to view themselves as conservative relative to blacks and Hispanics (see Figure 5-5). Whereas blacks and Hispanics have mean ideological scores to the left of center, in the aggregate

FIGURE 5-5   Race and Ideology

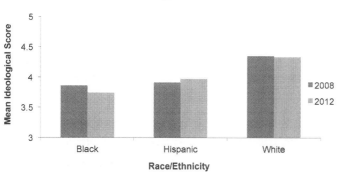

Definition: Self-Identification Scale from 1 to 7, with 1 = most liberal and 7 = most conservative.
Source: ANES 2008 and 2012 datasets.

whites see themselves as right of center. It is possible, however, that in practice whites may not be as conservative as is suggested by their mean ideological score because their ideological leanings are considerably less political than those of other groups.[48] Whites' identification as being relatively conservative, therefore, may be more philosophical than policy oriented.

An important reason for the relative liberalism of blacks and Hispanics is that these minority groups put much more of a premium on equality than whites do. Whereas nearly one-half of whites believe that we should worry less about equality, only two-fifths of Hispanics and one-third of African Americans agree with this sentiment.[49] A belief in egalitarian principles was a common thread that bound Barack Obama voters. A coalition of minorities and upscale whites who placed a higher priority on equality was critical to Obama's victory. In this respect the Democratic majority assembled by Obama represented the emergence of a Great Society electoral coalition. When Lyndon Johnson signed the Civil Rights Act of 1964, he reportedly said of the Democrats, "We have lost the South for a generation." The 2008 election, however, marked the possible emergence of a new Democratic coalition that rests upon historic changes brought about by Johnson's Great Society. These include the Civil Rights Act of 1964 and the Voting Rights Act of 1965, both of which enfranchised millions of African American voters; the Immigration and Nationality Act of 1965, which removed national-origin quotas and led to increased levels of immigration; and the Higher Education Act of 1965, which increased federal support for higher education.[50]

The tendency of racial and ethnic minorities—especially African Americans—to be strong believers in equality is unsurprising given the discrimination minorities historically faced. African Americans are especially sensitive to perceived inequalities in governmental policies. For example, the handling of Hurricane Katrina, which struck Louisiana and Mississippi in August 2005, appeared to demonstrate to many the inequalities of race and class in the United States. Some argued that the inability of the federal government to respond to the disaster called attention to a "politics of disposability" whereby certain people were deemed disposable and not worthy of care and help.[51] Others argued that the tragedy of Katrina was the result of policies that encouraged segregation and thus increased inequality.[52]

The Race Gap in Economic Issues

With regard to economic issues, there is a strong relationship between race and policy preferences. African Americans and Latinos tend to be to the political left of whites on economic issues, sometimes substantially so (see Figure 5-6). Whites are consistently more conservative about government spending than blacks and Hispanics, and there is no evidence of significant changes in the mass opinion of whites since the 1980s.[53] The relative conservatism of whites is derived in part from their perception that they are less likely to benefit from an increase in government services. After Congress enacted Obama's health care reforms, for example, a majority of whites believed that the new law would help the uninsured and low-income families but not them.[54] Contrarily, many African Americans viewed Barack Obama's election as president as a personal achievement that would now enable them to live the American Dream.[55] As a result, even though living conditions for African Americans remained largely the same after Obama was sworn into office, African Americans believed that their standard of living significantly improved after his election to the presidency.[56]

FIGURE 5-6   The Race Gap: Economic Issues

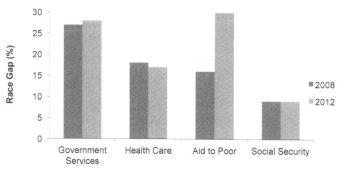

Definitions: Race gap = largest differential among whites, blacks, and Latinos. Government services = government should provide more services. Health care = favor universal health insurance. Aid to poor = aid to the poor should be increased. Social Security = favor Social Security invested in stocks and bonds. Source: ANES 2008 and 2012 datasets.

On government services, health care, aid to the poor, and Social Security privatization, African Americans are significantly more liberal than whites, which is a consequence of the fact that as a group they are poorer than whites and Hispanics. Despite dramatic changes in education and occupational opportunities for African Americans, the black-white earnings gap has remained stubbornly large. In part this is due to considerable differences in racial earnings inequality between the public and private sectors. Whereas the earnings gap in the public sector has vanished, in the private sector it is still significant.[57]

The economic preferences of Hispanics are consistently in between those of blacks and whites—they are more liberal than whites but not as liberal as African Americans. The large number of Hispanic immigrants to the United States since the 1970s has changed the relationship of income to voting because those ineligible to vote are substantially poorer than eligible citizens. Though international studies have found that immigrants are no more likely to support increased social spending or redistributive measures than natives,[58] this does not appear to be the case among Hispanics in the United States.

African Americans and Hispanics tend to have greater faith in the government to provide services, and in the case of Social Security are more skeptical of privatization. In the past Republicans suggested that blacks should favor Social Security reform because they have relatively lower life expectancy and thus are less likely to maximize their potential benefits. Given their low levels of support for putting Social Security in stocks and bonds, however, this argument appears to have garnered little support among African Americans.

The Race Gap in Domestic and Foreign Policy Issues

The race gap is by no means limited to economic issues; there is also a significant race gap on noneconomic issues (see Figure 5-7). Whites are more conservative than Hispanics and African Americans on such issues. African Americans are the most liberal on gun control, the environment, and defense spending, while Hispanics are the most liberal on immigration. Given that many Hispanics currently living in the United States are relatively recent

FIGURE 5-7   The Race Gap: Domestic and Foreign Policy Issues

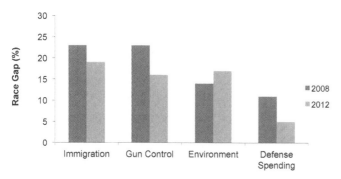

Definitions: Race gap = largest differential among whites, blacks, and Latinos. Immigration = immigration levels should be reduced. Gun control = buying a gun should be made more difficult. Environment = favor increased regulation to protect the environment. Defense spending = defense spending should be reduced.
Source: ANES 2008 and 2012 datasets.

immigrants, it is unsurprising that they are less supportive than blacks and whites of reducing immigration levels. Recent immigration has changed the face of America and considerably increased the number of people living in the country who are not citizens—the proportion of the population that is noncitizen today has tripled since the 1970s to 8 percent.[59] African Americans' relatively strong support for restricting immigration may be because they view immigrants as competition in the marketplace with respect to local political power and jobs.[60]

The politics of immigration has potentially important demographic consequences for the future strength of the parties. Immigration has divided Republicans, with probusiness interests favoring fewer restrictions on immigration and social conservatives favoring more. Most social conservatives in the country are wage earners, so the economic impact of competing with immigrants is undoubtedly a factor in their hostility toward immigrants. Probusiness Republicans, in contrast, feel that immigration keeps American's businesses supplied with cheap labor.[61] Social conservatives appear to have been winning the debate within the Republican Party in recent years, and as a result immigration has become a much more important issue for Hispanics, to the Democratic Party's advantage.[62]

That whites are less supportive of environmental regulation seems to contradict the premise that whites would be stronger environmentalists because they are relatively wealthier than blacks and Hispanics; previous investigations found a strong relationship between one's income and one's support for environmental protection measures.[63] On gun control, the relative lack of support among whites for making the buying of a gun more difficult is at least partially a consequence of the fact that whites are more likely to own guns. Whites are also less likely to live in urban areas than minority racial and ethnic groups are, and support for gun control is much higher in urban areas of the country than in rural areas.[64]

In regard to defense spending, whites are more conservative than African Americans and Hispanics. White voters, in fact, have been more supportive of increased defense spending since the 1980s.[65] Interestingly, even though Hispanics are more likely than whites to encourage young people to enlist in the military, they are relatively less supportive of military spending. Consequently, it has been suggested that such an ethnic gap in public opinion toward military spending may lead to future difficulties in securing funding.[66]

The Race Gap in Values and Social Issues

In many respects the race gap seems to contradict some of the premises of the religion gap. Even though African Americans are overwhelmingly Democratic, they also tend to be more religious than whites and Hispanics.[67] Not only are African Americans more likely than whites and Hispanics to attend religious services weekly, but also less than one-fifth of African Americans claim to never attend church, a figure considerably lower than the three-tenths of Hispanics and two-fifths of whites who never attend religious services. Though Protestants tend to be solidly Republican, some of the most religious people in the United States—African American Protestants—are overwhelmingly Democratic.

The movement of religious conservatives to the Republican Party has been strongest among whites because, influenced by their particular social and racial/ethnic histories, African Americans and Hispanics have religious interpretations that differ from those of whites. Thus, even though African Americans are much more likely than others to be evangelicals and biblical literalists, they are much less likely to identify with the Republican Party. As the Republican Party has become more associated with evangelicals and religious conservatives, white biblical literalists have strongly gravitated to the Party, but among African Americans there has been no movement whatsoever among biblical literalists to the Republicans.[68]

Among Hispanics, however, Republicans have made some gains among the most religious. Religious identity has an independent effect on the vote among Hispanic evangelicals. Religion is an important explanation of political differences among Hispanics, as Catholic Hispanics are considerably more likely than Protestant Hispanics to support Democratic candidates.[69] The existence of a religion gap among Hispanics suggests that the Hispanic electorate may become much less cohesive as a voting bloc as religious affiliation becomes more pluralistic in the Hispanic community.[70]

White evangelicals have typically been reluctant to support black candidates, which had led to implications that the white evangelical vote has racist overtones. Though white evangelicalism is associated with higher levels of racial resentment, these attitudes have been found to be steeped in ideological beliefs, not in an antiblack effect based on religious values. Evangelicals are not necessarily fundamentally racist; rather, their lack of support for black candidates is driven by differences in policy preferences.[71] Yet in 2008 the counties with the largest increases in the Republican share of the presidential vote from 2004 tended to be small towns and rural areas with relatively high concentrations of white southern Baptists, even though the policy differences between the Democratic nominees John Kerry and Barack Obama were relatively insubstantial.[72]

That African Americans and Hispanics are more regular churchgoers than whites shapes their views on social issues (see Figure 5-8). In regard to gay marriage, for example, African Americans are the most conservative group. The relative lack of support for gay marriage from African Americans is consistent with the 2008 vote in California on Proposition 8, a ballot measure to ban same-sex marriage. Although the measure won only

FIGURE 5-8   The Race Gap: Values and Social Issues

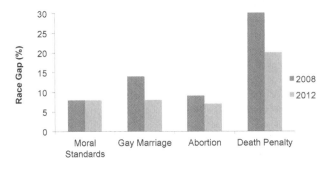

Definitions: Race gap = largest differential among whites, blacks, and Latinos. Moral standards = should be more tolerant of people with different moral standards. Gay marriage = agree that gays should be allowed to marry. Abortion = abortion should never be permitted/permitted only in cases of rape and incest. Death penalty = favor death penalty.
Source: ANES 2008 and 2012 datasets.

narrowly statewide, 70 percent of blacks voted for the proposition. The racial divide on gay marriage has been found to be a function of African Americans' ties to sectarian Protestant religious denominations and a high rate of church attendance.[73] Whereas blacks have consistently shown relatively less support for gay marriage, Hispanics have shown considerably more support for gay marriage.[74] Hispanics, in fact, are actually more likely to support gay marriage than whites.

On abortion, however, Hispanics tend to be more conservative as they are more likely to believe that abortion should never be permitted or permitted only in cases of rape and incest; blacks and whites take the prolife position at about the same rate. This similarity of views among blacks and whites on abortion is not a consequence of varying abortion rates among the races; abortion rates are considerably higher for blacks than for whites, largely because they have a higher number of unintended pregnancies.[75] Among whites, public opinion on abortion has remained remarkably consistent, and there has been no evidence of significant changes in mass opinion on the issue since the 1980s.[76] The relative liberalism of whites on abortion (and, to a lesser degree, gay marriage), however, does not translate to their views on moral standards in general. On the question of tolerance toward people with different moral standards, whites are the most conservative group.

Whites are also considerably more likely to support the death penalty. Because blacks and Hispanics are more religious than whites, their opposition to the death penalty may be based at least partially on moral grounds. Racial prejudice, however, has been found to be a strong predictor of white support for the death penalty. The percentage of African Americans in a state shapes the rate at which that state applies capital punishment.[77] As the black percentage of county residents rises, so, too, does the impact of racial prejudice on white support for capital punishment.[78] An explanation for the race gap on the death penalty is that whites see the death penalty as a means for justice and crime control, not a symbol of racism, whereas African Americans consider the death penalty to be administered unfairly and disproportionately toward their racial group.[79]

The ideological inconsistency of whites, Hispanics, and blacks on social issues—no one group is consistently the most liberal or conservative—seems to indicate that economic issues are better determinants for vote choice among the different racial groups than noneconomic issues. The strong preference of African Americans and Hispanics for Democratic candidates, therefore, is more a reflection of their views on economic issues—where they tend to be comparably liberal—than their views on social issues, where they tend to be relatively more conservative. Therefore, in regard to the race gap, economic issues appear to be a much more salient indicator of vote choice than social issues are.

The Significance of the Race Gap

The race gap has important implications for the future of American politics. As the United States becomes less white as a nation, the changing demographics of the electorate inevitably will affect future elections. Of particular importance in the changing demographics of the American electorate is the increasing number of Hispanic voters.

Historically, whites turned out to vote at higher rates than blacks and Hispanics did, though in both 2008 and 2012 African Americans—encouraged by Obama's attempt to become the first African American president—were actually slightly more likely to vote than whites (see Figure 5-9). The overall

FIGURE 5-9   Voter Turnout Rates in Presidential Elections by Race

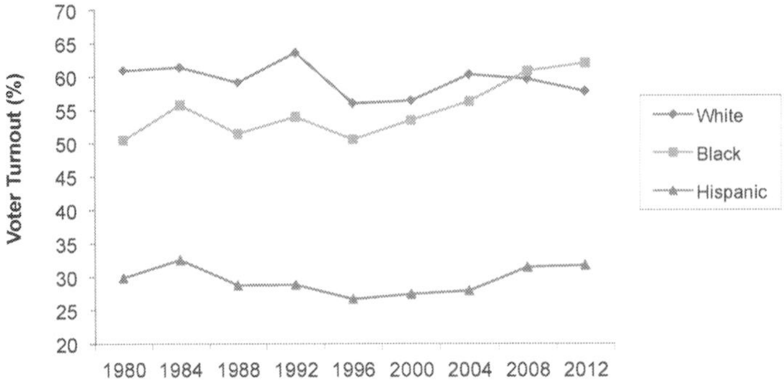

Source: US Census.

voter turnout rate was about the same in 2004 as in 2008 and 2012. But the composition of the electorate changed, as the turnout among eligible whites declined slightly but rose among eligible blacks. Voter turnout for Hispanics lagged considerably: in every presidential election since 1980, less than one-third of adult Hispanics voted, and in 2008 and 2012 the voter turnout rate of Hispanics was about one-half of what it was for blacks and whites. Though part of the reason for the lower voter turnout rate of Hispanics is the presence of Hispanic noncitizens legally unable to vote, even among citizens less than one-half of Hispanics voted in 2012. Hispanics thus remain severely undermobilized as a share of the electorate.[80]

Obama's victories in 2008 and 2012 were partly the result of the gradual transformation of the electorate since the 1990s. In 2012 whites accounted for 72 percent of the overall electorate, a 13-point drop from 1988. Obama's overwhelming support from nonwhites was thus crucial to both of his victories. If the racial composition of the electorate had been the same in 2008 and 2012 as in 1988, McCain and Romney would likely have defeated Obama. Obama's deficit among white voters, in fact, was remarkably similar to that of other recent Democratic presidential nominees. In every presidential election since 1988, Democrats consistently won between 39 percent (Obama in 2012) and 44 percent (Clinton in 1996) of the white vote. Yet in 2012, despite losing to Romney among whites by more than

17 million votes, Obama won the election by carrying nonwhites by more than 20 million votes. Obama's ability to win so many nonwhite votes derived largely from the growing numbers of Hispanics in the electorate. As recently as the first election of Bill Clinton as president in 1992, Hispanics made up only 2 percent of the electorate, far smaller than their 10 percent share of the electorate in 2012.

The changing demographics of the American electorate pose a dilemma for the Republican Party. Nearly 90 percent of McCain's and Romney's total vote came from whites. Obama's electoral coalition was much more diverse: in 2012 56 percent of his supporters were white, nearly 25 percent were black, and 16 percent were Hispanic. The majority of American children under three years old are now nonwhite. America's white, non-Hispanic population grew by only 1.2 percent from 2000 to 2010, and in fifteen of the fifty states it actually shrunk. Among children under eighteen, however, this drop was much more dramatic: the number of white children fell in forty-six states, for an overall decrease of 10 percent.[81] As a result of these demographic changes, the nonwhite share is projected to grow to become about one-third of the U.S. electorate by 2020. Under these circumstances, even a 60 percent share of the white vote would not be enough to give a Republican candidate a majority of the popular vote given the party's current support among nonwhites.[82] Since the Republican Party's devastatingly poor performance among nonwhites in the 2012 presidential election, many Republicans have become acutely aware of their party's dilemma, and some have sought to modify the Republican Party's image by embracing issues such as immigration reform.

Critical to Republican success in future elections will be the party's ability to increase vote share among Hispanics. Although Hispanics disproportionately voted Democratic in the past, given their continuing upward mobility and social conservatism on issues such as abortion, Latinos may become more Republican over time.[83] With generation replacement, changes in the dynamics of vote choice across immigrant generations may indicate long-term changes in the mechanisms of vote choice. Among Mexican Americans, for example, it has been found that generation replacement does shape vote choice both directly and indirectly.[84]

Nevertheless, Hispanics may be poised to become even stronger supporters of Democratic candidates. In the past, politically less knowledgeable Hispanics tended to favor Republicans more often than did those who
were more politically knowledgeable. Where issues counted, the majority
of Hispanic voters weighed strongly in favor of the Democrats.[85] Thus, as
Hispanics become more integrated into the fabric of American politics and
become more aware and knowledgeable about politics, this may lead them
to be even more Democratic in their vote choices. Of particular importance
is the issue of immigration because Latinos tend to be significantly more
supportive of immigration than blacks and whites. If Hispanics view the
Republic Party as anti-immigrant, this could be disastrous for the party's
prospects long term.[86]

The increasing diversity of the American population is not simply a reflection of immigration from Latin America. The number of Americans
who identify as Asian and as multiracial has also been steadily increasing,
and both groups have become solidly Democratic constituencies. Asian
Americans gave Obama 62 percent of their vote in 2008, a figured that increased to 73 percent in 2012. Those who identify themselves as multiracial
tend to develop political opinions that parallel those of their minority counterparts. Multiracial Americans consistently adopt political attitudes that
reveal they are more aware of racialized experiences than their monoracial
counterparts.[87] As a result, multiracial Americans have become strongly
Democratic in their vote preferences. This will be important as the multiracial proportion of the American population increases.

Native Americans, though negligible at the national level due to their relatively small population levels and low voter participation rates, represent
a potentially important voting bloc in some western states because of the
concentration of Native American communities there. In 2004, for example,
Democrat Tim Johnson of South Dakota won reelection to the Senate by
524 votes, a margin that was much smaller than the Native American votes
for Johnson. Because Native Americans are overwhelmingly Democratic in
their voting, this offers Democrats a potentially underutilized group of supporters in some parts of the country.[88]

The Republican Party potentially faces electoral peril unless it does a better job in the future of winning the votes of minorities. Increasing the Republican share of the nonwhite vote, however, will probably require the party to move closer to the ideological center on issues such as government services, health care, and immigration. Such a shift would certainly arouse intense opposition from conservative activists. In fact, led by Tea Party activists, the Republican Party appears to be moving in the opposite direction. Tea Party supporters have been found to exert a strong authoritarian pulse, and Tea Party members' judgments about aid to the poor are influenced considerably by racial attitudes.[89] Racial resentment stokes Tea Party fears about generational societal change and fuels the Tea Party's strong opposition to Obama. Many Tea Partiers are deeply concerned that the country they live in is not the country of their youth and that they themselves are no longer represented by the US government.[90] Republican leaders, therefore, will inevitably face a difficult choice between reaching out to nonwhite voters or continuing to cater to their party's shrinking base.[91] Thus, the Southern Strategy the Republican Party adopted beginning with Richard Nixon's presidential run in 1968, though successful for a number of decades by increasing the party's appeal to white voters, may backfire in the long run as the electorate becomes increasingly nonwhite.[92]

The only way Republicans can continue to be competitive without increasing their vote totals among nonwhites is to win the votes of whites by even greater margins. This, however, is probably not a viable strategy as younger whites are more willing to support Democratic candidates than older whites are. If the Republicans continue failing to make inroads in winning the votes of nonwhites as younger whites become increasingly Democratic in their vote preferences, the Republicans will indeed be in trouble.

Notes

1. Technically, Hispanics have been defined by the US Census as an ethnic group and can be of any race. The Census Bureau, however, in August 2012 proposed making Hispanics a distinct category regardless of race. For the purposes of linguistic simplicity, I will define the

race gap as the differences in political behavior and attitudes of African Americans, whites, and Hispanics

2. Hanes Walton and Robert Smith, *American Politics and African American Quest for Universal Freedom* (New York: Pearson Longman, 2006).

3. Michael S. Lewis-Beck, William G. Jacoby, Helmut Norpoth, and Herbert F. Weisberg, *The American Voter Revisited* (Ann Arbor: University of Michigan Press, 2008), 322–323.

4. Donald Kinder and Lynn Sanders, *Divided by Color: Racial Politics and Democratic Ideals* (Chicago: University of Chicago Press, 1996).

5. Walton and Smith, *American Politics*, 126.

6. Thomas B. Edsall and Mary D. Edsall, *Chain Reaction: The Impact of Race, Rights, and Taxes on American Politics* (New York: Norton, 1991).

7. Alan I. Abramowitz, *The Disappearing Center* (New Haven, CT: Yale University Press, 2010), 73.

8. Michael C. Dawson, *Behind the Mule: Race and Class in African-American Politics* (Princeton, NJ: Princeton University Press, 1994).

9. Tasha S. Philpot, *Race, Republicans, and the Return of the Party of Lincoln* (Ann Arbor: University of Michigan Press, 2007).

10. Barack Obama, *The Audacity of Hope* (New York: Three Rivers Press, 2006), 253.

11. Nolan McCarty, Keith T. Poole, and Howard Rosenthal, *Polarized America* (Cambridge, MA: MIT Press), 90.

12. "More Than 6 of 10 Very Religious Whites Identify with GOP," Gallup, October 31, 2011. Poll conducted July 1–October 26, 2011.

13. Julia Preston, "Poll Finds Hispanics Returning to Earlier Preference for Democrats," *New York Times*, December 7, 2007.

14. Eric L. McDaniel and Christopher G. Ellison, "God's Party? Race, Religion, and Partisanship over Time," *Political Research Quarterly* 61 (2008): 180–191.

15. James G. Gimpel and Jason E. Schuknecht, *Patchwork Nation: Sectionalism and Political Change in American Politics* (Ann Arbor: University of Michigan Press, 2003), 46.

16. Atiya Kai Stokes-Brown, "Racial Identity and Latino Vote Choice," *American Political Research* 34 (2006): 627–652.

17. Peter N. Skerry, *Mexican Americans: The Ambivalent Minority* (New York: Free Press, 1993).

18. Alan I. Abramowitz, "Beyond 2010: Demographic Change and the Future of the Republican Party," March 11, 2010, www.centerforpolitics.org.

19. Matt Barreto et al., "Should They Dance with the One Who Brung 'Em? Latinos and the 2008 Presidential Election," *PS: Political Science and Politics* 41 (2008): 753–760.

20. Donald Kinder and Lynn Sanders, *Divided by Color: Racial Politics and Democratic Ideals* (Chicago: University of Chicago Press, 1996), 217–218.

21. "2008 Electorate: European Americans—Tribal Politics Persist," November 11, 2009, www.openleft.com.

22. Adolph Reed, "The 2004 Election in Perspective: The Myth of 'Cultural Divide' and the Triumph of Neoliberal Ideology," *American Quarterly* 57 (2005): 1–15.

23. Brian K. Arbour, "Unhyphenated Americans in the 2010 U.S. House Election," *Forum* 9 (2011): article 4.

24. Warren Miller and Merrill Shanks, *The New American Voter* (Cambridge, MA: Harvard University Press, 1996).

25. Alan Abramowitz and H. Gibbs Knotts, "Ideological Realignment in the American Electorate: A Comparison of Northern and Southern White Voters in the Pre-Reagan, Reagan, and Post-Reagan Eras," *Politics and Policy* 34 (2006): 94–108; Mark D. Brewer and Jeffrey M. Stonecash, "Class, Race Issues, and Declining White Support for the Democratic Party in the South," *Political Behavior* 23 (2001): 131–155.

26. William D. Schreckhise and Todd G. Shields, "Ideological Realignment in the Contemporary U.S. Electorate Revisited," *Social Science Quarterly* 84 (2003): 596–612.

27. Abramowitz, *Disappearing Center,* 73.

28. James M. Glaser, "Back to the Black Belt: Racial Environment and White Racial Attitudes in the South," *Journal of Politics* 56 (1994): 21–41.

29. Regina P. Branton, "Voting in Initiative Elections: Does the Context of Racial and Ethnic Diversity Matter?," *State Politics and Policy Quarterly* 4 (2004): 294–317.

30. V. O. Key, *Southern Politics in State and Nation* (New York: Knopf, 1949).

31. Hurbert Blalock, *Toward a Theory of Minority-Group Relations* (New York: Riley, 1967).

32. Byron D'Andra Orey, "White Racial Attitudes and Support for the Mississippi State Flag," *American Politics Research* 32 (2004): 102–116.

33. Earl Black and Merle Black, *Politics and Society in the South* (Cambridge, MA: Harvard University Press, 1987), 138–142.

34. Benjamin Highton, "Prejudice Rivals Partisanship and Ideology When Explaining the 2008 Presidential Vote Across the States," *PS: Political Science and Politics* 44 (2011): 530–535.

35. Baodong Liu, "Obama's Local Connection: Racial Conflict or Solidarity," *PS: Political Science and Politics* 44 (2011): 103–105.

36. Benjamin G. Bishin and Casey A. Klofstad, "The Political Incorporation of Cuban Americans: Why Won't Little Havana Turn Blue?," *Political Research Quarterly* 65 (2012): 586–599.

37. J. Salvador Peralta and George Larkin, "Counting Those Who Count: The Impact of Latino Population Growth on Redistricting in Southern States," *PS: Political Science and Politics* 44 (2011): 552–561.

38. Matt Barreto et al., "Should They Dance?," 753–760.

39. Chuck Todd and Sheldon Gawiser, *How Barack Obama Won* (New York: Vintage Books, 2009), 41.

40. Valeria Sinclair-Chapman and Melanye Price, "Black Politics, the 2008 Election, and the (Im)possibility of Race Transcendence," *PS: Political Science and Politics* 41 (2008): 739–745.

41. Spencer Piston, "How Explicit Racial Prejudice Hurt Obama in the 2008 Election," *Political Behavior* 32 (2010): 431–451.

42. Abramowitz, *Disappearing Center,* 116.

43. Michael S. Lewis-Beck, Charles Tien, and Richard Nadeau, "Obama's Missed Landslide: A Racial Cost?," *PS: Political Science and Politics* 43 (2010): 69–76.

44. Charles Tien, Richard Nadeau, and Michael S. Lewis-Beck, "Obama and 2012: Still a Racial Cost to Pay?," *PS: Political Science and Politics* 45 (2012): 591–595.

45. Patrick Fisher, "The Gapology of the Obama Vote in the 2008 Democratic Presidential Primaries," *Society* 48 (2011): 502–509.

46. Philip A. Klinkner and Thomas Schaller, "LBJ's Revenge: The 2008 Election and the Rise of the Great Society Coalition," *Forum* 6 (2008): article 9.

47. Paul M. Sniderman and Edward G. Carmines, *Reaching Beyond Race* (Cambridge, MA: Harvard University Press, 1997).

48. R. M. Alvarez and L. G. Bedolla, "The Foundations of Latino Voter Partisanship: Evidence from the 2000 Election," *Journal of Politics* 65 (2003): 31–49.

49. Author calculations of responses to questions V081103a and V085165 in the ANES 2008 dataset.

50. Klinkner and Schaller, "LBJ's Revenge."

51. Douglas Kellner, "The Katrina Hurricane Spectacle and Crisis of the Bush Presidency," *Cultural Studies/Critical Methodologies* 7 (2007): 222–234.

52. Brian Barry, *Culture and Equality: An Egalitarian Critique of Multiculturalism* (Cambridge, MA: Harvard University Press, 2001).

53. Larry Bartels, *Unequal Democracy* (New York: Russell Sage, 2008), chap. 3.

54. Ronald Brownstein, "Dems Caught in a Populist Crossfire," *National Journal*, March 27, 2010.

55. Rakim Brooks, "A Linked Fate: Barack Obama and Black America," *Politics and Power* 3 (2012): 42–45.

56. "Black Optimism About Their Standard of Living Top Whites," Gallup, July 8, 2010. Poll conducted June 1–30, 2010.

57. Moshe Semyonov and Noah Lewin-Epstein, "The Declining Racial Earnings' Gap in the United States: Multi-Level Analysis of Males' Earnings, 1960–2000," *Social Science Research* 38 (2009): 296–311.

58. Rafaela Dancygier and Elizabeth N. Saunders, "A New Electorate? Comparing Preferences and Partisanship Between Immigrants and Natives," *American Journal of Political Science* 50 (2006): 962–981.

59. Nolan McCarty, Keith T. Poole, and Howard Rosenthal, *Polarized America: The Dance of Ideology and Unequal Riches* (Cambridge, MA: MIT Press, 2006), 115–116.

60. Paula D. McClain and Albert K. Karing, "Black and Hispanic Socioeconomic and Political Competition," *American Political Science Review* 84 (1990): 535–545.

61. Gary Miller and Norman Schofield, "The Transformation of the Republican and Democratic Party Coalitions in the U.S.," *Perspectives on Politics* 6 (2008): 433–450.

62. John Kenneth White, *Barack Obama's America* (Ann Arbor: University of Michigan Press, 2009), 206.

63. Ronald Inglehart, "Changing Values Among Western Publics from 1970 to 2006," *Western European Politics* 31 (2008): 130–146.

64. Robert J. Spitzer, *The Politics of Gun Control*, 3rd ed. (Washington, DC: CQ Press, 2004), 102.

65. Bartels, *Unequal Democracy*, chap. 3.

66. David L. Leal, "American Public Opinion Toward the Military Differences by Race, Gender, and Class?," *Armed Forces and Society* 32 (2005): 123–138.

67. Author calculations from questions V081103a, V083185, and V083186 in the ANES 2008 dataset.

68. Eric L. McDaniel and Christopher G. Ellison, "God's Party? Race, Religion, and Partisanship over Time," *Political Research Quarterly* 61 (2008): 180–191.

69. Nathan J. Kelly and Jana Morgan Kelly, "Religion and Latino Partisanship in the United States," *Political Research Quarterly* 58 (2005): 87–95.

70. Lee Jongho and Harry P. Pachon, "Leading the Way," *American Politics Research* 35 (2007): 252–272.

71. Brian Robert Calfano and Philip Paolino, "An Alan Keyes Effect? Examining Anti-Black Sentiment Among White Evangelicals," *Political Behavior* 32 (2010): 133–156.

72. Abramowitz, *Disappearing Center*, 99.

73. Darren E. Sherkat, Kylan Mattias de Vries, and Stacia Creek, "Race, Religion, and Opposition to Same-Sex Marriage," *Social Science Quarterly* 91 (2010): 80–98.

74. Christopher G. Ellison, Gabriel A. Acevedo, and Aida Ramos-Wada, "Religion and Attitudes Toward Same-Sex Marriage Among U.S. Latinos," *Social Science Quarterly* 92 (2011): 35–56.

75. Susan A. Cohen, "Abortion and Women of Color: The Bigger Picture," *Guttmatcher Policy Review* 11 (2008): 2–5.

76. Bartels, *Unequal Democracy*, chap. 3.

77. Barbara Norrander, "The Multi-Layered Impact of Public Opinion on Capital Punishment Implementation in the American States," *Political Research Quarterly* 53 (2000): 771–793.

78. Joe Soss, Laura Langbein, and Alan R. Metelko, "Why Do White Americans Support the Death Penalty?," *Journal of Politics* 65 (2003): 397–421.

79. James D. Unnever and Francis T. Cullen, "The Racial Divide in Support for the Death Penalty: Does White Racism Matter?," *Social Forces* 85 (2007): 1281–1301.

80. Charles S. Bullock and M. V. Hood, "A Mile-Wide Gap: The Evolution of Hispanic Political Emergence in the Deep South," *Social Science Quarterly* 87 (2006): 1117–1135.

81. "Minority Report," *The Economist*, April 1, 2011, 25.

82. Abramowitz, "Beyond 2010."

83. Rodolfo O. De La Garza and Jeronimo Cortina, "Are Latinos Republicans but Just Don't Know It?," *American Political Research* 35 (2007): 202–223.

84. Louis DeSipio and Carole Jean Uhlaner, "Immigrant and Native," *American Politics Research* 35 (2007): 176–201.

85. Stephen P. Nicholson, Adrian D. Pantojy, and Gary M. Segura, "Political Knowledge and Issue Voting Among the Latino Electorate," *Political Research Quarterly* 59 (2006): 259–271.

86. White, *Barack Obama's America*, 206.

87. Natalie Masuoka, "Political Attitudes and Ideologies of Multiracial Americans," *Political Research Quarterly* 61 (2008): 253–267.

88. Thomas F. Schaller, *Whistling Past Dixie* (New York: Simon and Schuster, 2006), 181–183.

89. Kevin Arceneaux and Stephen P. Nicholson, "Who Wants to Have a Tea Party? The Who, What, and Why of the Tea Party Movement," *PS: Political Science and Politics* 45 (2012): 700–710.

90. Vanessa Williamson, Theda Skocpol, and John Coggin, "The Tea Party and the Remaking of Republican Conservatism," *Perspectives on Politics* 9 (2011): 25–43.

91. Abramowitz, "Beyond 2010."

92. The phrase "Southern Strategy," popularized by Kevin Phillips, a political strategist for Richard Nixon, refers to the tactic of gaining political support for candidates in the South by appealing to racial resentment toward African Americans.

6

The Age Gap

Age and American Political Behavior

Age can be an important dynamic in political behavior. Though an age gap is not always a feature of the American political landscape, age has proven to be an important determinant of political attitudes. Not only are there variances in the way that different age groups vote in a particular election, but also the generation one comes of age in politically can play an important role in structuring political views over the course of an entire life. So there are two age gaps: a short-term age gap, meaning the voting differences among age cohorts in a particular election, and a long-term age gap, or the voting differences among generations over the course of their lives.[1] The development of specific orientations to politics and experiences with the political system are critical to one's political maturity.[2]

People develop values and assign priorities to their values based in large part on their socioeconomic conditions during their formative years. Due to the changing nature of society's socioeconomic conditions, people from different generations end up emphasizing different political values.[3] Changes in societal experiences may, therefore, alter citizens' political orientations and produce a disparity of political attitudes from one generation to the next. And as younger Americans replace older Americans in the electorate, there is potential for major partisan and policy changes in the future.

FIGURE 6-1   Partisan Vote for President by Age

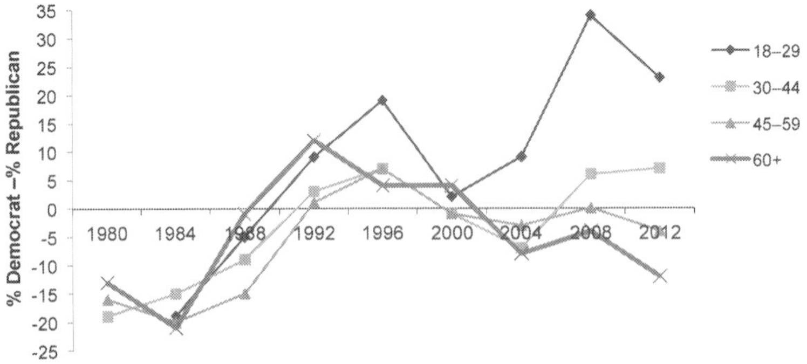

Note: For 2012 the oldest group is age 65+ and the next oldest group is age 45–65.
Source: Exit polls, 1980–2012.

In the past the age gap varied considerably from election to election. Presidential elections since 1980 witnessed large age gaps in voter preference in some years and relatively small age gaps in others (see Figure 6-1). Far and away the largest age gap occurred in Barack Obama's election in 2008; the smallest age differential in vote preference was in 1984 when Ronald Reagan was reelected in a landslide. In the nine presidential elections from 1980 to 2012, the youngest (18–29) age cohort was the most Democratic in its vote preference five times (1980, 1996, 2004, 2008, 2012), the oldest (60+) age cohort was the most Democratic three times (1988, 1992, 2000), and in one election (1984) the 30–44 age cohort was the strongest supporter of the Democratic presidential nominee.

Thus, although there is a stereotype that younger Americans are more liberal than older Americans, this is not always so. Younger voters have tended to disproportionately support the Democratic nominee for president, but this is more pronounced in some years than in others. In fact, in some years younger voters support more conservative candidates than older voters do. This was the case, for example, when Reagan won reelection. In the seventeen presidential elections from 1948 to 2012, voters under 30 voted only slightly more Democratic (3 percent) than the electorate as a whole. This group was not the most distinct age cohort; those in their 60s were 4 percent more Republican than the electorate as a whole.[4] Prior to the George

W. Bush administration, most presidential elections did not have much of an age gap, and by the 1990s there was evidence that the age gap on public policy issues that had grown in the 1960s and 1970s was shrinking.[5]

Some generations lean Republican and others lean Democrat depending on the political climate in which they developed their formative political views. Party identification can be remarkably consistent as people age. Popular presidents are associated with above-average levels of party support among the generation that came of age during their time in office, whereas unpopular presidents are associated with below-average ones. There are distinct partisan trends to age cohorts. Those who turned 18 during the John Kennedy, Lyndon Johnson, Richard Nixon, Gerald Ford, Bill Clinton, and George W. Bush administrations tend to be disproportionately Democrat, and those who became adults during the Dwight Eisenhower, Jimmy Carter, Ronald Reagan, and George H. W. Bush administrations tend to be disproportionately Republican (see Figure 6-2).

In 2009 the most Democratic age cohort (in terms of partisan identification) comprised those who reached voting age during the George W. Bush presidency; on the other end of the partisan spectrum, the most Republican age cohort comprised those who came of age during the Reagan years. The

FIGURE 6-2   Partisan Identification Gap Based on President at Age 18

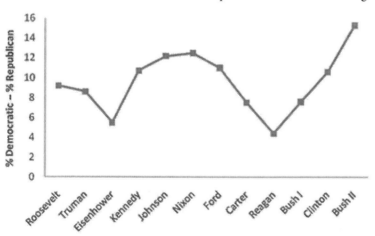

Source: Gallup Poll daily tracking, January 2–May 5, 2009.

Reagan generation has consistently supported the Republican Party since getting the right to vote.[6] Support for Republicans is also particularly strong among those currently in their 70s, a cohort of voters who came of age politically during the Eisenhower administration.[7] Those who came of age during the George W. Bush administration are associated with extremely low levels of Republican identification due to Bush's low levels of popularity. Voters who came of age politically during the eight years of the Bush administration are roughly 8 points more Democratic than the rest of the population.[8]

After a political party captures a generation, its members tend to remain loyal, contributing to electoral stability.[9] During the 1930s, for example, Franklin Roosevelt's popularity among younger voters was so strong that demographers began to speak of a New Deal generation.[10] There is thus considerable generational explanation for partisan preferences.[11] Most adults inherit partisanship from their parents, but because they lack political experience, they enter the electorate with weak partisan attachments.[12] Psychologists have found, however, that partisan identities that are adopted in early adulthood stabilize quickly and thereafter become highly resistant to more than transient change.

The influences of the political environment are most noticeable among younger voters. Political events and personalities have the greatest and most lasting influence during the stage of life when partisan identities are being formed.[13] During the Vietnam War, for example, those with low lottery numbers (who had a greater chance of being drafted) were more likely than those with high lottery numbers to abandon the party identification that they had held as teenagers, and draft number effects on party identification continued to exceed those for preadult party identification more than two decades later.[14] In fact, throughout their lives baby boomers—those born between 1946 and 1964—have expressed more libertarian attitudes than their elders and less respect for authority, religion, and patriotism. Members of generation X—those born from 1965 to 1980—have an extremely personal and individualistic view of politics.[15] This differentiates them from millennials—adults born after 1981—who are civic minded and technologically savvy, embracing the Internet and new technology for multiple modes of self-expression. Millennials' technological exceptionalism, in fact, is what this generation considers to be the most important attribute of its distinctiveness from other generations.[16]

The Age Gap in the 2008 and 2012 Elections

The age gap in 2008 and 2012 was considerably larger than it had been in previous presidential elections. The youth vote's movement toward the Democrats began in 2004, when the under-30 vote went for John Kerry by a 9-point margin, his best age cohort. This, however, pales in comparison to Barack Obama's 34-point margin in this age group in 2008 and 23-point margin in 2012. The 2008 presidential election had by far the largest age gap since political scientists began measuring the effects of age on vote choice. The age gap in 2008 was perfectly linear, with each younger age cohort giving Obama a higher share of its vote; in 2012 the gap was perfectly linear with the exception of those in their 50s, who were slightly more likely to support Obama than those in their 40s (see Figure 6-3). In both 2008 and 2012 Obama did poorly among older voters, winning less than 45 percent of the 70+ vote in both 2008 and 2012. On the other end of the age spectrum, Obama won a staggering two-thirds of the under-30 vote in 2008 and maintained his strength among younger voters by getting more than three-fifths of the under-30 vote in 2012. Obama's strength among younger voters, in fact, was critical to his margin of victory in 2008 and 2012. In 2008 the vote among those aged 30+ was basically a dead heat. In 2012, though Obama won the under-30 vote by a smaller share than he had in 2008, younger voters were even more critical in his reelection as he lost the 30+ vote by a couple of percentage points.

It is important to note, however, that the age gap was not uniform across the nation and varied considerably from state to state. In both the 2008 and 2012 elections, under-30 voters in Mississippi and North Carolina were more than 30 percentage points likely to vote for Obama than voters 65+. North Carolina in 2008 represents perhaps the greatest impact of the age gap: Obama won the under-30 vote by a 74 to 26 percent margin; he won

FIGURE 6-3   Vote for Obama by Age, 2008 and 2012

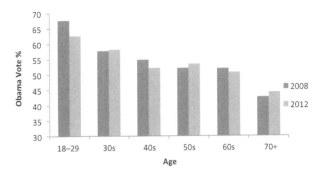

Source: ANES 2008 and 2012 datasets.

the state overall by just 0.4 percent. Joining Mississippi and North Carolina with large age gaps in 2012 were Arizona, Florida, and Nevada—all three with large and growing Hispanic populations. In both 2008 and 2012 Obama's percent of the under-30 vote tended to be extremely high in states considered to be safely Democratic and tended to be comparably low in states deemed to be safely Republican (even in a state such as Mississippi with a large age gap, Obama's share of the under-30 vote was considerably less than in the nation as a whole). Generally, the larger the age gap, the better Obama tended to do in the state. Blue states tended to have a much larger age gap than red states. At the extremes, one of Obama's best states in 2012 was Massachusetts, which he won overall with 61 percent of the vote. Obama, however, carried the 18–29 vote in Massachusetts by a huge margin, winning 73 percent of that vote. On the other end of the spectrum, one of Obama's worst states was Kansas, where his 41 percent share of the vote among younger voters was only slightly higher than the 38 percent he won overall.

The importance of the age gap at the state level is vividly displayed by the fact that in both 2008 and 2012 there were a number of important states Obama won that he would have lost without the overwhelming support of younger voters. In 2008 the 18–29 vote ended up giving him his margin of victory in North Carolina and Indiana; Obama lost the 30+ vote in both states. In North Carolina Obama lost the 30+ vote by a rather large 10 percentage points. In 2012 younger voters provided the margin of victory to Obama in three crucial battleground states: Ohio, Florida, and Virginia. Targeting younger voters in these three states, Obama was actually able to increase his share of their vote even though his margin among younger voters nationally was declining.

Importantly, the support of younger voters for Democratic candidates has proven to be not just a pro-Obama phenomenon. In the four House elections from 2006 to 2012, younger voters gave Democratic candidates 58 to 65 percent of their House votes. In Senate elections over the same time period, under-30 voters were consistently the best age group for the Democrats. Younger voters provided at least six Democratic senatorial candidates their margin of victory: Jon Tester (Montana) in 2006; Kay Hagen (North Carolina), Al Franken (Minnesota), and Mark Begich (Alaska) in 2008; Michael Bennet (Colorado) in 2010; and Tim Kaine (Virginia) in 2012.[17]

These trends suggest that if younger Americans follow other generations in keeping the same partisan voting patterns throughout their lives, the nation as a whole will progressively become more Democratic, with blue states becoming even bluer and red states becoming potentially more competitive. An electoral realignment may be occurring that will reinforce recent Democratic gains. Unquestionably, the youth vote in 2008 and 2012 broke overwhelmingly for Obama. Figure 6-4 displays Electoral College maps of the under-30 vote in 2008 and 2012. As you can see, if the electorate were limited to those voters, Obama would have won the presidential election both years in a landslide, with 481 Electoral College votes in 2008 and 437 in 2012.

In 2008 Barack Obama's performance among those in the middle of the age spectrum closely resembled his overall totals; among those aged 30–64, the only states that Obama ended up winning in which he did not win in this age group were North Carolina and Indiana. An Electoral College map of those aged 30–64 in 2008 thus has Barack Obama winning 338 Electoral College votes and John McCain, 200 (see Figure 6-5). In 2012, however, an Electoral College map of those aged 30–64 finds Obama doing considerably worse among this age group than he did with the population as a whole,

FIGURE 6-4   Electoral College Maps of 2008 and 2012 Presidential Votes: Ages 18–29

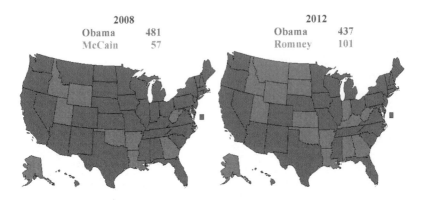

2008		2012	
Obama	481	Obama	437
McCain	57	Romney	101

Source: Exit polls, 2008–2012.

FIGURE 6-5   Electoral College Maps of 2008 and 2012 Presidential Votes: Ages 30–64

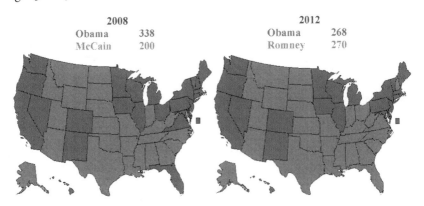

2008		2012	
Obama	338	Obama	268
McCain	200	Romney	270

Source: Exit polls, 2008–2012.

in fact, were these his only voters, Obama would have narrowly lost in the Electoral College 268 to 270.

Among older voters, neither of Obama's elections would have even been close (see Figure 6-6). If the electorate consisted only of those 65 and older, John McCain and Mitt Romney would have easily won the presidency with

FIGURE 6-6   Electoral College Maps of 2008 and 2012 Presidential Votes:
Ages 65+

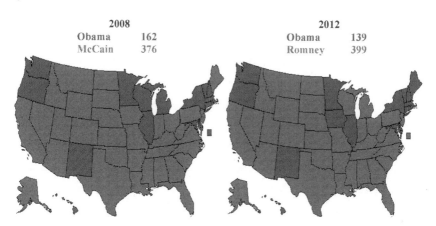

2008		2012	
Obama	162	Obama	139
McCain	376	Romney	399

Source: Exit polls, 2008–2012.

376 and 399 Electoral College votes, respectively. Both McCain and Romney
won the 65+ vote in a number a states that Obama won by fairly substantial
margins overall, including California, Pennsylvania, and New Jersey.

There are a number of potential explanations for the huge age gap that
emerged in Obama's elections. Recent trends unambiguously indicate that
younger voters tend to be more supportive of Democratic candidates than
other age groups as young Americans hold a markedly more positive view
of Democrats than they do of Republicans.[18] The Democratic Party has consistently had a favorability advantage over the Republican Party among un-
der-30 respondents that dwarfs that of 30+ respondents. Today's under-30
Americans are the most Democratic age group in the nation by a substantial margin in part because young voters react to the successes or failures
of the first politicians they know. The contemporary movement of younger
voters toward the Democrats may have begun in 2004, but John Kerry's
support among younger voters was to a considerable degree a function of
their contempt for Bush rather than of strong support for Kerry himself.
This was not the case in 2008. As his success among younger voters in the
Democratic primaries demonstrates, Obama himself was genuinely popular

among younger voters. Thus, the strong Democratic youth vote in 2008 was both pro-Obama and anti-Bush in nature.

Bush's second term in office proved to be the most unpopular term for a president since pollsters began measuring presidential job approval ratings. His popularity steadily declined to the point that when he left office, his approval ratings were in the low 20s. The only president in history to have left office with as dismal of an approval rating was Richard Nixon before he resigned over the Watergate scandal in 1974. Bush's unpopularity undoubtedly influenced the negative opinion that many younger Americans who were just becoming politically socialized and entering the electorate had of the Republican Party. Bush's second term, which provoked the longest period of low and downward-trending approval ratings on record, inflicted considerable damage on the Republican Party's popular support and electoral fortunes. Over the long run any lasting effect of the Bush presidency on the electorate will likely be the large Democratic advantage among voters who came of age politically during the Bush administration.[19]

The age gap in 2008, however, was not simply a consequence of younger voters' reaction against the Bush administration. Obama himself was enormously popular among younger voters, which could be seen right from the beginning of his campaign for president and in the nomination stage of his presidential run. The relative strength of Barack Obama's and Hillary Clinton's support among different age groups in the 2008 Democratic primaries goes a long way in explaining the political dynamics of the 2008 Democratic nomination. Although Obama won less than two-fifths of the over-60 vote in the 2008 primaries, he won more than three-fifths of the under-30 vote. Along with providing Obama their votes, younger voters gave him a further boost by turning out at record rates: the under-30 share of the electorate that voted in Democratic presidential primaries went up more than 50 percent from 2004 to 2008.[20] This increase in voter turnout among younger voters also provided a major boost to Obama in both the 2008 and 2012 general elections. In 2008 the share of those who voted who were under 30 was 18 percent, a figure that went up to 19 percent in 2012. To put that in perspective, in the 2006 and 2010 midterm elections the under-30 share was 12 percent. If the voter turnout shares of all age groups had been the same in 2008 as in 2006 and 2010, then Obama's victory margin would have been cut approximately in half; and if they had been the same in 2012 as in these midterm elections, then Obama might not have won the election.

Age and Public Policy Preferences

As the results of the 2008 and 2012 elections vividly demonstrate, younger voters today tend to be more supportive of Democratic candidates than other age cohorts are. Not only are younger Americans more likely to support the Democratic Party, but also they are ideologically more liberal to boot (see Figure 6-7). On the Michigan Scale of Ideology from 1 to 7, those under 30 are the only age group to have a mean ideological score of 4 or less, indicating that these voters are the only age group that identifies itself as being left of center ideologically.[21] Obama's overwhelming strength among younger voters, therefore, corresponds to the movement of younger voters to the ideological left of the overall population.

Younger Americans' relatively left-leaning—and older Americans' relatively right-leaning—ideological inclination is consistent with beliefs regarding equality. The elderly are much more likely to believe that the United States "should worry less about equality" than other age cohorts do, with

FIGURE 6-7   Age and Ideology

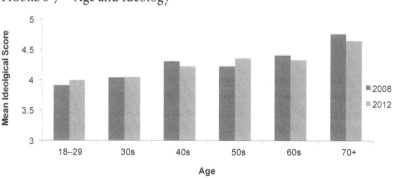

Definition: Self-Identification Scale from 1 to 7, with 1 = most liberal and 7 = most conservative.
Source: ANES 2008 and 2012 datasets.

younger Americans the most likely to disagree with this assertion. A majority of those born before 1940 believe that we "should worry less about equality"; this sentiment is shared by only about one-third of American adults born after the 1970s.[22]

The Age Gap in Economic Issues

Younger Americans' liberalism and support for egalitarianism can be demonstrated in their support for more government services (see Figure 6-8). The youngest age cohort is the most supportive of government providing more services, whereas the oldest age cohort is the least supportive. This is consistent with findings that those born after 1980 tend to be in favor of a more activist government.[23] Since the Great Depression the Democrats have generally been the party supporting a more activist government, so this could explain why younger voters have disproportionately supported Obama and identified with the Democratic Party in general.

On economic issues, younger voters are more liberal—and older voters more conservative—than the population as a whole. Although this dynamic is relatively unrelated to debate over aid for the poor, it very much pertains

FIGURE 6-8   The Age Gap: Economic Issues

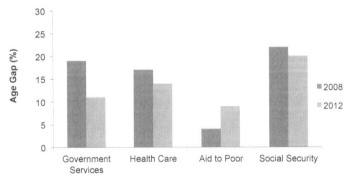

Definitions: Age gap = largest differential among those aged 18–29, 30–39, 40–49, 50–59, 60–69, and 70+. Government services = government should provide more services. Health care = favor universal health insurance. Aid to the poor = aid to the poor should be increased. Social Security = favor Social Security invested in stocks and bonds.
Source: ANES 2008 and 2012 datasets.

to the debate over health care: younger Americans are more likely to favor a government-run universal health care insurance system. Whereas more than two-fifths of Americans under 30 support such a system, less than three-tenths of Americans 70+ support universal health care. This is consistent with the observations made earlier about the differences in opinion on government services and the economy between age groups. Even though older Americans actually have universal governmental health insurance through Medicare, they are consistently less likely to favor more government spending on health care. Some of the people on Medicare may be suspicious of expanded government involvement in health care because they see it as competing with Medicare for federal funds.[24]

The relative conservatism of older Americans regarding government services even pertains—at least in one respect—to Social Security. Today the oldest Americans are actually the least likely group to support increased Social Security spending.[25] This is actually not a new phenomenon; younger Americans have historically expressed as strong a support for Social Security spending as elderly citizens.[26] Younger Americans may champion increased spending for Social Security, but they also tend to be more supportive of Social Security reform. Those under 30 were substantially more likely than other age groups to favor President George W. Bush's proposal to create private accounts in the Social Security system.[27] Social Security thus demonstrates that, even though younger Americans might be more liberal in regard to government spending in general, they are also influenced by the post-Reagan-era thinking that stresses the benefits of free markets.

Seniors tend to be much more skeptical than younger Americans about attempts to reform Social Security, and the elderly are overwhelmingly hostile to plans to privatize it. The farther one is from retirement age, the more likely one is to support at least partial privatization of Social Security, and those most supportive of putting Social Security in stocks and bonds are those in their 30s and 40s. This is one issue on which the Republican position has more support among younger Americans than among older Americans and a potential issue the Republican Party may be able to exploit in the future in its search to make gains among younger Americans. However, these gains may be limited because even though younger Americans are generally more supportive of putting Social Security funds in stocks and bonds, there is nowhere near majority support for this proposal in any age group. Even among those most supportive of privatization, the support level is less than 50 percent. At the same time, Social Security reform measures pose the risk of Republicans losing support among the elderly.[28]

The Age Gap in Domestic and Foreign Policy Issues

Another issue where younger Americans have significantly different attitudes than other age cohorts is immigration policy (see Figure 6-9). Younger Americans are more receptive to immigrants than their elders. Whereas only about one-third of those in the under-30 group say that immigration levels should be reduced, more than 40 percent of those in every other age cohort favor reducing immigration levels. This is consistent with a Pew Research Center finding that, whereas almost 60 percent of those under 30 say immigrants strengthen the country, just 43 percent of adults aged 30+ agree.[29] The different generational attitudes toward immigration are at least partly linked to experience. Younger and older Americans grew up in different demographic environments. Americans born after the civil rights

FIGURE 6-9   The Age Gap: Domestic and Foreign Policy Issues

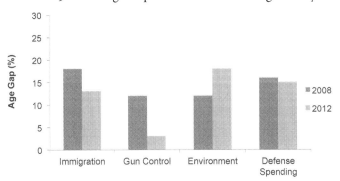

Definitions: Age gap = largest differential among those aged 18–29, 30–39, 40–49, 50–59, 60–69, and 70+. Immigration = immigration levels should be reduced. Gun control = buying a gun should be made more difficult. Environment = favor increased regulation to protect the environment. Defense spending = defense spending should be reduced.
Source: ANES 2008 and 2012 datasets.

era have lived in a country of relatively high rates of (both legal and illegal) immigration. Those born before the 1960s came of age in one of the most homogeneous eras in American history. In 1970 less than 5 percent of the country was foreign born; today that figure is about 13 percent, a rate similar to that of the late nineteenth and early twentieth centuries.[30]

Though not as prominent as is the case for immigration, there are also age gaps on gun control and the environment. Younger Americans are more likely to advocate making the buying of a gun more difficult. Opposition to gun control is strongly correlated with confidence in the federal government, and because younger Americans have more positive feelings toward government than other age groups do, this may help partially explain why younger Americans are more supportive of gun control.[31] In regard to the environment, younger Americans' relative support for increased environmental regulation may actually be a consequence of their relatively liberal leanings, not vice versa, because belief about global warming is significantly determined by partisan affiliation.[32] Younger Americans are more likely to express personal concern about global warming, which is consistent with Democratic and liberal positions on global warming relative to Republican and conservative ones.[33]

Even though younger Americans are consistently more liberal on domestic policy, this is not necessarily the case with foreign policy. Contrary to conventional wisdom, younger Americans historically were more likely to be supportive of what the president was doing in a time of war, as was the case during the Korean War and the Vietnam War. This proved to be the case with the Iraq War as well: in surveys taken in 2007 and 2008 at the end of the Bush administration, the under-30 age cohort was actually more supportive of the war than its elders were.[34] Thus, though it has been suggested that the unpopularity of the Iraq War may have disproportionately influenced younger Americans toward a negative view of Bush and Republicans, polling evidence suggests that the Iraq War was not the primary reason that younger voters soured on the Bush administration.

In general, however, younger Americans have somewhat lower levels of support for an assertive national security policy compared with other generations.[35] As a consequence, younger Americans are more supportive of reducing defense spending. Older Americans are notably to the right of the general public on foreign policy as well as domestic policy. Those 70+ tend to be considerably less supportive of reducing defense spending than other age cohorts. Whereas at least one-in-four people under 70 favored decreasing defense spending, the figure is closer to one in five for those 70+. Older Americans' relative support for a more robust military is consistent with prior findings that younger Americans are more likely to think globally and believe in international organizations than older Americans are.[36] Younger Americans may, therefore, be more sensitive to the criticism of US foreign policy levied against it by the rest of the world. Thus, even though younger Americans were not more hostile to the Iraq War, the unilateralist nature of Bush foreign policy in general was especially unpopular among younger Americans and probably influenced their negative impression of the Bush administration.

The Age Gap in Values and Social Issues

The political leanings of Americans of all ages are considerably influenced by their religious beliefs. As demonstrated in Chapter 3, the more religious one is, the more likely one is to vote for and identify as a Republican. Religion affects vote choice by moving the political focus to issues regarding values as opposed to issues regarding the economy. Younger Americans tend to be less religious and less conservative on social issues, whereas older Americans are generally more religious and more conservative on those issues.

There is a significant partisan divide along the lines of religious commitment among young people just getting the right to vote. From 1976 to 1978 the most religious high school seniors were only slightly more likely to identify as Republicans than those who were the least religious. By 1996, however, this gap increased dramatically to the point where the most religious high school seniors were twice as likely to identify with the Republican Party as those who were the least religious. Thus, there is clear evidence of an increasing relationship between religiosity and Republican Party identification among younger Americans. This suggests an electoral realignment as younger voters increasingly have their partisanship defined by the

FIGURE 6-10   The Age Gap: Values and Social Issues

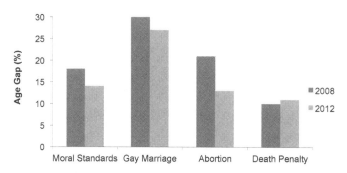

Definitions: Age gap = largest differential among those aged 18–29, 30–39, 40–49, 50–59, 60–69, and 70+. Moral standards = should be more tolerant of people with different moral standards. Gay marriage = agree that gays should be allowed to marry. Abortion = abortion should never be permitted/permitted only in cases of rape and incest. Death penalty = favor death penalty.
Source: ANES 2008 and 2012 datasets.

contours of this new cleavage.[37] Young evangelicals today are relatively politicized and overwhelmingly support the Republican Party.[38]

Yet as I discussed in Chapter 3, younger Americans as a cohort tend to be considerably less religious than the American populace as a whole. Politically, the important relationship is the degree by which younger Americans' relative lack of religiosity influences their positions on social issues and partisanship. Consistent with their stronger levels of secularism, young voters relative to other generations advocate being more tolerant of people with different moral standards (see Figure 6-10). The underlying political values of younger voters continue to be significantly more liberal than those of other generations on social values. Americans' tolerance of the activities of challenging political groups has increased over time as a new, more tolerant cohort of Americans has replaced an older, less tolerant one. In this respect younger Americans may be more like their counterparts in Europe.[39] That younger Americans are relatively more tolerant reinforces their support of the Democratic Party.

Social issues are, therefore, a critical reason that younger Americans have become comparably more Democratic. Younger Americans today say that Democrats, rather than Republicans, come closer to sharing their moral values.[40] Younger Americans with comparatively liberal social views are unlikely to see themselves in a party in which large and vocal segments favor constitutional bans on abortion and same-sex marriage, reject evolution, and deny the reality of human-induced global warming.[41] Since the 1990s there has been a greater emphasis placed on cultural issues by candidates and other political elites.[42] As a result, moral traditionalism has exerted a greater effect on vote choice through party identification and there has been a process of realignment in the electorate along a moral traditionalism divide. This insinuates a widening and deepening of a cultural-values-based realignment of the American electorate.

An important issue in the generational value divide is gay rights. The fact that younger Americans are significantly less likely to believe that there needs to be more of an emphasis on traditional values is consistent with younger Americans' attitudes toward gay rights. There is a huge generational gap on the issue of gay marriage—the age gap on gay marriage is the second largest gap (after the religion gap on abortion) that I will analyze in this book. Whereas older Americans have been very reluctant to embrace gay marriage, younger Americans have become strongly supportive of it. Support for gay marriage is strongly correlated with age: for every age cohort, as one gets older, support for gay marriage consistently goes down. The widening divide on gay marriage by age suggests that the potency of the marriage question may be in decline. Approximately one-third of the change in attitudes on gay marriage from 1988 to 2006 was due to later cohorts replacing earlier ones.[43] Gay marriage is one issue on which young voters and the Republican Party significantly diverge. Thus, though Republicans in the past (such as in the 2004 election) explicitly used the issue of gay marriage as a way to energize conservative religious voters, the gay marriage issue may eventually turn into more of a hindrance than a help to the Republican Party.

Younger Americans are also somewhat more liberal on the death penalty than older Americans: the age cohort least supportive of capital punishment is the youngest, and the age cohort most supportive is the oldest. All age groups, however, support the death penalty by large margins, so the age gap on the issue is not that pronounced. Abortion, however, presents a more muddled picture. Although overall younger Americans tend to be more liberal on social issues than the general population, one cultural issue on which young Americans are not significantly more liberal than other generations is abortion.[44] Despite the political prominence of the issue, younger Americans' views on abortion are generally reflective of the public at large. Whereas nearly a majority of those 70+ believe that abortion should never be permitted or be permitted only in cases of rape or incest, less than 40 percent of those under 70 agree. Those under 40, however, are actually slightly less inclined to take the prochoice position than those aged 40–70, although they are still more prochoice than the oldest voters. This is consistent with the findings of a study that showed whites who reached adulthood during the 1970s and 1980s tended to be less supportive of legal abortion than whites who came of age during the 1960s.[45] This is the case even though females born in the 1980s and 1990s are the most likely age cohort to actually seek an abortion today.[46] Abortion, therefore, is one issue on which younger generations have not necessarily become progressively more liberal. Consequently, the age gap is not a result of younger Americans being more supportive of abortion rights.

Abortion aside, the large age gaps in many areas of public policy indicate why younger Americans are notably to the left ideologically of older Americans. This fits the common stereotype of political differences between the generations. Yet as demonstrated previously, despite the common perception that older Americans are more conservative than the rest of the population, this has not always been the case. At the end of the twentieth century the country's oldest citizens were the most Democratic because as products of the New Deal, their earliest memories led them to have a lasting faith in government activism. In the 1992 and 2000 presidential elections, for example, the oldest age cohort was actually the most likely to vote Democratic.

Since 2004, however, older Americans have moved distinctly to the right of the general population. This is a new phenomenon. As the New Deal generation—which was overwhelmingly Democratic—dies off, it is replaced by seniors who have become more Republican. A 70-year-old American today would have no personal memory of FDR. Wooed by Ronald Reagan during their prime earning years, these voters are not as sympathetic to the Democrats' vision of an activist government. For the current generation of senior citizens, even the Social Security and Medicare on which they often rely may be viewed less as instruments of beneficial government than as partial repayment for decades of taxes.[47] Ironically, the declining loyalty of older voters to Democrats may be attributed to some degree to the success of the New Deal safety net programs. In the 1930s seniors were the age group most likely to live in poverty. Today they are the age group least likely to live in poverty and overall are the wealthiest age group. This relative affluence has spurred concern about taxes and inheritance, issues that may encourage the elderly to support the Republicans.[48]

More than economic issues, however, it is social issues that are motivating older Americans to support the Republican Party and younger Americans to give their support to the Democratic Party. The catalyst for the generational differences on social issues is religion. Older Americans are considerably more religious than younger Americans (see Figure 6-11). Whereas one-third of those in the 70+ age group attend religious services weekly, this figure is less than one-sixth for those in the under-30 group. Because religion strongly influences values, younger Americans' relative lack of religiosity is a critical component in understanding why they have relatively more liberal social views. Older Americans are more conservative due to the impact of religion in their lives.

Older Americans' movement to the Republican Party may also be a reaction against the Obama presidency. Obama's approval ratings as president among senior citizens during his first term in office were consistently lower than for other age groups.[49] Obama, in fact, has never done well among older Americans. Prior to the 2008 elections, surveys found that older Americans were substantially more skeptical about Obama's persona and style. In a poll conducted in early 2008, 73 percent of those aged 18–29 found Obama to be inspiring but only 53 percent of those 65+ did. Similarly, 67 percent of those 18–29 found Obama to be down to earth, while only 51 percent of those 65+ felt that way.[50] Obama did poorly among older Americans in both the 2008 primaries as well as in both the 2008 and 2012 general elections.

FIGURE 6-11   Age and Religious Attendance

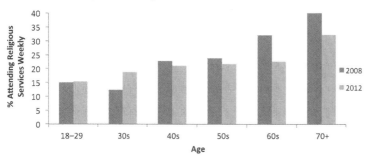

Source: ANES 2008 and 2012 datasets.

To put that in perspective, the last time a Democratic president first won the presidency, Bill Clinton actually did better among older voters than among any other age group. Of course, older Americans' movement to the Republicans is not simply an anti-Obama phenomenon; this group is substantially more conservative on a number of public policy issues.

The Significance of the Age Gap

The political power of today's younger Americans will only increase because their voting turnout rates will increase as they age. Even though the differences in the vote preferences of age groups vary from generation to generation, voting behavior is pretty clear cut in regard to whether or not people vote: turnout goes up dramatically as citizens get older. There is, therefore, a consistent generation gap when it comes to voter turnout. The voting turnout among those 65+ has consistently been much higher than the turnout of those 18–24 (see Figure 6-12). Since 1980 those 45+ have consistently voted in presidential elections at rates in the 60–70 percent range, whereas those under 25 have voted at rates ranging from 30 to 45 percent.

As the movement to lower the voting age to 18 grew in strength in the early 1970s, the general opinion was that doing so would ameliorate the problem of low youth turnout. In reality, however, it was made worse. In the first ten presidential elections after 18-year-olds got the right to vote in 1972, the turnout rate of those 18–20 averaged only 36 percent. The central reason that so many of today's young voters fail to vote is not their age but

FIGURE 6-12   Voter Turnout Rates in Presidential Elections by Age

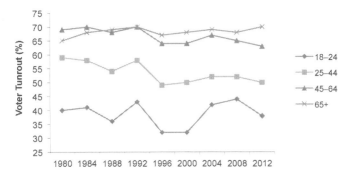

Source: US Census.

rather their lack of exposure to politics. Younger Americans struggle with becoming adults. College students and recent college graduates are consumed with nonpolitical concerns such as establishing a career and becoming financially independent.[51] Younger Americans are also much less likely to believe in the idea of voting as a citizen's duty. Yet the increased turnout levels by younger Americans in recent elections indicate that they are becoming more politically engaged than they previously had been. If feelings of citizen duty are eroding among the young, this is counterbalanced by new means of engaged citizenship: younger Americans have stronger participatory values than older Americans, and they have strong values of social justice, equality, and tolerance.[52] Those under 30 tend to be more optimistic about the condition of the country. In 2009 more than 40 percent of those 18–29 said they were satisfied with the way things were going in the country, compared to just about 25 percent of those aged 30+.[53]

The huge age gap in 2008 and 2012 suggests that there is an emerging realignment of the electorate along generational lines. George W. Bush's unpopular and divisive presidency helped to make the youngest generation of American voters increasingly Democratic in their vote preference.[54] Under Bush's guidance, the Republican Party became more identified with conservative Christianity just as younger Americans were becoming more secular and socially liberal.[55] The age gap of 2008 derived from a combination of Bush's extreme unpopularity among younger Americans and Barack Obama's unique appeal to them, something unmatched in the annals of the American presidency. Though Obama's totals among younger voters were not as impressive in 2012 as in 2008, Obama still won three-fifths of the under-30 vote and younger voters were a critical component of his reelection base.

Not all elections in the United States necessarily demonstrate an age gap, but as the 2008 and 2012 elections demonstrate, age can potentially be an important dynamic in vote choice. The youth vote may not always point in a more Democratic or liberal direction, but the results of the 2008 and 2012 elections clearly demonstrate that younger Americans' voting behavior can, when prodded, move in a significantly different direction from that of the population as a whole.

The long-term consequences of today's age gap appear to overwhelmingly favor the Democrats given the stability of partisan identification. In 2008 first-time voters made up 11 percent of the electorate and Obama won 69 percent of their vote. Of the 89 percent of the electorate that had previously voted for president, Obama won by only a 2-point margin. Party affiliation is habit forming. Many of those first-time voters who supported Obama will be Democrats for years to come. This move among younger voters toward the Democrats encompasses congressional elections as well. In 2002 voters 18–29 gave Democrats running for the House less than a majority of their votes, but by 2006 this figure was 63 percent, and in 2010—even as the Democrats were decisively losing control of the House of Representatives—it was still 55 percent.

The age gap between the parties is reinforced by the strength of the Tea Party movement within the Republican Party. There is considerable evidence to suggest that the Tea Party is further hurting the Republican Party among younger voters. Tea Party supporters are generally older than the general population and tend to describe today's youth as less responsible than earlier generations.[56] Not only do Tea Party supporters tend to be older than 50, but they are also overwhelmingly white.[57] Even among just whites, younger Americans are significantly less supportive of Republicans than the rest of the population: the white under-30 vote was 27 points more likely to support Obama in 2008 and 11 points more likely to support him in 2012 than whites 30+. One of the distinguishing features of the modern American population, however, is one of a growing, racially diverse younger age group juxtaposed against a largely white older population. Obama's strength among younger voters, in fact, was to an important degree a result of the country's changing demographics. Obama won a majority of the white under-30 vote in 2008 but lost this group in 2012. Yet he was still able to win three-fifths of the under-30 vote in 2012 by winning the votes of young African Americans and Hispanics by margins that were about as large as in 2008. In 2012 just 58 percent of voters under 30 were white, compared to 76 percent of voters older than 30. This suggests that eventually there will be an ascent of immigrant minorities as younger Americans age into adulthood.[58]

If history is any guide, as younger voters mature, they will vote at increasingly higher rates and they will generally maintain the partisan loyalties of their first vote choice for president. This means that those who identify themselves as Republicans are becoming relatively older and those who identify themselves as Democrats are becoming relatively younger. In 1990 the average age for those who identified themselves as Democrats was 46.8 and for the Republicans it was 44.1. Two decades later the Democrats had become slightly younger, with an average age of 46.6, while the Republicans had become, on average, more than four years older, with an average age of 48.3.[59] Over the long run this works to the Democrats' advantage because as older voters, who are disproportionately Republican, are replaced with a new cohort of young voters, who are disproportionately Democratic, the electorate as a whole becomes more Democratic. The Republicans desperately need to reverse the age gap, or the long-term consequences for the party could be severe.

Notes

1. Patrick Fisher, "The Emerging Age Gap in U.S. Politics," *Society* 45 (2008): 504–511.

2. Gabriel Almond and Sidney Verba, *The Civic Culture* (Boston: Little, Brown, 1965).

3. Ronald Inglehart, *Cultural Shift in Advanced Industrial Societies* (Princeton, NJ: Princeton University Press, 1990).

4. Author calculations from ANES data, 1948–2012.

5. National Opinion Research Center analysis of questions from the General Social Survey in 1973, 1985, and 1997.

6. John Kenneth White, *Barack Obama's America* (Ann Arbor: University of Michigan Press, 2009), 207–209.

7. Robert Binstock, "Older Voters and the 2008 Election," *Gerontologist* 49 (2010): 697–701.

8. Nate Silver, "Bush May Haunt Republicans for Generations," May 9, 2009, www.five thirtyeight.

9. Angus Campbell, Phillip E. Converse, Warren E. Miller, and Donald E. Stokes, *The American Voter* (New York: Wiley, 1960).

10. White, *Barack Obama's America*, 231–232.

11. Phillip E. Converse, *The Dynamics of Party Support: Cohort-Analyzing Party Identification* (Beverly Hills, CA: Sage, 1976).

12. Phillip E. Converse, "Of Time and Partisan Stability," *Comparative Political Studies* 2 (1969): 139–171.

13. Gary C. Jacobson, "The Effects of the George W. Bush Presidency on Partisan Attitudes," *Presidential Studies Quarterly* 39 (2009): 172–209.

14. Robert Erikson and Laura Stoker, "Caught in the Draft: The Effects of Vietnam Draft Lottery Status on Political Attitudes," *American Political Science Review* 105 (2011): 221–238.

15. Robert D. Putnam, *Bowling Alone* (New York: Simon and Schuster, 2000), 257–261.

16. "The Millennials: Confident. Connected. Open to Change," Pew Research Center, February 24, 2010.

17. Exit polls in 2006, 2008, 2010, and 2012.

18. Fisher, "The Emerging Age Gap," 504–511.

19. Jacobson, "The Effects of the George W. Bush Presidency," 172–209.

20. Patrick Fisher, "The Gapology of the Obama Vote in the 2008 Democratic Presidential Primaries," *Society* 48 (2011): 502–509.

21. The Michigan Scale of Ideology is a left-right ideological scale where 1 represents the far left, 7 represents the far right, and 4 indicates the ideological center.

22. Author calculations from responses to questions V083215a and V085165 in the ANES 2008 dataset.

23. "A Pro-Government, Socially Liberal Generation," Pew Research Center, February 18, 2010.

24. Andrew Gelman, "Seniors Skeptical on Health Care Spending," August 25, 2009, www.fivethirtyeight.com.

25. Author analysis of 2008 ANES data.

26. Debra Street and Jeralynn Sittig Cossman, "Greatest Generation or Greedy Geezers?: Social Spending Preferences and the Elderly," *Social Problems* 53 (2006): 75–96.

27. Scott Keeter, "Politics and the 'DotNet' Generation," Pew Research Center, May 30, 2006.

28. Susan A. MacManus, "Taxing and Spending Politics: A Generational Perspective," *Journal of Politics* 57 (1995): 607–629.

29. "The Millennials."

30. Damien Cave, "A Generation Gap over Immigration," *New York Times,* May 17, 2010.

31. Robert M. Jiobu and Timothy Curry, "Lack of Confidence in the Federal Government and the Ownership of Firearms," *Social Science Quarterly* 82 (2001): 77–88.

32. Christopher P. Borick and Barry G. Rabe, "A Reason to Believe: Examining the Factors That Determine Individual Views on Global Warming," *Social Science Quarterly* 91 (2010): 777–800.

33. Aaron M. McCright and Riley E. Dunlap, "The Politicization of Climate Change and Polarization in the American Public's Views of Global Warming, 2001–2010," *Sociological Quarterly* 52 (2011): 155–194.

34. Jacobson, "The Effects of the George W. Bush Presidency," 172–209.

35. "Democrats' Edge Among Millennials Slips," Pew Research Center, February 18, 2010.

36. Russell J. Dalton, *The Good Citizen: How a Younger Generation is Reshaping American Politics* (Washington, DC: CQ Press, 2008), 104–106.

37. David E. Campbell, "The Young and the Realigning," *Public Opinion Quarterly* 66 (2002): 209–234.

38. Corwin Smidt, "Evangelicals and the 1984 Election," *American Politics Quarterly* 15 (1987): 419–445.

39. Inglehart, *Cultural Shift*.

40. Adam Nagourney and Megan Thee, "Young Americans Are Leaning Left, New Poll Finds," *New York Times*, June 27, 2007.

41. Jacobson, "The Effects of the George W. Bush Presidency," 172–209.

42. Thomas E. Mann and Norman J. Ornstein, *It's Even Worse Than it Looks: How the American Constitutional System Collided with the New Politics of Extremism* (New York: Basic Books, 2012).

43. Dawn Michelle Baunach, "Decomposing Trends in Attitudes Toward Gay Marriage, 1988–2006," *Social Science Quarterly* 92 (2011): 346–363.

44. Nate Silver, "Is Public Opinion Changing on Abortion?," May 14, 2009, www.five thirtyeight.com.

45. Elizabeth Cook, Ted Jelen, and Clyde Wilcox, "Generational Differences in Attitudes Toward Abortion," *American Political Quarterly* 21 (1993): 31–54.

46. Rachel K. Jones, Jacqueline E. Darroch, and Stanley K. Henshaw, "Patterns in the Socioeconomic Characteristics of Women Obtaining Abortions in 2000–2001," *Perspectives of Sexual and Reproductive Health* 34 (2002): 294–303.

47. Matt Bai, "The New Old Guard," *New York Times Magazine*, August 30, 2009, 11–12.

48. Robert H. Binstock, "Older Voters and the 2004 Election," *Gerontologist* 46 (2006): 382–384.

49. Gallup Presidential Job Approval Center, www.gallup.com.

50. Scott Keeter, Juliana Horowitz, and Alec Tyson, "Gen Dems: The Party's Advantage Among Young Voters Widens," Pew Research Center, April 28, 2008.

51. Benjamin Highton and Raymond E. Wolfinger, "The First Seven Years of the Political Life Cycle," *American Journal of Political Science* 45 (2001): 202–209.

52. Dalton, *Good Citizen*, chap. 3.

53. "The Millennials."

54. Gary C. Jacobson, *A Divider, Not a Uniter: George W. Bush and the American People*, 2nd ed. (New York: Pearson Longman, 2011), 244–251.

55. White, *Barack Obama's America*, 208.

56. Vanessa Williamson, Theda Skocpol, and John Coggin, "The Tea Party and the Remaking of Republican Conservatism," *Perspectives on Politics* 9 (2011): 25–43.

57. Frederick R. Lynch, *One Nation Under AARP* (Berkeley: University of California Press, 2011), 93.

58. William H. Frey, "Baby Boomers and the New Demographics of America's Seniors," *Generations: Journal of American Society on Aging* 34 (2010): 28–37.

59. "Trends in Political Values and Core Attitudes: 1987–2009," Pew Research Center, May 21, 2009.

7

The Geography Gap

Geography and American Political Behavior

Where one lives is an extremely influential dynamic in the American polity. Localities have real and significant cultural and political differences.[1] There are important differences in identity politics and political culture along geographical lines, and some local political patterns deviate markedly from the national norm.[2] Even after group traits are accounted for, regional effects can often be detected because one is influenced by, and influences, those who are proximate.[3] This can be considered a "neighborhood effect," a tendency for people to be socialized by those they live around. In short, it can be said that "place matters" as a contextual influence on the strength and direction of relationships between social identity and political outcomes.[4]

The geography gap can be said to be either "compositional" or "contextual" in nature. The compositional approach suggests that regional patterns of political behavior are a reflection of the economic interests, races, and other politically relevant social groupings in a particular area. Geography is thus relevant to politics because it points to population traits that cause the people who live in a particular area to act the way they do at the polls. The contextual approach suggests that the geographic clustering of like-minded groups does not simply indicate the presence of particular social groups at those locations but in fact adds something extra to these communities through political socialization.[5]

The dominant political culture in a particular locality can influence ideological commitments and voting patterns in two ways. Firstly, there is the possibility of self-selection in migration patterns. People may be more likely to move to places where others tend to share their personal characteristics and political values. Those who are high on openness, for example, disproportionately relocate to major urban centers that are high on cultural diversity and that also tend to be liberal politically. Second, there is the prospect of social influence through social interaction because people are inevitably affected by their neighbors' traits and political orientations over time.[6]

Increasingly, liberals are identifying with the Democratic Party and conservatives with the Republican Party. Since 1980 differences between rank-and-file Democrats and rank-and-file Republicans have increased dramatically across a wide range of issues. Democratic voters have been moving farther to the left, and Republican voters have gone farther to the right. As the parties become more polarized, this allows people to "sort" themselves into the correct parties more easily.[7]

This trend has important implications for political geography. As a result of this ideological realignment, it has become more difficult for a conservative or moderate to win a Democratic primary and it has become more difficult for a liberal or moderate to win a Republican primary. Thus, partisan polarization among elites reflects increasing geographical polarization among the electorate.[8] The communities that Americans live in are increasingly becoming more Democratic or Republican. Americans have been clustering in communities of sameness, among people with similar ways of life, beliefs, and politics.[9]

There are numerous ways to measure political behavior based on where someone lives. Units of analysis could be on the basis of neighborhood (a micro level unit of analysis), city or town, county, state, or region (a macro level unit of analysis). For the purposes of this chapter I will focus on two different geography gaps in American politics:

1. The regional gap: the difference in political behavior between those living in the South relative to those living in the rest of the country (what I will term the "non-South")
2. The urbanism gap: the difference in political behavior among those living in urban, rural, and suburban areas

The Regional Gap

Sectionalism has always been a prominent feature of American politics, and a significant regional gap existed before the country was even born. At the Constitutional Convention in 1787 there were such major differences between Southern slave states and Northern states that the union of the thirteen colonies into the United States almost failed to materialize. After the country was founded, sectionalism became the dominant feature of American politics. In the early days of the country, sectionalism to a large degree dominated the political landscape, with members of Congress and the federal government being largely defined by region, not party.[10] Eventually, strong regional divides tore the country apart during the Civil War, and since Reconstruction the South has remained a distinct region politically. Historically, when the national government acted in ways that could be construed as territorially discriminatory, geographical clusters in opposition to its policies formed in response.[11] As a result, regionalism was often a feature of national economic debates, such as those over tariffs on foreign goods that were commonplace in American politics in the later part of the nineteenth century.

Partisan regional differences have defined American politics since political parties were formed after the George Washington administration. Geographical sections in the United States vote in stable patterns, with states in particular regions generally supporting the same political party in presidential elections.[12] If one takes a long enough historical view, regional political differences on many dimensions are declining due to increased ease of transportation, residential mobility, communication, and technology.

There is also evidence, however, that the regions have diverged politically since 1980, intensifying the regional gap in American politics. Though the boundaries of the regions are not necessarily an exact science and people disagree about which states (or parts of states) should be considered part of a particular region, for the purposes of this book the regions will be defined by the standards of the American National Election Studies (ANES), which divide the country into South (the eleven secession states during the Civil War) and non-South regions.[13]

The South has long been a political outlier in the United States. When the Republicans dominated national politics for seven decades after the Civil War, they did so with virtually no support from the South. The South was essentially a one-party region, and Republicans were not competitive at all in the South until the civil rights movement. That the South today is by far the most Republican region of the country is, therefore, a relatively recent development occurring over the course of one generation. As Figure 7-1 demonstrates, as late as 1980 the South was actually slightly less Republican than the nation as a whole in presidential vote preferences. By 2012, however, the South was 20 points more Republican than the rest of the country, and the South has been at least 10 points more Republican than the non-South in every presidential election since 1984.

Southerners hold distinctly conservative values and have long prided themselves for being socially and politically different from the rest of the country.[14] This is in part a consequence of the South having the highest concentration of evangelicals in the country.[15] Southerners are so different, in fact, that one study found that 10 percent of white southerners thought that the South would be better off as an independent nation.[16] Parochialism is much stronger in the South than it is in the rest of the country, and the South historically strongly favored southern candidates. This trend can be seen in presidential primaries: southern candidates in presidential primaries tend to do better than "home region" candidates in other parts of the country, meaning that southern candidates are more likely to win southern states than midwestern candidates are to win midwestern states, eastern candidates are to win eastern states, and western candidates are to win western states.[17]

FIGURE 7-1   Partisan Vote for President by Region

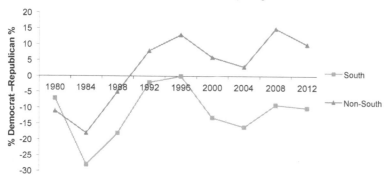

Source: Exit polls, 1980–2012.

Despite the Democrats' dominance in the South for a century after the Civil War, the one-party system in the South prior to the 1960s was purely a national-level-only situation. At the presidential level, all the states looked the same (Democratic) but in reality they were divided among many different factions. The South had no real political parties, and localism was very important in the South's factionalist politics.[18] The civil rights movement of the 1960s, however, ended this arrangement by catalyzing a realignment that reversed these long-held partisan electoral patterns. The parties' geographical bases today are almost the exact opposite of what they were prior to the 1960s.[19] In fact, by winning the presidency twice despite his relatively poor performance in the South, Barack Obama was the first Democratic president ever to assemble a governing coalition that did not include the South.[20]

Though the South may be less politically exceptional than it used to be,[21] the South still remains in many ways a political outlier. The South now accounts for a greater share of Republican strength than at any time since the party's founding. The Democrats once had a monopoly on elected officials in the South. As late as 1950 all the senators and governors in the region were Democrats. After the 2012 elections, however, Republicans held twenty of the twenty-six Senate seats and eleven of thirteen gubernatorial offices in the South. At the same time, outside the South the Republican Party has been shrinking. Voters both inside and outside the South have been responding to the increasing southern influence on the Republican

Party and the decreasing southern influence on the Democratic Party.[22] In the South the twin effects of race and religion have produced a socially conservative, electorally hostile environment for most Democrats. Political attitudes and demographic changes in other parts of the country, however, have become more favorable to Democrats.[23]

The strength of the Republicans in the South today is the product of efforts that began with an overt "southern strategy" that the party adopted during Richard Nixon's campaign in 1968. The goal of the Southern Strategy was to appeal to conservative whites in the South who had previously reliably voted Democratic.[24] Indeed, one of the Democratic Party's electoral Achilles' heel today is its weakness among southern white voters. Southern whites are considerably more Republican than whites elsewhere in the country. As Figure 7-2 reveals, in every presidential election since 1980 whites in the South have voted more Republican than whites elsewhere, since 2000 by overwhelming margins. Obama did particularly poorly among white southerners, losing them by 38 points in 2008 and 44 points in 2012 even as he won the national vote by 7 points. In the Deep South whites' overwhelming preference for the Republican Party exists even among younger voters. Even though Obama won two-thirds of the under-30 vote nationally in 2008, in Alabama, Louisiana, and Mississippi Obama won less than 20 percent of the white under-30 vote.

FIGURE 7-2   Partisan Vote for President Among Whites by Region

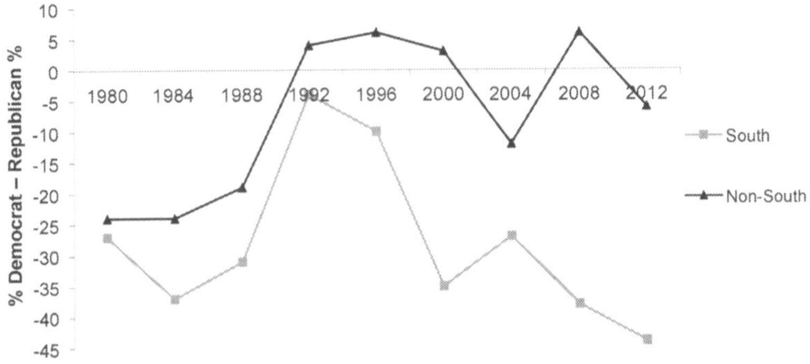

Source: ANES, 1980–2008; Pew Research Center, 2012.

The Republicans' dominance in the South has largely been considered a result of the region's cultural conservatism, especially on issues of race and religion. That conservatism appeared to be greater when southerners lived in racially heterogeneous areas, as articulated by the racial threat hypothesis.[25] Economic issues, however, are becoming more important in the partisan divisions of the South as there has been a sharply increasing income effect there since the 1990s. Today it is one's income level, rather than the racial composition of the community where one lives, that is the better predictor of political attitudes for southern whites.[26] Whereas income has steadily become a better predictor of white southerners' partisan identification, the income effect for white nonsouthern voters has actually declined.[27]

The Republicans have dominated the South even though the pro-Republican shift by southern whites was counterbalanced by a large growth in Democratic pluralities among newly mobilized black citizens.[28] The transformation of the Democratic Party during the past century has completely altered southern politics. Once the unchallenged majority party in the region, the Democratic Party has become a minority party in the South as most white conservatives and moderates have abandoned it. As a result, southern Democrats have had to learn how to compete effectively as a biracial party attractive to only a minority of whites.[29] As the number of Democratic elected officials has declined, southern elected officials have become more diverse. The region is electing not only more Republicans but also more women and African Americans. Two generations ago white southern Democrats would have made up nearly all elected officials in the Deep South. Today white southern Democrats make up a relatively small proportion of all elected officials in this region.

In general, the swings toward the Republicans in the 2008 and 2012 presidential elections were disproportionately in areas with a large number of southern whites who were natives of the region.[30] In particular, John McCain and Mitt Romney managed to do better than George W. Bush had in 2004 in an area called the Jacksonian Belt, a swath of counties from southwestern Pennsylvania along the Appalachian chain and extending to Oklahoma and Texas that were largely settled by Scottish and Irish immigrants who came to American before the Revolutionary War and their descendants.[31] This was the one area of the country that distinctly voted more Republican for president in 2008 than in 2004. In 2008 voters in the Jacksonian Belt voted heavily against Barack Obama in both the Democratic primaries and the general election, and it has been suggested that the Jacksonian Belt is fertile territory for the Republicans to pick up even greater support in the future, a premise that was supported by Obama's continued weak showing in the area in 2012.

The Urbanism Gap

Another aspect of the geography gap is the urban-rural divide in American politics. The existence of an urbanism gap in American culture and politics is one of the oldest concepts in the study of American politics.[32] There is a strong relationship between population density and partisanship. Republicans tend to live in areas where people are farther apart, and Democrats tend to cluster in places where people live closer together.[33]

The urbanism gap has long been a feature of American politics. In the East and Midwest, the rural-urban cleavage increased dramatically in 1928 when Al Smith, the urban, Catholic, and "wet" (favoring the repeal of Prohibition) Democratic candidate, drew strong support from urban areas while disproportionately Protestant rural areas strongly supported Republican Herbert Hoover.[34] The post–World War II movement of African Americans from the South into northern cities, along with the consequent move of whites to the suburbs—what became known as "white flight"—altered considerably the political landscape of cities. The inward migrants were generally poorer, and the outward movers were generally richer. This led to a downward trend in the wealth held in most cities and, as a result, substantially decreased the political power that they held.[35]

The divide between rural and urban voters has widened in part because the North-South sectional cleavage among rural voters has narrowed. Southern rural voters have become not only substantially more Republican than urban voters, but also more Republican than northern rural voters. This is a remarkable development in American politics when one considers that southern rural voters were the most loyal Democrats during the history of the one-party Democratic Solid South.

Though the urbanism gap is not new, the political differences between urban and rural areas are considerably more pronounced than they used to be. To critics of this development, the result is a "political balkanization" where inequalities across space in the propensity to vote or identify with one party or the other have reached a troubling level. [36] In most states the electorate has become more dispersed as residents have fled cities for suburbs. This has balkanized states into Republican and Democratic strongholds. At the same time, many rural areas have been abandoned and farms have been consolidated, creating a countervailing centralizing force within many states. As a result, there are fewer jurisdictions where the parties are competing to mobilize the same voters.

The prominence of the urbanism gap in American politics can be seen in Figure 7-3.[37] Urban areas have long been strongholds for the Democratic Party, and in all presidential elections since 1980 the Democratic nominee won cities (defined by the Census Bureau as having at least 50,000 residents) by at least 9 percentage points. Obama did particularly well in urban areas, winning cities by more than 25 points in 2008 and 2012. Suburban areas used to be more Republican than rural areas, but since 1992 rural areas have consistently been more Republican than the suburbs in presidential elections.

FIGURE 7-3   Partisan Vote for President by Degree of Urbanism

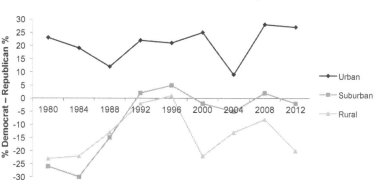

Source: ANES, 1980–1984; exit polls, 1988–2012.

Though voters in rural areas have consistently supported Republican presidential nominees (with the exception of 1996, when Bill Clinton narrowly carried rural areas), suburban voters have emerged as a key swing group.

The urbanism gap was large in the 1980s, declined in the 1990s, and once again increased beginning in 2000. In the 1992 and 1996 elections Clinton was able to win the presidency in part because he held his own with the rural vote. Similarly, in 2000 and 2004 Bush would not have won the presidency if not for the overwhelming support he received among rural voters even as he was decisively losing the urban vote. Contrarily, Obama twice successfully won the presidency despite his weak performance in rural areas: even as he was winning the election nationally, he lost rural areas by 20 points in 2012.

The red versus blue election-night maps mask the sometimes large urban-rural divide within states. There are important state differences between how the parties fare in urban, rural, and suburban areas. It is clear that the polarization of rural and urban voters has contributed to lopsided outcomes in solid red or blue states. Obama won the urban vote in all but the reddest states, but he lost the rural vote in all but the bluest states. The suburbs, in contrast, have proven to be a key swing constituency. Electoral College maps of just the suburban vote in 2008 and 2012 (Figure 7-4) closely resemble the full Electoral College maps, only a bit more Republican. In 2008 Obama won a plurality of the suburban vote in every state he carried with the exceptions of Indiana, Minnesota, and North Carolina, and in 2012 he won the suburban vote in all the states he carried with the exceptions of Minnesota, Ohio, Oregon, Pennsylvania, and Wisconsin. That Obama actually narrowly lost in the Electoral College in 2012 among suburban voters indicates just how important his large margins in urban areas were to his victory.

In red states rural voters are decidedly more Republican in their vote choice relative to urban voters. In blue states rural voters are also more likely to vote Republican than are urban voters, but not to the degree that is the case in red states. Thus, in blue states the rural-urban split is not quite as large as it is in red states, and the generally lower percentage of rural voters

FIGURE 7-4   Electoral College Maps of 2008 and 2012 Presidential Votes:
Suburbs

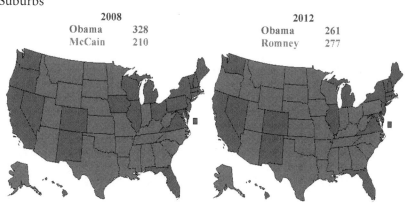

2008		2012	
Obama	328	Obama	261
McCain	210	Romney	277

Source: Exit polls, 2008–2012.

in blue states aids the Democratic cause. The most competitive states, however, exhibit a much smaller rural-urban divide in vote choice than either
solidly red or solidly blue states do.[38]

Cities have been an important part of the Democratic Party's base since
the New Deal. Yet since 1968 many urban counties—even among some that
leaned Republican in the 1960s and 1970s—have tended to become overwhelmingly Democratic (see Table 7-1). In three urban counties that have
long been strongly Democratic—New York (Manhattan), San Francisco, and
Philadelphia—the 1968 Democratic presidential nominee, Hubert Humphrey, won between 59 and 70 percent of the vote. By 1988 each of these
counties had become somewhat more Democratic as the party's presidential nominee, Michael Dukakis, won between 67 and 76 percent of the vote
there. As impressive as these margins were, however, Barack Obama easily
bested these totals in 2012, winning at least 80 percent of the vote in each.

In four urban counties that would have been considered swing areas in
1968—Cook (Chicago), Multnomah (Portland), King (Seattle), and Los
Angeles—Humphrey took between 46 and 51 percent of the vote. By 1988
each had become more Democratic but not necessarily overwhelmingly so,
as Dukakis won between 54 and 62 percent of the vote in these counties.
In 2012, however, Obama won more than 67 percent of the vote in each of

TABLE 7-1   Democratic Vote for President in Urban Counties (%)

County	1968	1988	2000	2012
New York (NY)	70	76	80	84
Philadelphia (PA)	62	67	80	85
San Francisco (CA)	59	73	76	83
Multnomah (OR)	51	62	64	76
Cook (IL)	51	56	69	74
King (WA)	47	54	60	69
Los Angeles (CA)	46	52	64	69

Source: Dave Leip, "Atlas of U.S. Presidential Elections," http://uselectionatlas.org.

these counties. The transformation of these once swing urban counties into overwhelmingly Democratic strongholds has had important implications for national politics: the states where these counties are located (Illinois, Oregon, Washington, and California) have all moved from being key swing states in national elections to being solidly blue states. California has become bluer even as more of its counties have become redder: thirty counties in the state have become more reliably Republican since 1976; only seventeen counties have become more reliably Democratic.[39]

Results in the 2010 midterm elections indicate that the continued concentration of the Democratic vote in urban areas is not simply a characteristic of presidential elections. In Illinois the Democratic candidate for Senate, Alexi Giannoulas, won 46 percent of the statewide vote, but 64 percent of the vote in Cook County. He actually won only three other counties in the whole state. In Pennsylvania a similar trend can be seen: Joe Sestak, the Democratic candidate for Senate, won 49 percent of the statewide vote but a huge 84 percent of the vote in Philadelphia County. Even though Sestak lost the state only by the narrowest of margins, he carried only seven counties in the entire state. As the 2010 races in Illinois and Pennsylvania indicate, even in relatively blue states rural voters have increasingly become more Republican while people in large cities have headed in the opposite direction.

A logical reason for the differences in urban and rural politics is that there are obvious demographic differences between urban and rural areas of the country. Racial composition, education, and income all vary widely by size of the place of residency. In the United States rural voters are—on average—more white, Christian, evangelical, religious, elderly, less educated, and less affluent than urban and suburban populations. Rural voters also own more guns, are more likely to oppose abortion rights, and have more traditional family arrangements than those living elsewhere. This suggests that rural voters share some set of inherent values with each other that leads them to identify with the Republican Party.

However, looking at the urbanism gap from just an urban-rural perspective is overly simplistic because more Americans actually live in the suburbs than in urban or rural areas. The United States is very much a suburban nation. Since the end of World War II, the suburban portion of the population has doubled, and more than one-half of Americans now live in a Census-classified suburban area. This transformation has fundamentally altered the American landscape as the geographic center of political power in the United States now lies in suburban areas.[40] Naturally, the face of the urban political landscape did not change overnight. Instead, it is an ongoing process, and what defines urban-suburban-rural is in constant flux.

Suburbs have been a feature of the United States since the early twentieth century, driven by the transportation revolutions of the streetcar and then the automobile. After World War II widespread car ownership combined with a government-subsidized home-building boom helped to produce an accelerated movement to the suburbs. The suburbs fragmented into a sociological mosaic, collectively heterogeneous but individually homogeneous, as people fleeing the city sorted themselves along the lines of race, class, life stage, and education.[41]

Suburbs historically drew upper- and middle-class residents out of central cities, leading to racial and class segregation. White flight from inner cities to the suburbs eventually produced staunchly Republican communities reinforced by class consciousness.[42] Life in the suburbs reminded voters that their interests were those of the middle class, not those of the cities.[43] Social issues also played a role in the movement of the suburbs toward the Republicans. Residents of the suburbs typically favored traditional

American culture, leading them to sympathize with Republican politicians who advocated traditional cultural values.[44] As a result, large central cities became overwhelmingly Democratic and suburbs, particularly growing suburbs, moved strongly toward the Republicans. Consequently, there were fewer and fewer truly competitive electoral contests in metropolitan areas.[45]

As a whole, however, suburbs have become more competitive and, as mentioned previously, have become the key swing geographical area in American politics. Part of the reason for this is that suburban voters tend to be less partisan than their counterparts in urban and rural areas. Suburban voters are more likely to base their decisions on the candidates' stances on specific issues rather than on party affiliation or personal traits.[46]

It is important, however, not to generalize too much about suburban political behavior because suburban areas across the nation vary considerably demographically. Suburban electoral behavior is differentiated by the composition of a particular suburb, with some suburbs exhibiting more "urban" characteristics (relatively high population density, more minorities) and others exhibiting more "rural" attributes (relatively low population density, less minorities). In particular, there tend to be significant political differences between suburbs relatively close to inner cities and so-called exurbs, a ring of low-density, sprawling residences on the edge of metropolitan areas. Exurbs are a new form of settlement space that exhibits a distinctive politics.[47]

The suburbs as a whole have moved away from the Republicans and have become politically competitive in part because of a recent movement of city dwellers, who tend to be more demographically diverse and Democratic leaning than historical suburbanites, to the suburbs.[48] Demography and density, therefore, have combined to help Democrats in the suburbs. Today Democrats dominate the urbanized suburbs that contain the largest share of the suburban population. Democratic strength in the counties that surround Philadelphia, around Detroit, and in the DC suburbs of northern Virginia has been a key to Democrats' success in Pennsylvania, Michigan, and Virginia.

Meanwhile, the exurbs have become a bastion of Republican votes. In the 2004 presidential election, for example, the locus of the Republican victory was in the exurbs. Of the one hundred fastest-growing counties, Bush won ninety-seven. These growing areas are for the most part in the exurbs and filled largely with younger families fleeing urban centers in search of affordable homes. Identification with the Republicans in these areas has become a kind of cultural and social statement.[49] Yet as impressive as exurban growth has been, the relatively small size of the exurbs compared to older suburbs as well as the tendency of exurbs themselves to become less conservative as their rapid growth brings higher population density and a more diverse population, limits the ability of the Republican Party to rely too heavily on exurban votes.[50] As a result of the growing political clout of the exurbs, Democrats and Republicans have different mobilization priorities than they had in the 1960s. Due to exurbanization, which has flung only certain types of voters to the metropolitan fringe, Democrats have developed a highly concentrated base of support in the cities and older suburbs near inner cities. Republicans have had to go farther afield in search of their voters, combing a larger geographic territory than do the Democrats.[51]

Geography and Public Policy Preferences

Politically, where people live is more important than ever.[52] Ideologically, those in the South tend to be more conservative than those living in other regions of the country (see Figure 7-5). The regional mean ideological scores closely parallel the regional variation in belief in equality: the South

FIGURE 7-5   Region and Ideology

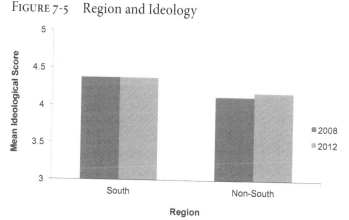

Definition: Self-Identification Scale from 1 to 7, with 1 = most liberal and 7 = most conservative.
Source: ANES 2008 and 2012 datasets.

FIGURE 7-6   The Regional Gap: Economic Issues

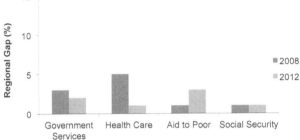

Definitions: Regional gap = difference between those living in the South and those living in the non-South. Government services = government should provide more services. Health care = favor universal health insurance. Aid to the poor = aid to the poor should be increased. Social Security = favor Social Security invested in stocks and bonds.
Source: ANES 2008 and 2012 datasets.

is less egalitarian than the rest of the country.[53] And as mentioned above, the urbanism gap has widened in recent years, and the political differences between urban and rural dwellers are considerably more distinct than ever.

The Geography Gap in Economic Issues

Economic policy preferences vary only slightly in terms of the regional gap. Southerners' attitudes on government services, aid to the poor, and Social Security privatization closely resemble those of nonsoutherners (see Figure 7-6). The South, despite its Republicanism, is not an outlier by any means on economic issues.

In terms of the urbanism gap, rural voters might be expected to be more Democratic than urban voters because voters with lower income cast their ballots overwhelmingly for Barack Obama—but this assumes that economic concerns are the driving force behind rural Americans' vote. Of course, the exact opposite occurs: rural Americans are more Republican than their higher-income counterparts in large cities. This suggests that the profile of rural Americans contains potential cross-pressures, but that noneconomic issues are increasingly driving their vote.

To some critics, the moral focus of modern American politics has distracted rural voters from economic issues. The Republican Party's emphasis on social issues, according to this argument, has led rural Americans to vote against their own economic interests. As a result, the economic vulnerability of rural voters has been displaced as an issue by business-oriented Republican elites. The result has been the creation of a Republican coalition consisting of working-class rural voters and corporate business interests, with the latter wielding the greater influence.[54]

Yet many rural Americans doubt whether typical Democratic economic positions fit with their own economic priorities. The lack of correlation between income and voting behavior in rural areas may in part occur not because of the relative economic situation that rural residents find themselves in, but because of the different way that they perceive their economic state. Rural residents see their income situation differently because their reality is different: having a lower income than urban residents does not necessarily mean that someone living in the country does not own a home or hold land. Despite making less money, more rural dwellers say that they are "satisfied" with their financial situation than do urban residents.[55] Thus, when it comes to the correlation among economy, geographic location, and voting, absolute income may be only a small part of the equation.

Rural voters have a strong sense of self-reliance anchored in an individualistic ethic. This ethic is tied closely to a preference for small government and a belief that those who succeed in the competitive marketplace owe nothing to those who fail. Economic individualism shows up not only in the conservative attitudes of rural Americans but also in the fact that rural dwellers are more likely to be self-employed and to own property. Home ownership is an especially strong predictor of individualistic attitudes favoring less government intrusion and greater resistance to egalitarianism. Rural residents are more likely to own their own home or own land than are urban residents, thereby increasing their level of support for private property rights.[56]

The Geography Gap in Domestic and Foreign Policy Issues

The South's conservatism is more evident on noneconomic issues than on economic issues. Southerners hold more conservative views on immigration, gun control, the environment, and defense spending (see Figure 7-7).

FIGURE 7-7   The Geography Gap: Domestic and Foreign Policy Issues

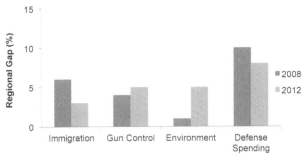

Definitions: Regional gap = difference between those living in the South and those living in the non-South. Immigration = immigration levels should be reduced. Gun control = buying a gun should be made more difficult. Environment = favor increased regulation to protect the environment. Defense spending = defense spending should be reduced.
Source: ANES 2008 and 2012 datasets.

Of these issues, the one where the South is most distinct is defense spending: southerners are considerably less supportive of cutting defense spending than those living in rest of the country. In part this is due to the demographic overrepresentation of southerners in the armed forces and the traditional cultural importance of the military in southern history. The South has long been the most hawkish region of the country in foreign policy, and southerners (especially white southerners) supported the Iraq War effort to a much greater degree than people living outside the South.[57]

The Geography Gap in Values and Social Issues

The regional gap on cultural issues is for the most part consistent with popular stereotypes of the regions. Where people live is as important as ever in cultural conflicts such as gay marriage, abortion, and the death penalty.[58] The growing importance of values and the cultural divide in the United States reinforces the nationalization hypothesis concerning vote choice, with voters more willing to cast their ballots for all office levels on the basis of national issues that used to be thought to affect only presidential vote choice.[59] Interestingly, the regional divisions on cultural issues may be related to a region's different attitudes regarding openness to new experiences. Such openness has been found to be the strongest regional personality predictor of the percentage of the statewide vote cast for Democratic versus Republican candidates in presidential elections. States with higher mean-level openness scores have been significantly more likely to have cast votes for the Democratic presidential nominee.[60]

Southern exceptionalism on public policy preferences is most evident on social issues. It is social issues that give the South a distinctly conservative hue in the modern American political landscape. On the question of tolerance of people with different moral standards, the South is somewhat less tolerant than the rest of the country (see Figure 7-8). On the specific cultural issues of gay marriage and abortion, however, the South is noticeably less supportive of gay marriage than the rest of the country. Whereas gay marriage has the support of about one-half of those in the East and West, only about one-third of those in the South support it. Those states that have legalized gay marriage or civil unions are disproportionately in the East or the West, and for decades these regions have had cities (such as San Francisco, New York, Los Angeles, and Seattle) that have had a large and politically powerful gay population. On abortion, the same pattern exists: the South is considerably less supportive of abortion rights, with nearly one-half of southerners taking a prolife position compared to less than four in ten elsewhere. Probably not coincidently, the South has lower abortion rates than the rest of the country.[61]

FIGURE 7-8   The Regional Gap: Values and Social Issues

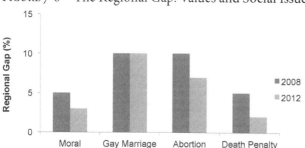

Definitions: Regional gap = difference between those living in the South and those living in the non-South. Moral standards = should be more tolerant of people with different moral standards. Gay marriage = agree that gays should be allowed to marry. Abortion = abortion should never be permitted/permitted only in cases of rape and incest. Death penalty = favor death penalty.
Source: ANES 2008 and 2012 datasets.

The death penalty is supported in all regions, but again the views of southerners are notable as southerners are somewhat more likely to support the death penalty than nonsoutherners. The South, in fact, has always been very supportive of capital punishment, and studies have consistently found that living in the South or being a native southerner increases the level of support for the death penalty.[62] This is not surprising: 80 percent of all executions since 1976 have taken place in the South. The South's support for capital punishment has its roots in both racism and the prevalence of violence in the region. The South has long been considered the most violent region of the United States. From the end of the Civil War until the 1930s, the South's subculture of violence can be seen in its preponderance of lynchings, which accounted for more than 1,000 deaths in the 1890s alone. Lynchings began to decline after the turn of the century as court-ordered executions supplanted them. The increase in executions in the South can thus be considered the result of a movement away from ad hoc mob lynchings to so-called legal lynchings. The result is that by "the end of the 1930s, the death penalty, like lynching, already had a peculiarly Southern stamp."[63]

The South's relative conservatism on cultural issues is undoubtedly a consequence of the region's religiosity. Religion plays a critical role in the formation of people's attitudes on cultural issues, and the South is considerably more religious than elsewhere in the country. Southerners are much more likely to attend religious services weekly and occasionally, whereas nonsoutherners are much more likely to never attend religious services.[64] Vote by frequency of religious attendance is relatively similar throughout the country; what varies is overall level of religious attendance. For Obama's initial election, his overall vote total was 13 to 17 percent higher than his vote among those who attended religious services weekly in all regions of the country.[65] Republican strength in the South is, therefore, enhanced by the region's religious commitment. The fact that the South is the most Republican region of the country is a consequence of its relatively high levels of religiosity. The values—influenced by relatively higher levels of religiosity—of the South are not the same as those of the rest of the country. In this respect the conservatism of the South is distinct from those who lean to the right outside the South. Southerners, for example, are much more likely to consider themselves evangelical Christians than those living in some western red states, such as Wyoming. Even in solidly red states, those in the individualistic West tend to be far more libertarian and secular than those in the traditionalistic South.

When it comes to the urbanism gap, rural voters are considerably more conservative on social and morality issues. Not only do rural populations tend to be more homogeneous ethnically, religiously, and culturally than urban areas, but rural areas are also, on the whole, older. The country has not been aging uniformly by place of residence. The gap between the younger urban areas of the country and the older rural areas has widened slightly in the past thirty years and seems poised to continue to do so.[66] This is at least partially due to factors such as increased life expectancy, migration of younger workers to cities, and the flow of older people toward more rural areas. The urbanism gap thus may be at least in part a consequence of age differences.

The classic policy difference between urban and rural areas is gun control. Rural areas are far less likely to have negative impacts from guns and gun-related crimes than cities. People in rural areas are also more likely to own guns and to be involved in hunting and sports that require guns; rural dwellers, therefore, express greater support for laws that allow freer access to them.[67]

Those residing in rural areas are also considerably more conservative than their urban counterparts on the issue of abortion. Not only is support for abortion rights contingent on place of residence, but so, too, is access to abortion providers. Women who obtain abortions are overwhelmingly more likely to be from metropolitan areas, with nine in ten women obtaining abortions residing in urban areas.[68] Similarly, those in rural America are also less likely to be supportive of gay marriage. The support of rural voters for gay marriage is not growing nearly as quickly as it is for those in urban areas. This could also be evidence of the cultural isolation that rural voters experience, causing their values to be more firm and slower to change.

The Significance of the Geography Gap

Where one lives has an important influence on one's political attitudes. There are significant differences in the lifestyles and beliefs of people living in solidly Republican and in solidly Democratic areas of the country. Strongly Republican areas tend to be whiter and poorer and to have lower education levels, more married couples, and more churchgoers than strongly Democratic areas. Such divisions will exist in any true democracy. The consequences of these differences, however, are magnified by the fact that American legislators are elected in plurality elections to represent specific geographical areas.[69] For example, that the Senate is malapportioned— that is, senators represent states of vastly different sizes—has very important consequences for American public policy.[70] In terms of urbanism, that each state has two senators greatly amplifies the relative power of less populous states. The regional bases of the Democratic and Republican parties also greatly affect national public policy. This is magnified by the fact that traditionally Republican areas of the country, such as the Sun Belt (the South and Southwest), have been generally growing much more rapidly than the Democratic strongholds in the Northeast, northern Midwest, and the cities.

The regions do not vary only by partisan and policy preferences, but also by voter turnout rates. Voter turnout has never been uniform across the country—some places have always had relatively high voter turnout rates and other places relatively low ones. Figure 7-9 displays the voter turnout rates by geographical area in presidential elections since 1980. Historically, southern voting rates were low compared to the rest of country, even among white voters.[71] Prior to the civil rights movement, suffrage limitations in the South were commonplace, and as late as 1988 the South had the lowest voter turnout rates. Since 1992, however, the South's turnout rates have surpassed those of the West, and in 2008—spurred by record African American turnout—the South had the second-highest turnout rate, higher than the West and the East as well (though that was not the case in 2012). On the other end of the voter turnout spectrum, the Midwest has consistently had the highest voter turnout: in every presidential election since 1980, the Midwest had a presidential turnout rate at least 5 points higher than that of any other region. The states with the consistently highest voter turnout rates—Minnesota, Wisconsin, North Dakota—are all Midwest states. The high voter turnout rates of the Midwest are related to the region's relatively robust communitarian values and strong sense of civic culture.

FIGURE 7-9   Voter Turnout in Presidential Elections by Geography

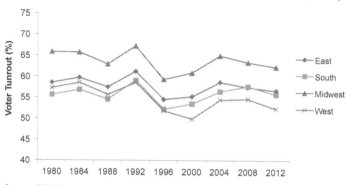

Source: US Census.

The geography gap is symbolically the most prominent feature of the increased polarization in American politics. The whole notion of a red-blue divide is based on the idea that people's political behavior is related to where they live. And from a geographical perspective, it is clear that the country is more polarized than it used to be. A county-by-county analysis of presidential returns since 1948 finds that Americans increasingly resided in "landslide counties" in which a presidential candidate received at least 60 percent of the vote. As a result of population movement, immigration, and party realignment within the electorate, Republicans are increasingly surrounded by other Republicans and Democrats by other Democrats. Red states, counties, and congressional districts have been getting redder, and blue states, counties, and congressional districts have been getting bluer.[72]

Political segregation in the United States—both interstate and intrastate—has grown significantly since the 1970s. The new geographical polarization of the American electorate can be seen in a comparison of two close presidential elections: those in 1976 and 2012. The 1976 and 2012 presidential elections were both competitive, but there were far more swing states in 1976 than in 2012. In 1976 twenty states with 299 electoral votes were decided by a margin of less than 5 percentage points. In 2012 only five states with 84 electoral votes were decided by a margin of less than 5 percentage points. Thus, the red and blue areas of the election maps are turning into darker shades of their own color as Republicans and Democrats grow more geographically segregated.[73]

Americans are increasingly choosing to live among like-minded neighbors. The idea of community has been miniaturized. People are picking and choosing their values on an individual basis in ways that link them with smaller communities of like-minded people.[74] Whereas nearly one-half of the population in heavily Republican counties attend regular Bible study or group prayer meetings, for example, only about one-quarter of the population in heavily Democratic counties participate in such activities.[75]

Conservatives are choosing to live near other conservatives and liberals near other liberals. To some, the sorting of Americans based on geography is counterproductive to American democracy. Face-to-face contact between groups on different sides of an issue defines a self-governing people. As Americans are less exposed to contrary views, the culture wars become more bitter and political consensus is harder to achieve. As Democrats and Republicans separate geographically, they become more distrustful of each other.[76]

As the country is becoming more geographically polarized, it is also undergoing important demographic changes. From an urbanism perspective, more Americans are living in the exurbs at the fringes of metropolitan areas and fewer are living in rural areas. From a regional perspective, the South and West have for decades been growing much faster than the East and Midwest, a trend that is evident with every decennial apportionment of seats to the House of Representatives. After the 1940 census, for example, New York had 45 House seats and Texas had 21. After the 2010 census, New York was apportioned 27 House seats and Texas was given 36.

The changing demographics of where Americans live inevitably leads to the question of whether or not this is helping either the Democrats or Republicans. Clearly, some demographic changes appear to be helping the Republicans, in particular, the rapid population growth rates of the South and the exurbs. The South's growth in particular seems to bode well for Republicans in the future as the region has become easily the most Republican in the nation. Yet some fast-growing states in the South—such as Florida, North Carolina, and Virginia—appear to have become more competitive politically as nonsouthern migrants have flocked to these states. Obama, in fact, won all three states in 2008, suggesting that they are far from the

Republican bastions (at least at the presidential level) that they were a generation ago. Thus, some demographic trends seem to be working in favor of the Democrats. In particular, new-growth cities built upon some combination of light industry, soft technology, university and research centers, and growing retail and service sectors—so-called ideopolises—have moved strongly toward the Democrats.[77]

One development that seems to benefit the Democrats is the increasing clout of cities relative to rural areas. Rural America is especially conservative on the social issues that have driven the culture wars of recent decades, and the Democratic Party has had difficulties winning the votes of those in rural areas, especially outside the East and Midwest. As late as 1900 a majority of Americans lived in rural areas; by 2010 this figure was one in five. As fewer and fewer Americans live outside metropolitan areas, an important part of the Republican base shrinks.

The urbanism gap will probably remain a major cleavage in American politics for the foreseeable future. The differences among urban, rural, and suburban areas in race, religion, age, and employment opportunities are simply too large to suggest that they will be going away anytime soon. Demographic trends, however, suggest that rural America will continue to steadily lose its political clout to the cities and suburbs. Over the long run, given the Democratic Party's relative weakness in rural areas, this should be a boon to the Democrats.

Notes

1. Andrew Gelman, *Red State, Blue State, Rich State, Poor State* (Princeton, NJ: Princeton University Press, 2008), 20–23.

2. Richard E. DeLeon and Katherine C. Naff, "Identity Politics and Local Political Culture," *Urban Affairs Review* 39 (2004): 689–719.

3. Diana Mutz, "Cross-Cutting Social Networks: Testing Democratic Theory in Practice," *American Political Science Review* 96 (2002): 111–128.

4. DeLeon and Naff, "Identity Politics," 689–719.

5. James G. Gimpel and Jason E. Schuknecht, *Patchwork Nation: Sectionalism and Political Change in American Politics* (Ann Arbor: University of Michigan Press, 2003).

6. John T. Jost, "The End of the End of Ideology," *American Psychologist* 61 (2006): 651–670.

7. Alan Abramowitz and Kyle Saunders, "Ideological Realignment in the U.S. Electorate," *Journal of Politics* 60 (1998): 634–652.

8. Alan I. Abramowitz, "Rejoinder," in *Red and Blue Nation?*, ed. Pietro S. Nivola and David W. Brady (Washington, DC: Brookings Institution Press, 2006), 111–114.

9. Bill Bishop, *The Big Sort* (Boston: Houghton Mifflin, 2008).

10. James S. Young, *The Washington Community* (New York: Columbia University Press, 1966).

11. V. O. Key, *Public Opinion and American Democracy* (New York: Knopf, 1961), chap. 5.

12. John Heppen, "Racial and Social Diversity and U.S. Presidential Election Regions," *Professional Geographer* 55 (2003): 191–205.

13. The ANES defines the South as Alabama, Arkansas, Florida, Georgia, Louisiana, Mississippi, North Carolina, South Carolina, Tennessee, Texas, and Virginia.

14. Thomas F. Schaller, *Whistling Past Dixie* (New York: Simon and Schuster, 2006).

15. Ted Jelen, "The Political Consequences of Religious Group Attitudes," *Journal of Politics* 55 (1993): 178–190.

16. William P. McLean and Tom W. Rice, "Support for Independent South Among Contemporary White Southerners," *American Review of Politics* 24 (2003): 307–320.

17. Nate Silver, "How a Southerner Could Sweep to the G.O.P. Nomination," nytimes.com, May 18, 2011.

18. V. O. Key, *Southern Politics in State and Nation* (New York: Knopf, 1949).

19. Arthur Paulson, *Electoral Realignment and the Outlook for American Democracy* (Boston: Northeastern University Press, 2007).

20. John Kenneth White, *Barack Obama's America* (Ann Arbor: University of Michigan Press, 2009), 214–215.

21. Joseph A. Aistrup, "Southern Political Exceptionalism? Presidential Voting in the South and Non-South," *Social Science Quarterly* 91 (2010): 906–927.

22. Alan Abramowitz and H. Gibbs Knotts, "Ideological Realignment in the American Electorate: A Comparison of Northern and Southern White Voters in the Pre-Reagan, Reagan, and Post-Reagan Eras," *Politics and Policy* 34 (2006): 94–108.

23. Schaller, *Whistling Past Dixie.*

24. Kevin Philips, *The Emerging Republican Majority* (New Rochelle, NY: Arlington House, 1969).

25. Michael W. Giles, "Percent Black and Racial Hostility: An Old Assumption Reexamined," *Social Science Quarterly* 58 (1977): 412–417.

26. D. Stephen Voss, "Beyond Racial Threat: Failure of an Old Hypothesis in the New South," *Journal of Politics* 58 (1996): 1156–1170.

27. Nolan McCarty, Keith T. Poole, and Howard Rosenthal, *Polarized America: The Dance of Ideology and Unequal Riches* (Cambridge, MA: MIT Press, 2006), 93–95.

28. Warren E. Miller, "Party Identification, Realignment, and Party Voting: Back to the Basics," *American Political Science Review* 85 (1991): 557–568.

29. Merle Black, "The Transformation of the Southern Democratic Party," *Journal of Politics* 66 (2004): 1001–1007.

30. Philip A. Klinkner and Thomas Schaller, "LBJ's Revenge: The 2008 Election and the Rise of the Great Society Coalition," *Forum* 6 (2008): article 9.

31. Michael Barone, "A Jacksonian Republican Sweep?," *Washington Examiner*, November 11, 2009.

32. V. O. Key, "A Theory of Critical Elections," *Journal of Politics* 17 (1955): 3–18.

33. Bishop, *Big Sort*, 203–206.

34. Seth C. McKee, "Rural Voters and the Polarization of American Presidential Elections," *PS: Political Science and Politics* 41 (2008): 101–108.

35. William H. Frey, "Central City White Flight: Racial and Non-Racial Causes," *American Sociological Review* 44 (1979): 425–448.

36. Gimpel and Schuknecht, *Patchwork Nation*.

37. The ANES phased out the coding of urban-rural-suburban after the 2000 elections due to the Office of Management and Budget changing its definition of metropolitan and nonmetropolitan areas following the 2000 Decennial Census. Thus, using ANES data for the urbanism gap for the 2004 and 2008 elections was not possible. Also, exit polls did not differentiate by urban-rural-suburban in 1980 and 1984. As a result, the data in Figure 7-5 are a combination of exit polls (1988–2008) and ANES data (1980–1984).

38. McKee, "Rural Voters," 101–108.

39. Bishop, *Big Sort*, 44.

40. J. Eric Oliver and Shang E. Ha, "Vote Choice in Suburban Elections," *American Political Science Review* 101 (2007): 393–408.

41. Robert D. Putnam, *Bowling Alone* (New York: Simon and Schuster, 2000), 207–210.

42. Bishop, *Big Sort*, 53.

43. Herbert Gans, *The Levittowners: The Life and Politics in New Suburban Community* (New York: Random House, 1967).

44. Matthew D. Lassiter, "Suburban Diversity and Economic Inequality," *Dissent* 57 (2010): 37–41.

45. James Gimpel, *Separate Destinations* (Ann Arbor: University of Michigan Press, 1999), 12–15.

46. Oliver and Ha, "Vote Choice," 393–408.

47. Nicholas A. Phelps and Andrew M. Wood, "The New Post-suburban Politics?," *Urban Studies* 48 (2011): 2591–2610.

48. Bernard Lazerwitz, "Suburban Voting Trends: 1948–1956," *Social Forces* 39 (1961): 29–36.

49. Ronald Brownstein and Richard Rainey, "GOP Plants Flag on New Voting Frontier," *Los Angeles Times*, November 22, 2004.

50. Ruy Teixeira, "Beyond Polarization? The Future of Red, Blue, and Purple America," in *Red, Blue, and Purple America*, ed. Ruy Teixeira (Washington, DC: Brookings Institution Press, 2008), 1–22.

51. Gimpel and Schuknecht, *Patchwork Nation*.

52. Michael Brown, Larry Knopp, and Richard Morrill, "The Culture Wars and Urban Electoral Politics: Sexuality, Race, and Class in Tacoma, Washington," *Political Geography* 24 (2005): 267–291.

53. According to author calculations from responses to questions V081204 and V085165 in the ANES 2008 dataset, 48 percent of southerners thought we "should worry less about equality" while 42 percent of nonsoutherners agreed with this statement.

54. Thomas Frank, *What's the Matter with Kansas?* (New York: Metropolitan Books, 2004).

55. James G. Gimpel and Kimberly A. Karnes, "The Rural Side of the Urban-Rural Gap," *PS: Political Science and Politics* 39 (2006): 467–472.

56. Rold Pendall, Ronald Wolanski, and Douglas McGovern, "Property Rights in State

Legislatures: Rural-Urban Differences in Support for Anti-Takings Bills," *Journal of Rural Studies* 18 (2002): 19–33.

57. Karen M. Kaufmann, "The Gender Gap," *PS: Political Science and Politics* 39 (2006): 447–453.

58. Brown et al., "The Culture Wars," 267–291.

59. Jonathan Knuckey, "A New Front in the Culture War?," *American Politics Research* 33 (2005): 645–671.

60. Jost, "The End of the End," 651–670.

61. Lawrence B. Finer and Stanley K Henshaw, "Abortion Incidence and Services in the United States in 2000," *Perspectives of Sexual and Reproductive Health* 35 (2003): 6–15.

62. James D. Unnever and Francis T. Cullen, "The Racial Divide in Support for the Death Penalty: Does White Racism Matter?," *Social Forces* 85 (2007): 1281–1301.

63. James Clarke, "Without Fear or Shame: Lynching, Capital Punishment, and the Subculture of Violence in the American South," *British Journal of Political Science* 28 (1998): 287.

64. According to author calculations from the ANES 2012 dataset, 25 percent of southerners attended religious services weekly compared to only 20 percent of nonsoutherners while 36 percent of southerners never attended religious services, much less than the 47 percent of nonsoutherners who never attended religious services.

65. Author calculations from questions V083185, V083186, V081204, and V085195 in the ANES 2008 dataset.

66. Annabelle Kirschner, E. Helen Berry, and Nina Glasgow, "The Changing Faces of Rural America," in *Population Change and Rural Society*, ed. William Kandel and David Brown (New York: Springer Books, 2006), 53–74.

67. Robert J. Spitzer, *The Politics of Gun Control*, 3rd ed. (Washington, DC: CQ Press, 2004), 102.

68. Rachel K. Jones, Jacqueline E. Darroch, and Stanley K. Henshaw, "Patterns in the Socioeconomic Characteristics of Women Obtaining Abortions in 2000–2001," *Perspectives of Sexual and Reproductive Health* 34 (2002): 226–235.

69. Patrick Fisher, "The Filibuster and the Nature of Representation in the United States Senate," *Parliaments, Estates, and Representation* 26 (2006): 187–195.

70. Frances E. Lee and Bruce I. Oppenheimer, *Sizing Up the Senate* (Chicago: University of Chicago Press, 1999).

71. Key, *Southern Politics*.

72. Alan Abramowitz, Brad Alexander, and Mathew Gunning, "Don't Blame Redistricting for Uncompetitive Elections," *PS: Political Science and Politics* 39 (2006): 87–90.

73. Ruy Teixeira, "The Future of Red, Blue, and Purple America," *Issues in Governance Studies* 11 (2008): 1–15.

74. Francis Fukuyama, *The Great Disruption: Human Nature and the Constitution of Social Order* (New York: Touchstone Books, 2000), 89.

75. Bishop, *Big Sort*, 179.

76. Ibid., 73.

77. John Judis and Ruy Teixeira, *The Emerging Democratic Majority* (New York: Scribner's, 2002).

8

The Implications of Gapology

Each of the gaps analyzed in this book is important in its own right. American political behavior unquestionably divides along income, religion, gender, race, age, and geographical fault lines. Political attitudes in the United States are not separate from the demography of individual Americans. One's demographic background strongly influences both vote choice and public policy preferences.

Collectively, these gaps greatly affect American public policy. The issues that emerge as important in American politics will inevitably have demographic underpinnings. Public opinion is created through the filter of political socialization, which is greatly influenced by one's demographic background. Public opinion then provides stimuli for the media that help frame the policy environment and for the elites who create public policy. To a significant degree, institutional factors help keep gaps going. The parties and candidates receive support from specialized interests—the National Rifle Association and the National Organization for Women, for example—that give staying power to the gaps in American politics and help perpetuate them.

Of course, not all gaps are of equal importance. Some will be more relevant, depending upon the election at hand and the policy context. The relative significance of the gaps is noteworthy because it tells us to which groups politicians and political elites are disproportionately catering. All groups, to put it simply, are not equal when it comes to their political prominence. Some groups are larger (i.e., women), some groups have more political resources (i.e., the wealthy), and some groups are relatively more influential because of their strong support for one political party or set of policy preferences (i.e., African Americans). Also important is the fact that not all groups turn out to vote at the same rates (older Americans turn out at much greater rates than younger Americans), skewing elections and policy disproportionately toward those who show up at the polls.

One of the most fascinating aspects of gapology is the fact that the gaps are not static; rather, they are constantly shifting in terms of their political magnitude. The religious affiliation gap—specifically whether or not one was Catholic or Protestant—was much more important in the 1960s than it is today. The religious attendance gap, in contrast, is much more important in understanding political behavior and policy preferences today than it was in the 1960s.

A critical component of gapology is thus the idea that the magnitude and relative importance of the gaps today will transform in the future. Though we cannot be exact, we can extrapolate from current demographic and political trends which gaps may become more (or less) important. The implications are potentially significant: if one of the parties fails to adjust to the changing demographics of the country and the relative importance of the gaps, a political realignment advantaging to the other party is possible.

The Gaps and Vote Choice

Even though all the gaps that I have analyzed throughout this book tell us notable characteristics of American politics, some gaps are unquestionably more important than others. The relative strength of Barack Obama's support among different demographic groups explains much of the political dynamics of his victories. Figure 8-1 demonstrates that there were noteworthy gaps in the presidential vote in 2012 on the basis of race, religion, age, income, gender, and region. Defining each gap as the largest difference between demographic groups that were classified for each category in exit

FIGURE 8-1   Ranking of Demographic Gaps in the 2012 Presidential Election

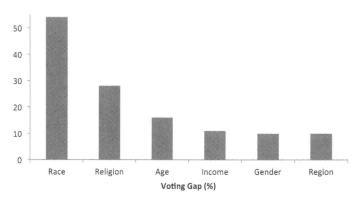

Definitions: Race gap = Obama black vote versus Obama white vote. Religion gap = Obama no-religion vote versus Obama Protestant vote. Age gap = Obama 18–29 vote versus Obama 65+ vote. Income gap = Obama $100,000+ vote versus Obama under $50,000 vote. Gender gap = Obama female vote versus Obama male vote. Geography gap = Obama vote outside of the South versus Obama vote in the South.
Source: Exit polls, 2012.

polls, we can see that Obama's demographic bases of support were African Americans, those with no religious affiliation, younger voters, poorer voters, females, and the non-South. Romney's strongest demographic groups were whites, Protestants, older voters, wealthier voters, males, and the South.

The largest gap in contemporary American politics is the race gap between blacks and whites. In 2012 the difference in the vote for Obama among blacks and whites was a staggering 54 percentage points. After race, religion had the most prominent gap as those with no religious affiliation gave Obama 70 percent of their vote while Protestants gave him only 42 percent of their vote. There was a notable drop-off in the size of voting gaps after race and religion, though there were significant age, income, gender, and region gaps, as each of these demographic groups had a gap of at least 10 points.

Demographic divides have long characterized American politics. Since the election of Ronald Reagan in 1980, the gaps studied in this book have been a regular feature of American politics. Though there have been strong correlations of demographic characteristics and presidential vote choice, these relationships are not necessarily constant from election to election.

FIGURE 8-2   Gap Correlations with Presidential Vote

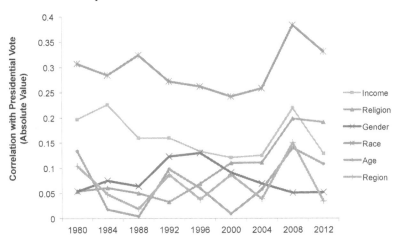

Correlations are Pearson Correlations, where income is family income, religion is frequency of church attendance, gender is male/female, race is white/nonwhite, age is the respondent's age, and region is South/non-South.
Source: ANES, 1980–2012.

This can be seen in Figure 8-2, which displays correlations for income, religion, gender, race, age, and region with presidential vote choice from 1980 to 2012. The correlations are presented in absolute value terms to give a sense of the relative importance of the correlation regardless of partisan direction (i.e., favoring the Democrats or Republicans). The variation in the degree by which demographics are correlated with presidential vote choice suggests that the relative importance of the gaps varies from election to election.

Some gaps are consistently crucial determinants of vote choice in all presidential elections. In particular, race (defined for the correlations in Figure 8-2 as white or nonwhite) stands out as consistently being highly correlated with vote choice. In all nine presidential elections from 1980 to 2012, race had by far the strongest correlation with presidential vote among the gaps. Though race appeared to be slowly declining in its importance from 1980 to 2004, Obama's presence on the ballot was a catalyst in making race an extremely strong predictor of one's vote. Thus, despite all the talk of Obama's victory representing a new postracial era in the United States, race was as important as ever. Income also was consistently correlated with vote choice, and in Obama's first election the correlation of income with vote choice was larger than it had been in any election since 1984. Religion (defined by frequency of attending religious services) appears to be the gap that has gained the most in importance since 1980. In the elections from 1980 to 1992, the correlation of religion and vote choice was relatively small, but after 1992 the correlations consistently went up in each presidential election to the point where religion was almost as highly correlated with presidential vote choice as income. This reinforces the culture war contention that social issues are becoming more important vis-à-vis economic issues. The correlations with vote choice of age and region demonstrated uneven trends, varying considerably from election to election. This is particularly the case with age: even though Obama's strong support among younger Americans generated a strong correlation of age with vote choice, for some elections (1984, 1988, and 2000) there was very little correlation between age and presidential vote. The one gap that appears to be declining in importance is gender: the correlation of gender and presidential vote choice consistently went down after peaking in 1996.

People, of course, belong to more than one group. They might be white, affluent, and religious, for example. Though all the gaps are correlated with presidential vote choice, they clearly are interconnected and overlap. There is a strong correlation, for example, between family income and race, to name just one of many important correlations between the various gaps. Yet at the same time people can be cross-pressured. An African American who is religious may be pulled in one direction politically by her race and another by her religion. If the gaps are cross-cutting, such as the aforementioned example, this suggests that the gaps may pose fewer negative implications for the United States. But if the gaps are overlapping, such as someone who is white and affluent, there is potential concern for the nature of contemporary American politics. Overlapping gaps would indicate the possibility of groups polarizing into two distinct and uncompromising forces, something that Americans have feared ever since James Madison argued in "Federalist Paper #10" that the best way to guard against "factions" was to have many different groups of citizens checking one another's power.

The possible link among the different demographic gaps examined in this book poses the question of whether or not each gap has an independent effect and to what degree. To determine the answer, a multivariate model was utilized. The analysis in Table 8-1 displays the results of binary logistic regression models, which measure the relationship between a binary categorical dependent variable (a variable that has two categories) and continuous independent variables (variables whose range is countable). Thus, in a binary logistic regression model the observed outcome can have only two possible types (major party vote for president—i.e., Democratic or Republican— from 1980 to 2012 in my models), and continuous independent variables (each of the gaps with a chapter dedicated to it in this book in my models) are utilized to convert the dependent variable into probability scores.

Statistical significance, the *p*-value, indicates the probability that observations as extreme as the data would occur by chance. In 2008 and 2012 all the gaps were statistically significant at the $p < .05$ level, indicating that there was less than a one-in-twenty chance that the gaps would have occurred by chance, and income, religion, and race were all statistically significant for both elections at the $p < .001$ level, indicating that there was less than a one-in-a-thousand chance that these gaps would have occurred by chance. This indicates the significance of each gap independent from any other. All the gaps unquestionably were important determinants of vote choice in their own right.

For the other presidential elections (1980–2004), the relative importance of the gaps in the regression models was fairly stable, though not always statistically significant. The race, income, and religion gaps were statistically significant in all models, representing each presidential election between 1980 and 2012; the race gap for each election was at the $p < .001$ level. Though there is a strong correlation between race and income in the United States, the consistent importance of both race and income on their own appears to undermine the argument that economic interests drive the construction of a racialized American identity.[1] The gender gap also proved to be consistently important, as it was statistically significant for all elections except 1988 and 1992.[2] The age and regional gaps, however, tended to be considerably less consequential in 2008 and 2012; the regional gap was

TABLE 8-1   Significance of Gaps in Presidential Vote Choice

Gap	2012	2008	2004
Income	0.194 (0.045)***	0.376 (0.059)***	0.176 (0.072)**
Religion	-0.667 (.048)***	-0.275 (0.035)***	-0.178 (0.048)***
Gender	-0.291 (.072)***	-0.338 (0.124)**	-0.499 (0.164)**
Race	-2.177 (.124)***	-2.416 (0.190)***	-1.429 (0.206)***
Age	0.032 (.011)**	0.080 (0.035)*	-0.020 (.049)
Region	-0.194 (.078)*	-0.656 (0.126)***	-0.160 (0.187)
Constant	1.584 (.219)***	3.638 (0.488)***	2.865 (0.655)**
Nagelkerke R^2	.224	.322	.155
Cases predicted correctly	66.7%	71.3%	63.0%

Gap	2000	1996	1992
Income	0.180 (0.070)**	0.267 (0.076)***	0.273 (0.060)***
Religion	-0.165 (.042)***	-0.272 (0.044)***	-0.300 (0.035)***
Gender	-0.484 (0.149)***	-0.614 (0.153)***	-0.186 (0.126)
Race	-1.454 (0.202)***	-1.820 (0.235)***	-1.384 (0.178)***
Age	-0.105 (0.046)*	-0.044 (0.046)	-0.026 (0.038)
Region	-0.776 (0.170)***	-0.217 (0.168)	-0.130 (0.144)
Constant	4.054 (0.630)***	3.154 (0.629)***	1.885 (0.496)***
Nagelkerke R^2	.160	.223	.179
Cases predicted correctly	65.3%	67.5%	67.4%

Gap	1988	1984	1980
Income	0.172 (0.068)*	0.393 (0.062)***	0.233 (0.076)**
Religion	-0.113 (.038)**	-0.138 (0.036)***	-0.100 (.044)*
Gender	-0.259 (0.135)	-0.259 (0.127)*	-0.336 (.159)*
Race	-1.835 (0.190)***	-1.652 (0.185)***	-1.984 (0.264)***
Age	0.015 (0.041)	-0.040 (0.038)	-0.017 (0.046)
Region	-0.315 (0.158)*	-0.327 (0.153)*	0.082 (0.171)
Constant	3.019 (0.567)***	2.568 (0.536)***	2.572 (0.628)***
Nagelkerke R^2	.172	.170	.171
Cases predicted correctly	65.3%	66.6%	66.2%

Notes: Binary logic regression estimates with standard errors are in parentheses.
Significance levels: ***$p < .001$; **$p < .01$; *$p < .05$.
Definitions: Income gap = respondent's family income. Religion gap = respondent's frequency of church attendance. Gender gap = respondent's gender (1 = male, 2 = female). Race gap = respondent's race (1 = white, 2 = nonwhite). Age gap = respondent's age. Region gap = respondent's region (1 = South, 2= non-South).
Source: ANES, 1980–2012.

statistically significant five times (in 1984, 1988, 2000, 2008, and 2012); and the only other year that the age gap was statistically significant besides 2008 and 2012 was 2000.[3]

Although different life situations may shape people's vote in their own way, people's life experiences essentially operate independently of group membership, which has a unique effect.[4] The regression models not only demonstrate how important each gap is in relation to the other gaps, but also prove the gaps' collective importance as the models correctly predict at least 63 percent of the cases for every presidential election from 1980 to 2012.

The Gaps and Public Policy Preferences

There are important implications regarding the theoretical relationship between gapology and public policy. Issues are a critical determinant in understanding people's vote choice.[5] Although individual-level attitudes may be inconsistent, aggregate public opinion is coherent and responsive to political events.[6] The consistency of aggregate public opinion has been congruent with the increase of political polarization. There is evidence that the growing ideological polarization at the elite level has made it easier for voters to choose a party identification on the basis of their ideological preferences.[7] Polarized elite opinion on abortion, for example, was the catalyst to mass partisan polarization on abortion among Republican and Democratic identifiers.[8] Public policies thus powerfully influence both expectation and perceptions.[9] Public opinion, in turn, is of major importance for the determination of public policy.[10]

Public opinion is especially important in economic issues because economic concerns are often the electoral focal point. In the 2012 presidential election, for example, when voters were asked which of four issues was the most important facing the country, nearly three-fifths said the economy. Yet there is also a built in bias in the political system favoring those of higher social economic status. Special-interest groups disproportionately represent wealthy business interests and consist of upper-class members.[11] Thus, despite the prominence of economic issues, economic policy seems to be

TABLE 8-2   The Gaps and Public Policy Preferences: Economic Issues

	Income Gap	Religion Gap	Gender Gap	Race Gap	Age Gap	Regional Gap
Government Services *Government should* *provide more services (%)*	18	9	6	**28**	15	3
Health Care *Favor universal* *health insurance (%)*	**21**	16	6	18	16	3
Aid to the Poor *Aid to the poor should* *be increased (%)*	23	4	5	**25**	7	2
Social Security *Favor Social Security* *in stocks and bonds (%)*	20	3	4	9	**21**	0

Notes: **Bold italics** denotes largest gap for that issue.
Each gap represents the mean for 2008 and 2012.
Definitions: Income gap = largest differential among lower, middle, and upper thirds of household income. Religion gap = largest differential among those who attend religious services weekly, occasionally, and never. Gender gap = difference between men and women. Race gap = largest differential among whites, blacks, and Hispanics. Age gap = largest differential among those aged 18–29, 30–39, 40–49, 50–59, 60–69, and 70+. Regional gap = difference between those living in the South and those living in the non-South.
Source: ANES 2008 and 2012 datasets.

especially vulnerable to being biased toward the distinct interests of the upper class. This would not necessarily be problematic if the wealthy had the same policy preferences as the rest of the population, but in reality individualists are unusually prominent among the American upper class.[12] This is evident in a comparison of the income gap to other gaps on economic issues. Table 8-2 displays the largest gap (averaged for 2008 and 2012) on economic issues for each of the demographic groups investigated for Chapters 2–7 of this book. For all four economic issues, the income gap—in each case the difference in policy preferences for the wealthiest third of the population and the poorest third of the population—is the largest or second-largest gap. One's income is obviously a critical influence on economic policy public opinion.

With regard to government services, race is the largest gap by a strong margin, followed by the age gap and the income gap. African Americans prefer the government to be more active than whites do. The attitudes of whites regarding public services, however, is the dominant one in American political culture as American public services are modest by comparative standards. African Americans aside, large portions of the American political elites and ordinary citizens do not want public-sector revenues anywhere near as large as those that are collected in other democracies.

With regard to health care, the income gap is larger than any other gap. Wealthier Americans are obviously much less supportive of universal health insurance than poorer Americans. Obama won the votes of three-fourths of those in 2012 exit polls who stated that health care was the most important issue facing the country, demonstrating the potency of this issue for those with less means economically. It also indicates why Obama made health care reform a primary cause after he assumed office. Yet the reluctance of the United States to adopt universal health insurance coverage, which has been adopted in all other developed democracies, shows how effective wealthier Americans have been in blocking health care reform. Future changes to the American health care system may be assisted by the changing political views of doctors. Once a solidly conservative group politically, doctors now increasingly identify themselves as liberal. One study, in fact, found that medical students in the class of 2003 were considerably more liberal than the general public, with 40 percent of medical students characterizing themselves as liberal, 33 percent characterizing themselves as moderate, and 26 percent characterizing themselves as conservative. This indicates that future US physicians may be more receptive to liberal messages and their political orientation may profoundly affect their health system attitudes.[13]

Health care is also the only economic issue that had much of a religion gap: those who regularly attend religious services are considerably less supportive of universal health insurance than those who rarely or never attend

TABLE 8-3   The Gaps and Public Policy Preferences: Domestic and Foreign Policy Issues

	Income Gap	Religion Gap	Gender Gap	Race Gap	Age Gap	Regional Gap
Immigration						
Immigration levels should be reduced (%)	6	4	3	*21*	18	9
Gun Control						
Buying a gun should be made more difficult (%)	9	6	17	*20*	7	5
Environment						
Favor increased regulation to protect the environment (%)	10	*19*	3	16	15	3
Defense Spending						
Defense spending should be reduced (%)	3	9	4	8	*16*	9

Notes: **Bold italics** denotes largest gap for that issue.
Each gap represents the mean for 2008 and 2012.
Definitions: Income gap = largest differential among lower, middle, and upper thirds of household income. Religion gap = largest differential among those who attend religious services weekly, occasionally, and never. Gender gap = difference between men and women. Race gap = largest differential among whites, blacks, and Hispanics. Age gap = largest differential among those aged 18–29, 30–39, 40–49, 50–59, 60–69, and 70+. Regional gap = difference between those living in the South and those living in the non-South.
Source: ANES 2008 and 2012 datasets.

religious services. However, when it comes to aid to the poor, there is virtually no religion gap and there are only small gender, age, and regional gaps on this issue. But income and race gaps on aid to the poor are notable, indicating the degree to which this issue is intertwined with class and race.

Social Security privatization does not show nearly as large a race gap as income gap. If fact, only the age gap is anywhere near as large as the income gap when it comes to putting part of Social Security in stocks and bonds. That the age gap is larger on Social Security reform than on any other economic issue suggests that it is one of the few issues where the Republican Party might be able to win the votes of younger Americans.

The income gap is not nearly as pronounced when it comes to domestic and foreign policy (see Table 8-3). The domestic and foreign policy issues studied throughout this book have a number of distinct gaps. The race gap is the largest gap in immigration policy, largely due to the views of African Americans, who are substantially more supportive of reducing immigration than Hispanics and whites are. The race and gender gaps are prominent in gun control as gun owners are disproportionately white males, and this is reflected in these gaps along racial and gender lines.[14]

The largest divide on the environment is the religion gap, as those who regularly attend religious services are considerably more skeptical of the merits of environmental regulation than those who attend religious services less often. Though environmental policy may at first glance seem to be an odd issue to have a large religion gap, environmental policy has been an issue on which there is significant polarization of both partisan elites and mass partisans.[15] The number of everyday environmental policies adopted by governments in the United States, in fact, is closely related to political culture.[16] Based on public opinion, environmental issues seem to benefit the Democratic Party, but unfortunately for the Democrats, environmental issues seldom shape individual vote preferences because of low issue salience.[17]

The gapology of defense spending suggests that the political dynamics of this issue in the United States may be changing to become more like that of other democracies. It has been found that the effects of defense cuts in democracies generally are not as politically sensitive as cuts in social programs because polls indicate that citizens in most countries consider military defense one of the few policy areas on which government spends too much money.[18] The United States, however, has been an exception: defense spending tends to be relatively popular in the United States. Yet the fact that defense spending has seen a significant age gap, as younger Americans are more supportive of cutting spending for defense than older Americans, indicates that the days of the United States being an extreme outlier on this issue may be dwindling. Globally, anti-Americanism is much greater than it used to be, due to the impact on foreign societies of American popular culture, a resentment toward American-style business practices, and the world's reaction to American foreign policy.[19] The age gap on defense spending may be in part a reflection of the fact that younger Americans, growing up in an era of increasing globalization, are much more sensitive to perceptions of the nation by non-Americans.

The idea of American exceptionalism influences views not only of defense spending but also of American foreign policy in general. Americans, more than other westerners, tend to view international politics in nonnegotiable moralistic and ideological terms. Europeans, in contrast, are more disposed to perceive international conflicts as reflections of interest differences and, therefore, subject to negotiation and compromise.[20] American exceptionalism in foreign policy was evident at the beginning of the Iraq War, but this masked the substantial differences between Republicans and Democrats on the issue. Republicans' views on the Iraq War were determined by commitment to George W. Bush. Democrats and most Independents had no such commitment, and they were largely responsible for Bush's decline in popularity. Bush's approval ratings were dominated between 2003 and 2007 by popular evaluations of the Iraq War. Only when the economy fell into recession in 2008 did his job approval ratings decouple somewhat from views of the war.[21] By the time of the 2008 presidential election, it was obvious that the Iraq War differentiated Americans much less than had been the case four years earlier. Exit polls in 2008 found that 63 percent of voters disapproved of the Iraq War, and of those voters Obama won three-fourths of the vote. The age gap on cutting defense spending arose in part because younger Americans became more hostile to the Iraq War and Bush's foreign policy in general. As a result, the backlash against the Iraq War may have long-term consequences for the conduct of American foreign policy.

If it is the income gap that is the most prevalent in economic issues, it is the religion gap that dominates social issues (see Table 8-4). To critics, social issues distract voters from more important issues. Social issues such as gay marriage, abortion, and the death penalty are said to be "easy" issues—that is, issues that people respond to on a fundamental or "gut" level. Only

TABLE 8-4 The Gaps and Public Policy Preferences: Values and Social Issues

	Income Gap	Religion Gap	Gender Gap	Race Gap	Age Gap	Regional Gap
Moral Standards *Should be more tolerant of people with different moral standards (%)*	6	**25**	6	8	16	4
Gay Marriage *Agree that gays should be allowed to marry (%)*	5	**40**	6	11	33	9
Abortion *Abortion should never be permitted/permitted only in cases of rape and incest (%)*	9	**42**	2	8	17	9
Death Penalty *Favor death penalty (%)*	4	7	7	**29**	10	3

Notes: **Bold italics** denotes largest gap for that issue.
Each gap represents the mean for 2008 and 2012.
Definitions: Income gap = largest differential among lower, middle, and upper thirds of household income. Religion gap = largest differential among those who attend religious services weekly, occasionally, and never. Gender gap = difference between men and women. Race gap = largest differential among whites, blacks, and Hispanics. Age gap = largest differential among those aged 18–29, 30–39, 40–49, 50–59, 60–69, and 70+. Regional gap = difference between those living in the South and those living in the non-South.
Source: ANES 2008 and 2012 datasets.

a limited amount of political knowledge is required, and a person can form an opinion almost immediately.[22] Due to the perceived simplicity of these issues, their opponents can easily be demonized. The strength of the religion gap relative to other gaps on social issues displays the strong moral underpinnings of these issues. One's views on morality issues unquestionably are strongly related to one's religious beliefs.

On moral standards the only gap that is relatively close to the size of the religion gap is the age gap. Those who never attend religious services and younger Americans are considerably more likely to believe that one should be more tolerant of people of different moral standards. The religion and age gaps are even more prominent on gay marriage; in fact, these gaps are among the largest of any demographic group's position on any issue. Attitudes on gay marriage have significantly liberalized during the past twenty-five years: only 12 percent supported same-sex marriage in 1988, but by 2010 this figure had risen to 46 percent.[23] Approximately two-thirds of this change was due to individuals modifying their views over time, and one-third was due to later cohorts replacing earlier ones. This suggests that the use of an "equality/tolerance" framing of gay marriage by its supporters may have convinced some people who used to disapprove of gay marriage to approve of it.[24] Yet the sizable religion and age gaps demonstrate the degree by which there remains strong opposition to gay marriage among some groups.

As is the case with gay marriage, abortion is a very salient issue. Of all the issues in the American culture wars, none is more provocative than abortion.[25] This, however, was not the case before the Supreme Court's ruling legalized abortion nationally in *Roe v. Wade*. Before the Court's decision in 1973, there was no relationship between partisanship and views on abortion, but since 1988 self-identified Democrats in the population have become notably more prochoice on abortion than self-identified Republicans.[26] The politics of abortion, however, has always been closely tied to religious beliefs. Approval or disapproval of abortion is not a function of religious preference; rather, attitudes on abortion are a function of the intensity of religious adherence, regardless of specific religions.[27]

There is unquestionably a robust relationship between attendance at religious services and abortion attitudes. The religion gap on abortion, in fact, is larger than any other gap on an issue analyzed in this book: those who attend religious services weekly and those who never attend religious services are separated by 40 percentages points on the issue of whether or not an abortion should be permitted. Besides religion, there is also a large age gap on this issue, but much smaller gaps for other demographic groups. Despite the stereotype that women are significantly more prochoice on abortion than men, the gender gap on abortion is virtually nonexistent. There is also a relatively small difference on abortion on the basis of income, at least when compared to religion. This is consistent with the notion that the Republican Party's position on abortion has alienated the more affluent who support abortion rights. High-income voters who are troubled by the Republican Party's position may, therefore, represent a prominent group that is "suppressed" in terms of possible class voting.[28]

The religion gap is not nearly as prominent for the death penalty as it is for the other cultural issues of gay marriage and abortion. Rather, on the death penalty it is the race gap that is the outlier. African Americans are significantly less likely to support capital punishment than white Americans. African American opposition to the death penalty stems from the fact that many see it as being unfairly implemented on racial grounds. In fact, one-third of the racial divide in support for the death penalty can be attributed to the influence of white racism. When other factors are controlled, support for capital punishment among nonracist whites is similar to that of African Americans.[29] This underscores the degree to which attitudes toward the death penalty in the United States are filtered through the prism of race.

There is a significant demographic gap on all the issues that I have analyzed. The closest to a consensus issue that I found is on defense spending, but even that had an age gap of 16 percentage points, hardly insignificant. This is not to say that there are no consensus issues that unite the disparate groups in the United States; it is just that these issues are not the focal point of contemporary American politics. A greater emphasis on consensus issues that moderate conflict in the political system by bringing Americans together would no doubt be beneficial, but my findings seem to indicate that Americans are indeed extremely divided on the major issues of the day.

In contrast to the dominant political belief systems of most other societies, American values are liberal, individualistic, democratic, and egalitarian.[30] This is reflected in gapology. The gaps underscore these aspects of the nation's political culture, which are basically antigovernment and antiauthoritarian in character. Ultimately, the gaps are a reflection of the choices offered by American political institutions and political parties.[31] On their own, however, the gaps tell us quite a bit about the contemporary state of American politics. The demographic gaps in American politics are a good indicator of the current mood of the country: larger gaps point to greater political polarization.

Large gaps in groups' political behavior also point to a gulf between political ideals and political reality in the United States. That a majority of African Americans are against the death penalty despite the fact that three-fourths of whites support it, for example, makes many Americans uncomfortable because it goes against the egalitarian strain in American political culture. Large gaps indicate an inconsistency between the promise and the performance of government that creates an inherent discord in American society.

The Significance of Gapology

Whatever the angle of approach (income, religion, gender, race, age, or geography), indicators suggest political divisions are evolving in such a way that the expectations of American politics may be markedly transformed. Demographic divides have long characterized American politics, but these gaps are becoming even more distinct. The fact that the gaps are not static and can vary considerably over the long run has important implications for the future of American politics.

For the most part, the gaps that are the focus of this book are growing stronger, not weaker. Race, an important division in American politics since the civil rights movement of the 1960s, is becoming even more prominent. Income, which has helped to define American politics since the Great Depression, continues to exert as strong an influence as ever. Religion, age, and region, which as late as the 1980s were relatively negligible in presidential elections, have become much more important gaps and today help to define American political behavior. The only gap studied in this book that appears to be diminishing is the gender gap. It is important to note, however, that the gender gap is far from irrelevant: not only did the emergence of the gender gap in 1980 indicate a long-term shift in the parties' respective bases, but also in 2012 Obama won approximately 10 million more votes among women than men.

The dramatic increase in the relevance of the gaps leads one to ponder whether or not this will become a long-term predictor of American politics or if it is simply a fluke of the unique dynamics of the time. Certainly, the electorate turned strongly against the Republican Party due to the unpopularity of President Bush. Bush's approval rating varied more widely during his tenure as president—by a remarkable 65 percentage points—than any previous president.[32] In 2008 voters split 48–48 on the question of whether John McCain would continue Bush's policies. Those who said he would went for Obama by a 90 to 8 margin; those who said he would not went for McCain 85 to 13. Thus, not only did voters who thought a McCain administration would constitute a third Bush administration vote overwhelmingly for Obama, but also about 90 percent of those who voted for McCain did so in the belief that his administration would not be a continuation of Bush's. It is hard to imagine that Obama would have won either the Democratic nomination or the presidency had disaffection with Bush and the Iraq War not been so high.

Yet just two years after Obama's impressive victory in 2008, the electorate turned strongly against the Democrats in the 2010 midterm elections. The backlash against the Democrats was perhaps best reflected in the conservative and populist Tea Party movement. Obama ran on an explicit platform of change, in a campaign that appealed to the young and reached out to racial and ethnic minorities. For supporters of the Tea Party, as for many Americans, Obama's election symbolized the culmination of generation change. For his supporters, this was a matter of hope and pride. For many Tea Party supporters, however, the change Obama represented provoked deep anxiety.[33]

The Republican ascendancy, however, proved to be short-lived: Obama was reelected in 2012, and the Democrats made gains in the House and the Senate. Despite the Tea Party–led rebellion against Obama and the Democrats in 2010, the 2012 results suggest that over the long haul the gaps will work to the advantage of the Democrats. The enormous demographic changes in the American polity have left both major political parties in a state of transition but have undoubtedly benefited the Democratic Party.[34] The demographics of the supporters of the Tea Party—overwhelmingly older and white—actually highlight the dilemma for the Republican Party.[35] This suggests that the Tea Party may represent the past of the nation much more than its future.

Some of the gaps do not suggest much of a long-term partisan advantage. The gender gap, for example, does not appear to overtly favor the Democrats or the Republicans. Though it can be argued that the gender gap is the result of men abandoning the Democratic Party, and thus works to the advantage of the Republican Party, it can just as easily be argued that the weakness of Republicans with women limits their electoral capabilities. Given that there are roughly the same number of men and women in the United States (with women making up a slight majority due to their higher life expectancies), and the male-to-female ratio is expected to remain stable for the foreseeable future, the gender gap does not seem to be advancing either of the parties' standing. Similarly, the income gap in voting can be seen as the result of either the Democrats' relative strength with poorer Americans or their relative weakness with wealthier Americans, but long-term income trends do not currently appear to be favoring one party over the other. The Democrats have been making inroads in recent years with wealthier voters, with Obama doing particularly well among those on the higher end of the economic spectrum in 2008. However, Obama's weaker showing among this group in 2012 makes it unclear whether or not this is a sustainable trend.

Some gaps, however, do suggest at least somewhat of a long-term partisan advantage because of changing demographics. Currently, the regional gap appears to be favoring Republicans because the most Republican region—by a large margin—is the South, which is the fast-growing part of the country. As the population of the South grows, therefore, this would seem to favor the Republicans. Yet some of the fastest-growing states in the South (Florida, Virginia, North Carolina) have become much more supportive of Democratic presidential candidates over the past couple of decades, and though no southern state can be deemed a blue state, some might be more purple in nature as time goes on. Thus, the outlook for the region gap may be a decrease in importance.

The demographic trends in religion also seem to have important consequences for the future of American politics. The Democrats' strongest group in terms of religious attendance—those who never attend religious services—are increasing in numbers: 20 percent of Americans now report no religious affiliation, up from 8 percent in 1990.[36] Those who regularly attend religious services—a solidly Republican group—are decreasing in size relative to the rest of the population, mainly as a result of generation replacement. Thus, the growing secularization of the country advantages the Democrats.

The gaps with the greatest implications for the future of American politics, however, are the race and age gaps. The race gap has potentially dramatic consequences over the long haul as the country becomes less white and more diverse. Those from minority groups are projected to increase dramatically in numbers in upcoming decades, and given current political trends the increasing diversity of the American electorate considerably benefits the Democrats. Racial and ethnic minorities overwhelmingly supported Obama: in 2012 he won 93 percent of the black vote, 71 percent of the Hispanic vote, and 73 percent of the Asian vote. Republican weakness at appealing to nonwhites was also noticeable during the party's 2012 presidential primaries, where most of the Republican primary electorates were overwhelmingly white. In South Carolina, for example, although 68 percent of the state population was white, the percentage of the 2012 Republican presidential primary that was white was a staggering 98 percent.[37]

No state symbolizes the problems facing the Republican Party if the party continues its inability to pick up the votes of nonwhites more than California: non-Hispanic whites made up only 40 percent of California's population in the 2010 Census. Historically, California was a key swing state that, if anything, leaned a bit Republican at the presidential level: Republican presidential nominees won it every election from 1968 to 1988. As the share of the Hispanic and Asian populations increased from 21 percent in 1980 to 52 percent in 2010, however, California moved from being a purple state to being a solidly blue state. California went from being about as Republican as the nation as a whole in the 1984 presidential election to being 18 percentage points more Democratic than the nation as a whole in 2012. A current swing state that might present a similar quandary for Republicans in the future is Florida. The under-30 vote in Florida supported Obama by a 2

to 1 margin in 2012, and Latinos, whose current one-sixth of the state's electorate is projected to grow—potentially dramatically—in the future, gave
him 60 percent of the vote. As the third most populous state in the country,
Florida's 29 Electoral College votes are crucial, and if they move consistently
to the Democrats, the Republican Party's presidential aspirations will become significantly more difficult.

For Republicans to be more successful in future elections, they will need
to do better among minority voters, especially Hispanics. But younger
Americans, who have turned strongly against the Republicans, are more
ethnically diverse than other age cohorts. Hispanics in particular make
up a larger portion of younger Americans than of the general population
as a whole. Given that Republicans currently appear to be losing ground
among Hispanics, this poses a major problem for the party in the future. As
a more diverse younger population of Americans matures, the Democrats
are poised to pick up more votes.

The Republicans face a similar dilemma in regard to the generation replacement of older voters with younger voters. Historically, those over
60 have tended to distribute their votes among presidential candidates in
roughly the same proportions as the electorate as a whole, and they have
consistently favored the winner of the overall popular vote. Today, however, older Americans have by a good margin become the most Republican
leaning of all age groups. As the New Deal generation—which was overwhelmingly Democratic—dies off, it is replaced by older Americans who
have become distinctly Republican. Over the long run this works to the
Democrats' advantage. As the country ages, the most Republican age cohort—older Americans—will be replaced by younger Americans who are
considerably less conservative in their political outlook than the generation
they are replacing. In recent years younger Americans have been consistently to the left of the general population and have increasingly become
more likely to support the Democratic Party. The Republican Party desperately needs to reverse the age gap, but given the public policy preferences of
younger Americans, this will be difficult for the Republicans to do unless
the party moves toward the center ideologically.

The relative importance of the gaps is also interconnected with voter turnout. One of the important findings of gapology is that turnout varies considerably from group to group. Voter turnout is inexorably influenced by group membership. Incorporating the role of social groups helps us understand the individual's decision to cast a vote.[38] Thus, not only do the groups vary in terms of vote choice, but they also vary in terms of whether or not they vote in the first place.

It is widely believed that the Republican Party is helped by lower voter turnout. In fact, there is a saying that "rainy weather is Republican weather"—meaning that bad weather on Election Day tends to decrease voter turnout, which benefits the Republicans. The turnout rates of some groups back up this belief, but it is not true in all cases. That the wealthier, whites, and older Americans are more likely to vote all work in favor of the Republicans. That women vote at slightly higher rates than men works to the advantage of the Democrats. The Republican Party's overall advantage in voter turnout, however, is not necessarily sustainable, especially when the age gap is involved. The voting rates of younger Americans are expected to increase as they age, as happened with previous generations. As today's younger voters mature, they will vote more often at the same time the country becomes more racially and ethnically diverse. This bodes well for the Democrats.

The 2008 and 2012 elections suggest how changes in voter turnout may affect future elections by changing the demographic composition of the electorate. Instrumental to Obama's victories was the fact that the groups that favored Obama made up a larger share of the electorate than they historically had. In particular, African Americans, Hispanics, and young voters increased their share of the electorate, and all strongly favored Obama. If future Democratic candidates can muster the same turnout levels as Obama did among African Americans, Hispanics, and younger voters, the Democrats will be well positioned in future elections. To some degree the Republicans seem to be aware of these looming demographic problems: apparently, the party's recent promotion of stricter voter identification laws is an attempt to limit the turnout of those groups and individuals likely to give their votes to the Democrats.[39]

The Democratic debacle in the 2010 midterm elections shows how important younger voters and minority voters were to Obama's election victories in 2008 and 2012. Nonwhite voters made up 26 percent of the electorate in 2008 and 28 percent in 2012, but only 23 percent in 2010. The turnout drop was even more dramatic among younger voters: voters 18–29 made up 18 percent of the electorate in 2008 and 19 percent in 2012 but only 11 percent in 2010. The fortunes of the Democrats, therefore, were strongly tied to their ability (in 2008 and 2012) and inability (in 2010) to get the groups that strongly supported them to the polls.

There are also long-term group effects on vote choice to consider. Once a demographic group strongly moves toward one of the political parties, its loyalty to that party tends to be long lasting. A classic example of this is with African Americans, who moved overwhelmingly toward the Democrats in the 1964 Lyndon Johnson–Barry Goldwater election and have remained loyal Democrats ever since. An interesting question for future elections is the level of support Democrats will receive from Hispanics. Because the Hispanic population is projected to increase from 16 percent of the population in 2010 to 29 percent in 2050, this group is destined to become much more politically significant.[40] If Democrats continue to win the Hispanic vote at the 71 percent clip that Obama carried the group in 2012, the Republicans risk being annihilated in future elections.

Gapology is grounded in the concept that specific subsets of Americans' voting behavior can move in a direction distinct from the population as a whole. The gap trends suggest the parties' coalitions are in flux, which potentially provides a major opportunity (or risk) for the Democratic and Republican parties. The gaps exist in part due to policies that the parties have staked out through the years; opposition to civil rights by conservatives such as Barry Goldwater, for example, encouraged African Americans to move en masse to supporting the Democratic Party. How the parties adapt to the reality that they have gap problems will be critical to the parties' success in the future. If the parties do not make attempts to seek bigger umbrellas and appeal to broader coalitions, they run the risk of being marginalized.

The very fact that a person like Barack Obama—an African American whose mother was white, whose father was Kenyan, and who spend part of his childhood in Indonesia—could be elected president underlies the transformation of the American electorate.[41] Though different gaps can be interpreted as having different long-term consequences, the groups that are poised to play a greater role in American politics in the future are consistently to the left of the general population and have increasingly become more likely to support the Democratic Party.

The gap trends thus indicate that a significant realignment of the electorate in the future is possible. Demographics—especially in regard to race and age—strongly favor the Democrats, especially given the change in the issues that currently dominate political discourse. Though economic issues are still important, a new political culture has transformed American politics: social issues are increasingly distinguished and emphasized relative to economic issues. Even though elements of the parties—in particular the candidates and the national committees—are more concerned about electability than ideological purity, this not the case with party activists. The parties would rather support a candidate who is closer to the district's median voter than an ideological purist who would be more likely to lose an election. Warring ideological activists, however, are not generally willing to make ideological sacrifices in the interest of their parties' candidates. This makes it easier for social conservatives to dominate both the Republican primaries and the activists who give the party its image to the nation; the converse is true of the Democrats. The result is that it has become more difficult for social liberals to hope for a successful career within the Republican Party and social conservatives to succeed within the Democratic Party.[42] Consequently, as social liberals depart the Republican Party and social conservatives leave the Democratic Party, the parties have become more ideologically monolithic.

This transformation of the parties' bases appears to advantage the Democrats over the long haul because groups that have relatively liberal positions on social issues are poised to grow in political stature. In regard to public opinion, the Democrats seem to have future openings on a number of public policy issues, many of which have huge demographic gaps that appear to be breaking in favor of the Democrats over the long term. This may be best demonstrated with the age and religion gaps on gay marriage. Whereas younger Americans, who will become more politically important as they mature and replace older voters in the electorate, are strong proponents of gay marriage, religious Americans, who are declining as a share of the electorate, are solid opponents. The result is a demographic shift that works in the favor of gay marriage over the long term. Similarly, the gapology of public policy preferences on immigration, gun control, environmental regulation, defense spending, health care, abortion, and the death penalty all point to future trends that favor the Democratic positions on these issues relative to the Republican positions. One issue where demographics appear to be working in favor of the Republicans is Social Security privatization, though overall the population is still fairly opposed to putting Social Security in stocks and bonds.

The Democratic Party was the nation's dominant party for a generation after the New Deal, but since the civil rights movement of the 1960s, the party has lost as many presidential elections as it has won. The changing demographics of the country, however, suggest that the Democrats are well positioned to regain the dominant position in the electorate that they once held. The Democrats have not been in this strong a position with new voters entering the electorate since the Great Depression. The unpopularity of George W. Bush, especially among younger Americans, combined with the tremendous support Barack Obama managed to garner among younger Americans, has created a new overwhelmingly Democratic age cohort. As this new generation matures, the Democratic Party has the potential to dominate the next era of American politics.

All this, of course, is contingent on the successes and failures of future policymakers. Ironically, sometimes the best thing a party can do for its long-term success is to lose an election. Democrats, for example, were despondent after the 2004 elections. Many in the press talked about a permanent realignment advantaging the Republicans. But over the long run there is a good argument to be made that the Democrats were better off losing the presidency in 2004. By losing in 2004, they were well positioned to win control of Congress in the 2006 midterm elections, which would have been unlikely if John Kerry had won in 2004, as well the White House in 2008 once public opinion turned solidly against Bush.

The results of the 2008 and 2012 elections suggest that issues and tactics that worked for the Republican Party in helping them win control of the White House in 2000 and 2004 may prove to be detrimental to the long-term success of the party. Bush's move to more conservative stands, especially on social issues such as gay marriage, may have helped him pick up evangelical votes but at the cost of votes from other groups.[43] Yet groups that will be more politically influential in the future are much more supportive of gay marriage than groups that are declining in influence. As a result, the Republican Party risks being associated with positions that are highly unpopular with these more influential groups. Thus, its emphasis on social conservatism, though successful in 2000 and 2004, may end up costing the Republicans in the long run.

Since long-term trends in gapology are currently breaking away from the Republicans, their future success may rest on the party's ability to alter its positions. On immigration, for example, Republican support for reducing immigration levels damages the party's ability to win the votes of Hispanics, who are destined to become considerably more politically powerful. A less rigidly conservative stance in the future would work to the Republican Party's advantage on this issue as well as on gun control, the environment, defense spending, and gay marriage.

Notes

1. Ronald Takaki, *A Different Mirror: A History of Multicultural America* (Boston: Little, Brown, 1999).

2. In 1992 this was probably a consequence of the large vote for Ross Perot: he won 19 percent of the overall vote and did noticeably better among men, winning 21 percent of the male vote in 1992. In 1988 the gender independent variable just barely missed being statistically significant at the $p < .05$ level.

3. Importantly, the directions of the correlations were reversed for age in 2000 compared to 2008 and 2012. In 2000 age was in a negative direction, whereas in 2008 and 2012 it was in a positive direction, indicating that when other variables were controlled, being older made one relatively more likely to vote Democratic for president in 2000 but Republican in 2008 and 2012.

4. Michael S. Lewis-Beck, William G. Jacoby, Helmut Norpoth, and Herbert F. Weisberg, *The American Voter Revisited* (Ann Arbor: University of Michigan Press, 2008), chap. 11.

5. Charles Prysby, "Perceptions of Candidate Character Traits and the Presidential Vote in 2004," *PS: Political Science and Politics* 41 (2009): 115–122.

6. James A. Stimson, *Tides of Consent: How Public Opinion Shapes American Politics* (New York: Cambridge University Press, 2004).

7. Alan I. Abramowitz and Kyle Saunders, "Ideological Realignment in the U.S. Electorate," *Journal of Politics* 60 (1998): 634–652.

8. Greg Adams, "Abortion: Evidence of an Issue Evolution," *American Journal of Political Science* 41 (1997): 718–737.

9. Murray Edelman, *Politics as Symbolic Action* (Waltham, MA: Academic Press, 1971).

10. Robert Erikson, Gerald Wright, and John McIver. *Statehouse Democracy: Public Opinion and Policy in the American States* (New York: Cambridge University Press, 1993).

11. E. E. Schattschneider, *The Semisovereign People* (Chicago: Holt, Rinehart, and Winston, 1960).

12. Charles Lockhart, "American and Swedish Tax Regimes," *Comparative Politics* 35 (2003): 379–397.

13. Erica Frank, Jennifer Carrera, and Shafik Dharamsi, "Political Self-Characterization of U.S. Medical Students," *Journal of General Internal Medicine* 22 (2007): 514–517.

14. Stanley B. Greenberg, *The Two Americas* (New York: Thomas Dunne Books, 2004), 128–129.

15. Kara Lindaman and Donald P. Haider-Markel, "Issue Evolution, Political Parties, and the Cultural Wars," *Political Research Quarterly* 55 (2002): 91–110.

16. Brad T. Clark and David W. Allen, "Political Economy and the Adoption of Everyday Environmental Policies in the American States, 1997: An Exploratory Analysis," *Social Science Journal* 41 (2004): 525–542.

17. Deborah Lynn Guber, "Voting Preferences and the Environment in the American Electorate," *Society and Natural Resources* 14 (2001): 455–469.

18. B. Guy Peters, *The Politics of Taxation* (Cambridge, MA: Basil Blackwell, 1991), 88–89.

19. Andrew Kohut and Bruce Stokes, *America Against the World* (New York: Henry Holt, 2006), chap. 2.

20. Seymour Martin Lipset, *Continental Divide* (New York: Routledge, 1989), 220.

21. Gary C. Jacobson, "The Effects of the George W. Bush Presidency on Partisan Attitudes," *Presidential Studies Quarterly* 39 (2009): 172–209.

22. Edward G. Carmines and James A. Stimson, "The Two Faces of Issue Voting," *American Political Science Review* 74 (1980): 176–186.

23. 1988–2010 General Social Survey.

24. Dawn Michelle Baunach, "Decomposing Trends in Attitudes Toward Gay Marriage," *Social Science Quarterly* 92 (2011): 346–363.

25. Mark D. Brewer and Jeffrey M. Stonecash, *Split: Class and Cultural Divides in American Politics* (Washington, DC: CQ Press, 2007), 127–130.

26. Morris Fiorina, *Culture War? The Myth of a Polarized America* (New York: Pearson Longman, 2005).

27. Ross Baker, Laurily Epstein, and Rodney Forth, "Matters of Life and Death," *American Politics Quarterly* 9 (1981): 89–103.

28. Brewer and Stonecash, Split, 179–180.

29. James D. Unnever and Francis T. Cullen, "The Racial Divide in Support for the Death Penalty: Does White Racism Matter?," *Social Forces* 85 (2007): 1281–1301.

30. Samuel Huntington, *American Politics: The Promise of Disharmony* (Cambridge, MA: Harvard University Press, 1981), chap. 1.

31. Thomas Mann and Norman Ornstein, *It's Even Worse Than It Looks: How the American Political System Collided with the New Politics of Extremism* (New York: Basic Books, 2012).

32. Jacobson, "The Effects of the George W. Bush Presidency," 172–209.

33. Vanessa Williamson, Theda Skocpol, and John Coggin, "The Tea Party and the Remaking of Republican Conservatism," *Perspectives on Politics* 9 (2011): 25–43.

34. John Kenneth White, *Barack Obama's America* (Ann Arbor: University of Michigan Press, 2009).

35. Williamson et al., "The Tea Party," 25–43.

36. "'Nones' on the Rise: One-in-Five Adults Have No Religious Affiliation," Pew Research Center, October 9, 2012.

37. US Census Bureau and exit polls of South Carolina presidential primary, January 21, 2012.

38. Benny Geys, "Rational Theories of Voter Turnout: A Review," *Political Studies Review* 4 (2006): 16–35.

39. Alec MacGillis, "Holy Toledo," *New Republic*, November 8, 2012, 14–16.

40. "U.S. Population Projections 2005–2050," Pew Research Center, February 11, 2008.

41. Ruy Teixeira, "Beyond Polarization?: The Future of Red, Blue, and Purple America," in *Red, Blue, and Purple America*, ed. Ruy Teixeira (Washington, DC: Brookings Institution Press, 2008), 1–22.

42. Gary Miller and Norman Schofield, "The Transformation of the Republican and Democratic Party Coalitions in the U.S.," *Perspectives on Politics* 6 (2008): 433–450.

43. David E. Campbell and J. Quin Monson, "The Case of Bush's Reelection: Did Gay Marriage Do It?," in *A Matter of Faith*, ed. David E. Campbell (Washington, DC: Brookings Institution Press, 2007), 120–141.

Appendix: Exit Polls, 1980–2012

APPENDIX   Exit Polls, 1980–2012

	2012	2008	2004	2000	1996	1992	1988	1984	1980
Income									
$0–50,000	60–38	60–38	55–44	52–44	53–37	46–34	49–51	44–55*	44–49*
$50–100,000	46–52	49–49	44–56	46–51	46–47	40–41*	39–61	32–68*	33–59*
$100,000+	44–54	49–49	41–58	43–55	39–55	36–48*	33–67	31–69*	26–66*
Religion									
Protestant	42–57	45–54	40–59	40–58	41–50	36–45	38–61	32–67	35–59
Catholic	50–46	52–46	47–52	49–47	53–37	44–35	47–52	45–54	42–50
Jewish	69–30	78–21	74–25	79–19	78–16	80–11	64–35	67–31	45–39
Gender									
Men	45–52	49–48	44–55	42–53	43–44	41–38	41–57	37–62	36–55
Women	55–44	56–43	51–48	54–43	54–38	45–37	49–50	44–56	45–47
Race									
White	39–59	43–55	41–58	42–54	43–46	39–40	40–59	35–64	36–56
Black	93–6	95–4	88–11	90–8	84–12	83–10	86–12	90–9	85–11
Hispanic	71–27	67–31	56–43	62–35	72–21	61–25	69–30	62–37	56–35
Age									
18–29	60–37	66–32	54–45	48–46	53–34	43–34	47–52	40–59	44–43
30–44	52–45	52–46	46–53	30–44	48–41	41–38	45–54	42–57	36–56
45–59	47–51^	49–49	48–51	48–49	48–41	41–40	42–57	40–60	39–55
60+	44–56^	47–51	46–54	51–47	48–44	50–38	49–50	39–60	41–54

(continues)

APPENDIX   Exit Polls, 1980–2012 (continued)

	2012	2008	2004	2000	1996	1992	1988	1984	1980
Geography:									
Urban	63–36	63–35	53–46	61–36	56–34	53–31	55–44	N/A	N/A
Suburban	48–50	50–48	47–52	47–49	47–42	41–39	42–57	38–61	35–55
Rural	39–59	45–53	43–56	37–59	45–45	39–41	43–56	32–67	39–54

% Democrat for President–% Republican for President

* In 1992 the middle-income group is $50,000–$75,000 and the highest-income group $75,000+. In 1984 the income groups are $0–$35,000, $35,000–$50,000, and $50,000+. In 1980 the income groups are $0–$25,000, $25,000–$50,000, and $50,000+.

^ In 2012 the oldest age group is 65+ and the preceding age group is 45–64.

Source: Exit poll data for 2012 were collected by Edison Research for the National Election Pool. In 2008 the exit polls were conducted by Edison/Mitofsky; in 1996 and 2000, by Voter News Services; in 1992, by Voter Research and Surveys; and in earlier years, by the *New York Times* and CBS News.

Discussion Questions

Chapter 1: Introduction to Gapology

1. What is "gapology"?
2. How is political socialization related to gapology?
3. What does the "red" versus "blue" dichotomy in American politics imply?
4. How does gapology help us understand what it means to be American?
5. What important implications does gapology have for public policy?

Chapter 2: The Income Gap

1. What are the historical underpinnings of the income gap?
2. How large is the income gap?
3. How are the policy preferences of poorer Americans different from those of wealthier Americans?
4. What is the education gap in American politics?
5. Why is the income gap important for understanding policy outcomes?

Chapter 3: The Religion Gap

1. How has religious affiliation historically affected American politics?

2. What is the relationship between religious commitment and political leanings?
3. How important are evangelicals to the modern Republican Party?
4. How does religious commitment influence policy preferences?
5. What role does religion play in the notion of a culture war?

Chapter 4: The Gender Gap

1. When did the gender gap emerge in American politics?
2. Why are women more Democratic and liberal than men?
3. What issues have relatively large gender gaps?
4. Why does a political marriage gap exist?

Chapter 5: The Race Gap

1. Why is race the single most important divide within the contemporary American electorate?
2. What is the history of the race gap in American politics?
3. Why are African Americans such political outliers in American politics?
4. How are the political and policy preferences of Hispanics different from those of whites and African Americans?
5. How important were racial and ethnic minorities in the elections of Barack Obama in 2008 and 2012?
6. How important will the race gap be in the future of American politics?

Chapter 6: The Age Gap

1. How were the political leanings of younger Americans historically different from those of older Americans?
2. Why were younger Americans such strong supporters of Barack Obama in 2008 and 2012?
3. What public policies have especially large age gaps?
4. Why is the age gap important?

Chapter 7: The Geography Gap

1. Historically, how was the South a political outlier in American politics?
2. How are the policy preferences of southerners different from those in the rest of the country?
3. How are the political leanings of those who live in cities different from those who live in the suburbs or in rural areas?
4. Why is the urbanism gap growing?
5. How are exurbs politically distinct from suburbs in general?
6. How is the country becoming more geographically polarized?

Chapter 8: The Implications of Gapology

1. Why do the issues that emerge as important in American politics inevitably have demographic underpinnings?
2. Which gaps are relatively more important?
3. Which public policy issues have especially large demographic gaps?
4. Which gaps have the greatest implications for the future of American politics?
5. How do demographic trends appear to be working in favor of the Democrats?

Index

environmental regulations and, 128
Johnson receiving vote of, 114
Obama votes and Lincoln votes of,
119 (fig.)
Obama with black population by
state and, 118 (fig.)
Obama's support eroding of,
121–122
political behavior of, 113–116
presidential elections by region with,
172 (fig.)
suburbs move of, 174
2008 and 2012 election electoral
map of, 117 (fig.)
White evangelicals, 7, 54–55, 63, 129
Women
on abortion and gay marriage, 95–96
college-educated, 91

in Democratic Party, 84, 94–95, 101
education impacting, 102
Electoral College map vote of,
88 (fig.)
equality views of, 89–90
without health insurance, 92
labor force expansion including,
92–93
liberalism of, 89
in marriage gap, 97–98
Obama's votes from, 86–87
Reagan's opposition to rights of,
85–86
rights of, 94
2008 and 2012 Presidential elections
votes of, 88 (fig.)
voter turnout of, 85–86
Working class, 22, 183

Made in the USA
San Bernardino, CA
18 January 2017